Green Volunteers

The World Guide to Voluntary Work in Nature Conservation

Green Volunteers

Publications

Green Volunteers
The World Guide to Voluntary Work in Nature Conservation

Editor: Fabio Ausenda, assisted by Erin McCloskey
Cover design: Studio Cappellato e Laurent srl, Milano
Cover photo: Victoria Falls Lion Rehabilitation Programme, Zimbabwe
                        (See African Impact Lion Rehab. Progrs. in Project List)
                        Courtesy Umberto Pajarola, Switzerland (1st winner of the
                        Green Volunteers Photo Contest, see page 254).

This Guide is not an annual publication. Readers can keep it up to date and be constantly informed of new conservation volunteering opportunities through the *Green Volunteers Database* (see page 3 for access details) and its e-mail newsletter.

Published by: Green Volunteers di Fabio Ausenda
                        Via Canonica 72
                        I-20154 Milano, Italy
                        www.greenvol.com - green@greenvolunteers.org

US & Canada distribution: Universe Publishing
                           A division of Rizzoli International Publications, Inc.
                           300 Park Avenue South,
                           New York, NY 10010

UK distribution: Vacation Work Publications
                           An imprint of Crimson Publishing
                           Westminster House, Kew Road,
                           Richmond TW9 2ND, England
Australia and
New Zealand distribution: Woodslane Pty Ltd
                           Unit 7/5 Vuko Place
                           Warriewood NSW 2102

Printed in Jan. 2007 by: Consorzio Artigiano L.V.G. srl, Azzate (VA), Italy
ISBN: 978-88-89060-12-4
Library of Congress Control Number: 2006939728

PREFACE

In the last 20 years there has been a growing demand for volunteers for nature conservation projects in general and for wildlife related projects in particular. Volunteering provides wildlife and nature enthusiasts with an opportunity to become involved in worldwide conservation efforts. Students can gain experience allowing them to pursue a career in nature conservation as well as ideas for a thesis. Until recently, large organisations were mostly responsible for offering this kind of opportunity, but usually the financial contributions required limited the number of people who could afford them and become volunteers. However, there are many smaller nature conservation and wildlife protection projects with a constant shortage of funding which greatly need volunteers for research assistance and financial resources. Often these contributions by volunteers can maintain projects for years. The Gibbon Rehabilitation Project in Thailand, for example, has been running successfully for over 15 years exclusively on the contributions and help of international volunteers. Until now many of these projects throughout the world did not have a worldwide forum. With this guide these valuable projects have the opportunity to connect with prospective volunteers and vice versa.

The objective of *Green Volunteers* is to provide information to fill the communication gap between people who are willing to join interesting and valuable projects worldwide, and the projects in need of volunteers. For this reason, the Geneva-based World Conservation Union's Species Survival Commission (the body which publishes the "Red Lists" of endangered species) considers the *Green Volunteers* guide a useful instrument for supporting conservation projects throughout the world.

HOW TO BE LISTED IN THE *Green Volunteers Guide and Database*

If you are an organisation or project based anywhere in the world and you would like to be listed in the next edition of this guide and or on our website at **www.greenvounteers.org**, please contact *Green Volunteers* at the addresses on the previous page. Should you require any information on how to recruit and organise volunteers as a valuable instrument to support a nature conservation project *Green Volunteers* is willing to assist you.

INTRODUCTION

Green Volunteers is a directory. There are 2 sections: one dedicated to organisations and one to specific projects.

Organisations play an important role in providing opportunities for volunteer work; listed are those offering projects on a wide range of species, habitats and geographic locations, at various costs to volunteers (from zero to a few thousand dollars.) Organisations are listed in alphabetical order. Should an organisation have an acronym, as many do, the organisation is listed according to the alphabetical order of the acronym. For example, BTCV, CVA, WWF, are listed according to the acronym's alphabetical order. For some of the larger organisations, or for those offering interesting projects to prospective volunteers, a few projects have been described in greater detail in the second section. These projects are listed at the end of the organisations' descriptions under the heading: Selected Projects. For most of the organisations no projects have been described in the second section due to limited space in this guide. Prospective volunteers are therefore encouraged to contact the organisations directly (or visit their websites), and inquire for further information about available projects.

Projects are found in the second section of this guide. Greater detail about the projects offered by the organisations is provided, and many more independent projects, which are not part of major organisations, are listed.

MEANING OF ABBREVIATIONS

For each organisation and project the guide lists:

The **address** and the **telephone** and **fax** numbers with the international codes. Remember to change the local area code according to the country's telephone system. For example, to call The Monkey Sanctuary, (UK) phone number (listed as ++ 44 (1503) 262 532), people calling from the UK should not dial ++ 44 (the international code), but should add 0 (zero) before 1503 (the local area code). People calling from the Netherlands should add 00 before 44 to call the UK. Whereas people calling from the US should dial 011, then 44, the international access codes from the US to the UK. **E-mail** and World Wide Web (**www**) addresses are listed where available. If these references are not listed, a quick phone call to ask an organisation if they have recently activated an e-mail or www address will help you to communicate and get information much faster than through regular mail and will speed your selection of the right organisation for you. One project indicated its Skype ID, this very cheap (or even free) method of communication (voice via the internet) will be used more and more in the future.

Desc.: The main activity and objectives of the organisations or projects.

Spp.: The species or the group of species involved. The common name, and Latin name if necessary for clarification, is provided. For projects involving groups of species, families, classes or communities, these groupings are cited in more general terms such as marine mammals, tropical birds, African herbivores, etc. Abbreviations are occasionally used.

Hab.: Specific habitats or wider biogeographical areas an organisation is involved with, such as tropical seas and coasts, African savannah, Mediterranean islands, etc. Abbreviations are occasionally used.

Loc.: The countries, regions (such as Southeast Asia) or continents where an organisation conducts its projects.

Travel: A basic summary of travel directions. Organisations and projects will give full details to the volunteers once accepted.

Dur.: The duration of the volunteering time, either a set period or a minimum and maximum duration.

Per.:   The period of the year when a volunteer can join a project such as year round, the summer, July to August, etc.

L.term: Long-term volunteering is a longer stay than the set volunteer duration. Some projects do not allow long-term volunteering, others do, but they typically continue charging the volunteers the same contribution (per week, for example) without recognizing any discount for the additional experience acquired by the volunteer. Other organisations or projects encourage long-term volunteering for this benefit. The Ecovolunteer Network is one organisation that encourages a longer permanence on some of the projects by considerably decreasing the cost to the volunteer the longer a volunteer stays. Some projects or organisations require professionally qualified labour and staff and accept graduate students for their thesis work.

Age: Minimum and maximum age for joining a project. Elderly volunteers must always consider that most projects are located in remote areas and in developing countries where good quality health facilities are out of reach or non existing. The nature of the work expected from the volunteers, which can span from hard manual labor to data collection, and the climate conditions, must also be carefully considered.

Qualif.: The qualifications and skills required of a volunteer who wants to join a project. Most of the time no special qualifications are needed, other than a strong motivation and enthusiasm. Adaptation to harsh climates, long walks, hot or cold temperatures, basic accommodation and very little comfort is almost always required. Where possible, the Editor has specified particularly extreme working or lodging conditions present at a given project. However, specific information is to be obtained from the organisation or project. Other typical requirements include a strong flexibility to work with other people, a willingness to accept very little privacy (very rarely volunteers will be able to lodge in a single or even double rooms) and the ability to adapt to different cultures. These requirements apply to almost all projects but are not always stated. A volunteer may offer special skills, such as photography, good computer literacy, mechanical skills, etc. Never expect, nor impose these skills onto a project— there may already be very qualified people performing these duties with the accuracy required by the project.

For long-term volunteering, or for organisations or projects where little or no contribution is required, volunteers are often selected according to their qualifications or previous experience in related work. Contact the organisation directly for more information on the skills and qualifications required.

Work: The main activities performed by volunteers are listed for projects. Since most organisations manage several projects, the work performed by volunteers is not described in detail because it will vary with each project. Prospective volunteers can predict what kind of activities to expect from the description of an organisation and the projects it supports. Further details are given by the organisations directly.

Lang.: The languages that are required for a volunteer to work on a project. The importance of communicating with the project staff or with local or international researchers should not be overlooked. Prospective volunteers should never underestimate the importance of this aspect and never overestimate their ability to understand a foreign language in a working environment.

Accom.: (Not described within the organisation description.) The style of accommodation the volunteers will be lodged in. For most of the projects volunteers should be prepared for very basic accommodations such as bunk beds in research stations (rarely in houses) tents or hammocks. Bathroom facilities can also be very basic and hot showers, particularly in the tropics, can be quite rare. Chores such as housecleaning, cooking, washing dishes, etc., are often expected. Comfort and privacy is rare. The ability to do without these privileges must be considered for environmental volunteering.

Cost: Most of the projects require a contribution from the volunteers, which is often the major funding for a project. Projects are often conducted with the financial contribution and the work volunteers perform. The cost of projects may vary from a few hundred to a few thousands dollars US. The Editor has tried to list as many organisations as possible requiring little or no contributions. These organisations, however, are difficult to find; they are either small projects in developing countries that have no means for communication or until now did not perceive the importance of taking volunteers. It is fair, however, that even these small projects or organisations ask for a small contribution, especially in developing countries.

9

Usually, the volunteer's contribution covers food and accommodation or there may be a common kitty for food costs. Very rarely will the cost include the international airfare to reach a project site. Some projects have introduced a very useful 'progressively decreasing cost' policy, depending on the length of stay. The rationale is that the longer a volunteer stays with a project, the more useful he or she becomes because of the experience he or she gains. Long-term volunteers selected according to their skills are often reimbursed for their living expenses. This is typically the case for long-term volunteers with Government Agencies, such as the US National Park Service, the US Forest Service or The US Fish and Wildlife Service.

Part of the volunteer contribution likely pays for the project costs: marketing, reservation staff, rent, telephone, mail, etc. Money going towards an agency or larger organisation or overhead should not be considered money diverted from the conservation objective. Larger organisations perform a basic role in a world-wide conservation effort by providing volunteers and funding to projects that alone would not have been able to reach these important resources. However, when overhead costs are in excess of a reasonable percentage (max. 20–25%) an organisation should try to become more efficient by reducing costs, in order to devote a higher percentage of a volunteer's contribution to actual projects. It is perfectly in the right of a volunteer to know how much of his or her contribution goes into a project, and what is the organisation's overhead.

Agents: The agents or organisations where a prospective volunteer can or should apply. Many organisations have branches in other countries that act as agents for projects. Other organisations use outside agents such as travel agencies to recruit volunteers. Many organisations do not have agents and require direct application.

Applic.: This section briefly describes application procedures that may be required such as filling out an application form, sending a deposit or initial contribution, or becoming a member of a specific organisation.

Selected Projects are listed for some organisations. If detailed description of projects are not provided, volunteers should contact the organisation directly in order to receive further information.

WILDLIFE REHABILITATION CENTRES

To volunteer with wildlife you don't necessarily need to cross an ocean or stay away for weeks or months. You may indeed be able to volunteer and get in close contact with various species, mostly endemic but also exotic, in your own town, county, district, province or state at Wildlife Rehabilitation Centres. These centres, usually managed by local or national Non-Profit Organisations or private individuals – rarely local governments, take care and try to rehabilitate wounded or mistreated animals. Animals may have been wounded by hunters or car accidents or have been victims of plain cruelty. Often exotic wildlife that is confiscated by local authorities is handed over to Wildlife Rehabilitation Centres. Rare species illegally imported or detained against the CITES convention (International Convention on Trade of Endangered Species) cannot be released into a foreign habitat and rarely are re-exported to the country of origin.

Wildlife Rehabilitation Centres are always in need of volunteers. They often don't charge any fees and, if they are located near where you live, they may allow you to work just a few hours a week. There are several hundred Wildlife Rehabilitation Centres throughout the world, and they are mostly concentrated in First World countries. We did list a few in this guide as examples because we have had direct communication with them, but it would not be difficult to find a Rehabilitation Centre nearby where you can volunteer for a short period, a weekend or even a few hours a week.

We recommend that you do a web search with the key words "Wildlife Rehabilitation" and the name of the geographical area of your choice, such as Bedfordshire, Oregon, Alberta or New South Wales, depending on where you live or where would you like to volunteer. To help with your search, we have selected a few websites with a comprehensive international list of Wildlife Rehabilitation Centres.

www.catchat.org/adoption/notcats.html

A very thorough list of animal rescue centres in the British Isles, divided by species.

www.ispca.ie/content/links.html

The website of the Irish Society for the Prevention of Cruelty to Animals, a good list of Irish and non-Irish Wildlife Sanctuaries.

www.tc.umn.edu/~devo0028/contact.htm

The Wildlife Rehabilitation Information Directory. A complete list of Centres throughout the US, Canada and the world.

www.greenpeople.org/sanctuary.htm

A list of over 200 sanctuaries in the US, Canada, Australia and throughout the world.

www.wildliferehabilitators.com/links.htm

The link page of the Association of Wildlife Rehabilitators, it has a good list of Wildlife Rehabilitators and Rehabilitation Centres in the US, Australia, Canada and the UK.

Finally Yahoo has a good list of Wildlife Rehabilitation Centres under Wildlife > Rescue and Rehabilitation.

TIPS FOR CONTACTING
AN ORGANISATION OR PROJECT

1) **Have clear in mind what you want to do, the species or habitats you prefer, the geographical location, the duration of your volunteering period and the costs you can afford.** This will help you in selecting and reducing the number of organisations or projects you want to apply to. Select a list of both organisations and projects and divide them into your first and second priority. The first priority should include not only those organisations or projects that are of primary interest to you, but also those which are more remote and harder to contact.

2) **Use the fastest possible method to contact an organisation.** Remember that interesting projects or organisations also have many applicants, and they usually fill their available positions on a first come, first serve basis. Therefore, you want to be as fast as possible in letting them know that you are interested in taking a position with them. You may send via e-mail the *Green Volunteers Standard Application Form* found at page 255. Should you not receive a reply within 3–5 days, be prepared to send reminders or telephone them to confirm their e-mail address. These addresses often change, particularly when an organisation finds a cheaper internet server.

3) **Inform as much as possible the organisation or project you would like to work for about yourself.** With your request for information, send a description of your skills and interests and possibly a CV. You can find at page 255 the *Green Volunteers Standard Application Form*, modeled on the application forms of many organisations. This form may be sufficient for applying and it may help you to save time. The form (which is not an official application form but just a tool to help in the application process) is also available from the *Green Volunteers Database* at **www.greenvolunteers.org** (the Database is accessible with your User ID and password, see page 3 for details). Always enclose a cover letter (preferably typed and not handwritten) and ask if the organisation accepts the *Green Volunteers Standard Application Form*.

4) **Make an organisation's response easier.** Remember that organisations and projects often are short of funds. Therefore, help them by enclosing self-addressed stamped envelopes. If the organisation is located in a foreign country, enclose an international reply coupon. You may also offer an organisation to fax you collect (give them an appointment, because in order to receive a fax collect you should first be able to answer vocally, accept the call,

then switch on the fax mode). Better still, since a fax goes both ways regardless of who calls, you can offer the organisation to call them on their fax line, and have them fax back the information. Remember that you should arrange this over the phone. If you interact with a large organisation, well equipped for recruiting volunteers, they have all the means to contact you, particularly if they are in the more expensive range of projects. In general, the cheaper the project or organisation you want to volunteer for, the more you should try to help them by reducing their cost of contacting you. In the past few years, however, the diffusion of the Internet, also in developing countries, has considerably reduced communications costs.

5) **Do exactly what is required by an organisation for being accepted.** If they do not accept the *Green Volunteers Standard Application Form*, fill in the proper application form, pay the required deposit or membership fee and comply with other requirements. Once accepted, don't miss an opportunity by not paying a deposit on time. Inquire about the fastest method to transfer funds: by international telegraph money order, credit card, money wire from bank to bank, etc.

6) **Contact many projects and organisations.** Select the projects well in advance. Properly plan your vacation or time off, find the best air fares and select the best research period. Get detailed information on what to expect: the type of work, accommodation, food, climate, clothing and equipment necessary, etc. Owing to a lack of space this information is not included in the *Green Volunteers* guide. This guide aims to give a general overview of a given project or organisation. Do not show up at a project location without having applied first and having been accepted and confirmed. Most projects have limited positions, lodging and personnel. Very rarely are they equipped to take on an unexpected volunteer. If you want to do so, because you were already travelling in a certain area, do not be disappointed if you are rejected.

14

IMPORTANT NOTE AND WARNING

The Editor and Publisher of *Green Volunteers* has decided, both in order to offer prospective volunteers the widest possible choice and most valid conservation instrument, to cite, whenever possible, small projects and organisations, particularly in developing countries, for the following reasons:

1) **Without *Green Volunteers* many small projects and organisations would not be able to receive volunteers** from developed nations. We think that we should help as best as we can this conservation potential, particularly if it comes directly from local organisations, without an input from large organisations from our side of the world.

2) **Prospective volunteers**, by purchasing this guide, **expect to find something different and unique** from what is normally offered by large organisations in developed countries.

3) **Often small projects require non-paying and long-term volunteers**, which is what many of *Green Volunteers* readers expect. These opportunities are also usually offered at extremely affordable costs to the volunteers, which is not the case of projects offered from large organisations, which are often expensive and don't allow long-term volunteering.

BEFORE JOINING PROJECTS AND ORGANISATIONS, PROSPECTIVE VOLUNTEERS SHOULD CAREFULLY READ THE FOLLOWING CONSIDERATIONS AND WARNINGS:

1) **Because of obvious cost reasons**, which would then reflect on the cover price, **the Editor and Publisher cannot personally visit every project** listed in this guide but have to trust what projects and organisations (or the websites or previous volunteers) declare.

15

2) **Small projects and organisations**, particularly in developing countries, mainly because of shortage of funding or qualified personnel or because of conflicts with local populations and/or local authorities, **often change their programmes or even interrupt their activities without informing the Editor and Publisher of** *Green Volunteers*.

3) **Before joining a project volunteers should verify the validity of what is declared** on the project website (if one exists) or in this guide.

4) **Prospective volunteers should exchange frequent e-mails**, or even fax or phone calls, **with project leaders** and ensure that communication is always prompt and clear. They should also confirm the project details, such as the living, working and safety conditions, prior to departure.

5) **Prospective volunteers to any project should ask names** and addresses **of previous volunteers and correspond with them** to further verify the conditions of the projects.

6) **Volunteers should never join a project by going directly to the location** without previous correspondence and verification of existing conditions.

7) **Prospective volunteers should read carefully the WARNING on the third page of this book.**

ORGANISATION LIST

À PAS DE LOUP 'VOLUNTEERS FOR NATURE'

12, rue Malautières
26 220 Dieulefit France
Tel.: ++33 (4) 7546 8018
Fax: ++33 (4) 7546 8018
E-mail: info@apasdeloup.org
www.apasdeloup.org

Desc.: À Pas de Loup is a conservation volunteering organisation founded in 1994. Its objectives are to support local organisations in both developing and executing their schemes of nature conservation and to improve their local natural environment. 250 volunteers work in the field each year. During an assignment, volunteers are monitored by local staff to ensure quality results. À Pas de Loup volunteers are required to pay only for transportation and living costs.

Spp.: Some projects are wildlife related (seals, elephants, wolves, turtles), others are related to vegetation or reforestation (in France and in Africa).

Hab.: Coastal Mediterranean, African savannah and tropical forests.

Loc.: Europe, Africa and South America.

Dur.: From 1 to 6 weeks.

Per.: In Europe in the summer, year round elsewhere.

Age: Min. 18.

Qualif.: No qualifications required.

Work: Depends on the project, often is mostly manual, such as work planting trees in Togo or cutting young trees for recovering the Grouse habitats in the Alps. Scientific observation is also involved, such as of birds migration or turtles monitoring. Leisure activities and ecotours are also planned.

Lang.: English, French, Spanish, Italian.

Accom.: Always very simple; in a campsite or in local houses.

Cost : Volunteers must pay for travel and food and must join the organisation (EUR 20).

Applic.: Send CV with letter explaining interests and intents.

AFRICAN CONSERVATION EXPERIENCE

P.O. Box 206
Faversham, Kent. ME13 8WZ UK
Tel.: ++44 (1795) 590 105 – (870) 241 5816 (from the UK only)
Fax: ++44 (1795) 590 105
E-mail: info@conservationafrica.net
www.conservationafrica.net

Desc.: The organisation promotes Educational Work Experiences with conservationists, game rangers and biologists. Applicants may attend an optional Open Day to gain first hand information on the Game Reserves and Conservation Projects.

Spp.: Large and small game, including mammals, reptiles, birds, marine and freshwater life, plants.

Hab.: Sub-tropical coasts, seas, mountains; southern African savannah, plains, bushveld; semi-desert, fresh water marshes, wetlands; coastal lowlands, mountain ranges.

Loc.: South Africa, Zimbabwe, Botswana.

Travel: All travel arrangements included in the package.

Dur.: 4 – 12 weeks.

Per.: Year round.

L.term: Only in exceptional circumstances and by special arrangement.

Age: Min. 17, no maximum. Reasonably fit and healthy.

Work: Varies with Reserves. May include relocation or collaring of rhinos and elephants; capturing, tagging, releasing and game counts; animal monitoring and habituation. Whale and dolphin, seal and seabird research projects. Use of horses on conservation programmes. Volunteers usually work as part of a team under the supervision of experienced co-ordinators.

Lang.: English.

Accom.: Shared house in staff accommodation.

Cost: Approx. GB£2,700–4,000 (US$5,000–7,300); inquire for details.

Applic.: Request a free Application Pack.

Notes: Essential qualification required is enthusiasm for conservation and must be reasonably physically fit.

THE AMERICAN BEAR ASSOCIATION
The Vince Shute Wildlife Sanctuary
P.O. BOX 77, Orr, Minnesota 55771 USA
Tel.: ++1 (218) 757 0172
E-mail: bears@americanbears.org
www.americanbear.org

Desc.: This non-profit organisation is dedicated to promoting the well-being of the black bear, other wildlife and all natural resources through education and research. The Vince Shute Wildlife Sanctuary is the best place in North America to observe and photograph wild black bears. The VSWS features environmental education, conservation efforts, and wildlife co-existence.

Spp.: American black bear (*Ursus americanus*).

Hab.: Forest.

Loc.: Northwoods of Minnesota, USA.

Travel: Airplane to Duluth, Minnesota.

Dur.: Volunteers min. 1 week max. 4 months; interns (U.S. citizens or residents only) min.8 weeks max. 14 weeks.

Per.: Summer.

L.term: Volunteers can stay up to 4 months with director's approval.

Qualif.: All volunteers must read the Volunteer Handbook and complete a liability waiver. When possible, jobs will be matched to the specific interests and skills of the volunteer. Students are encouraged to apply.

Work: Greeting and visiting with visitors on and off the viewing platform, interpreting bear behaviour to visitors, assisting in construction projects, conducting daily clean-up chores, cooking, completing routine maintenance projects, grounds-keeping, maintaining records on bear activity, etc.

Lang.: English.

Accom.: All services available in the town of Orr. Campgrounds and numerous resorts are at nearby Pelican Lake. On-site lodging may be possible.

Cost: Volunteers are responsible for off-site lodging and extras.

Applic.: Contact the Association for more information.

APPALACHIAN TRAIL CONSERVANCY

P.O. Box 174
Blacksburg,
Virginia 24063 USA
Tel.: ++1 (540) 953 3571
Fax: ++1 (540) 552 4376
E-mail: crews@appalachiantrail.org
www.appalachiantrail.org

Desc.: The Appalachian Trail is America's best-known long-distance trail. Each year over 400 volunteers help with trail construction and rehabilitation. Volunteers can enjoy great scenery, and are provided with food, lodging, tools, equipment, training, and the opportunity for lots of fun.

Hab.: Appalachian Mountain Range.

Loc.: Great Smoky Mountains National Park, Southwest Virginia, Pennsylvania, Maine, and Vermont, USA.

Travel: Detailed access directions to base camp are provided.

Dur.: From 1 to 6 weeks.

Per.: May through October.

L.term: Volunteers can work up to 6 weeks.

Age: Min. 18.

Qualif.: Enthusiasm, good health, physical vigour, and adaptability. Willingness to follow instructions and safety rules and to share equally in camp chores. Experience is not necessary.

Work: Trail work is hard, physical labour, with hand tools. The crews work 8-hour days, rain or shine, hot or cold, regardless of black flies, mosquitoes, and other insects.

Lang.: English.

Accom.: Rustic cabins at base camp and tents out in the field.

Cost: Only transportation to base camp. Most expenses are covered including shelter, food, transportation to and from work projects, tools, safety equipment, and group camping gear. Crew members need to bring work clothing, sturdy boots, and their own basic camping gear.

Applic.: Download application form and see detailed Crews Programs in the 'Volunteers section' ('Trail Crews' page) on the website.

Notes: International applicants are responsible for necessary visas. Weather conditions can vary from very hot to below freezing.

ARCAS – Asociaciòn de Rescate y Conservaciòn de Vida Silvestre

4 Ave. 2-47, Sector B5, Zona 11, San Cristobal Guatemala
Tel./Fax: ++(502)2478 4096 – 2480 7270
E-mail: arcas@intelnet.net.gt – arcaspeten@intelnet.net.gt
www.arcasguatemala.com

Desc.: ARCAS'S flagship project is its Wildlife Rescue and Rehabilitation Centre, established in 1990, in order to rescue, rehabilitate and release wild animals confiscated from traffickers. It releases 300–600 animals of 35+ species per year into the Mayan Biosphere Reserve (MBR). The project is also a focal point for environmental education and awareness-raising in the MBR through its Environmental Education and Interpretation Centre. ARCAS' second big project is the Hawaii Sea Turtle Conservation Program on the Pacific coast of the country. The primary conservation activity at Hawaii is the collection and incubation of as many sea turtle eggs as possible. The Hawaii Program also includes a caiman and iguana breeding programme, mangrove reforestation, community development and environmental education activities. In 2003, ARCAS began co-managing the Cerro Alux Cloud Forest Reserve on the outskirts of Guatemala City. There, is carried out environmental education, research and conservation activities.

Spp.: The centre receives many different species from the MBR, which include: birds (parrots, scarlet macaws, toucans, aracaries), mammals (spider and howler monkeys, raccoons, coatimundis, pacas, margays, kinkajous, peccaries, bairds tapirs, jaguars) and reptiles (iguanas, turtles, crocodiles, caimans). The seaturtles are: Olive Ridley, Leatherback.

Hab.: Tropical forest, tropical beach, mangrove coastal wetland.

Loc.: The Wildlife Rescue Centre is near the city of Flores; the Seaturtle Conservation Project is on the Pacific Coast of Gutemala.

Travel: Airplane to Guatemala City, then bus or plane to Flores or bus to Monterrico, then by boat to the projects.

Dur.: For generic volunteers min. 1 week. For internships or research projects, min. 1 month.

Per.: Year round for the Rescue Centre. Seaturtle Nesting is July - December.

Age: Min. 18.

L.term.: Volunteers can stay for as long as they want. Volunteers can also spend some time in each project.

Qualif.: No specific skills required for generic volunteers. Candidates for internships or research projects must be students or researchers in a conservation related field.

Work: Volunteers help cleaning cages and feeding and caring for the animals. Special projects may include: observing the animals in the rehabilitation area, building cages, animal releases, etc. Research and internship opportunities are in the area of wildlife veterinary medicine, wildlife rehabilitation, nutrition, sea turtle conservation and environmental education. At Hawaii volunteers assist in patrolling beaches at night in search of nesting sea turtles, collection and burial of eggs in the hatcheries and collection of data. Volunteers can also take part in caiman breeding, mangrove reforestation, construction and upkeep of park facilities and environmental educational activities in area schools. Everyone is expected to help in house cleaning and dish washing.

Lang.: English, basic Spanish is highly desirable.

Accom.: Volunteers live in a confortable house with toilet and kitchen facilities and electricity (110V, 12 V in Peten). Sheets are provided, own sleeping bag useful in cooler months (Dec. – Feb.), mosquito net is otional.

Cost: US$100/week for room and board at the Rescue Center. US$50/week for room at the Seaturtle Project. Volunteers must pay all travel expenses.

Agents: Contact ARCAS directly for up-to-date information.

Applic.: No application needed. For the research and internship opportunities candidates shouold contact ARCAS directly.

Notes: Apart from the projects mentioned above, ARCAS carries out a range of other conservation and community development projects in which volunteers are always needed. Contact ARCAS for more information.

ASVO – Asociacion de Voluntarios para el Servicio en las Areas Protegidas

Programa de Voluntariado
P.O. Box 11384–1000 San José Costa Rica
Tel.: ++(506) 258 4430 – Tel./Fax: ++(506) 233 4989
E-mail: info@asvocr.org – lmatarrita@asvocr.com – alopez@asvocr.com
www.asvocr.org

Desc.: ASVO is the organisation providing volunteers to Costa Rican National Parks and Reserves. Volunteers are needed for research, construction and maintenance work, english teaching, tourist assistance and interpretation. They can also participate in seaturtle conservation programmes on the coasts. Biology or Ecology students can participate into special projects, such as "reintroduction of monkeys" in a given area.

Spp.: Primates, tropical birds and mammals, sea turtles.

Hab.: Tropical coast, rainforest, cloud forest, beaches.

Loc.: Parks and Reserves throughout Costa Rica.

Dur.: Min. 30 days, 2 months for special projects. Volunteers who stay at least 30 days can work in two different projects.

Per.: Year round.

L.term: Inquire with organisation.

Age: Min. 18.

Qualif.: Flexibility, motivation, a good physical condition and ability to tolerate the tropical climate. Two reference letters by Costa Rica residents or by organisations in the home country are required along with a copy of passport and two photos. Special qualifications are necessary for some research projects.

Work: Various tasks: construction and maintainance of park structures and trails, providing information to tourists, assisting in research on biodiversity or in wildlife surveys, etc.

Lang.: Spanish. Inquire for English.

Acc.: In general in rangers' lodges.

Cost: Approx. US$15/day for room and board. Application fee of US$30

Applic.: Contact ASVO.

Notes: Health and repatriation insurance required.

BIOSPHERE EXPEDITIONS

Sprat's Water, near Carlton Colville,
The Broads National Park, Suffolk NR33 8BP UK
Tel.: ++44 (870) 446 0801
Fax: ++44 (870) 446 0809
E-mail: info@biosphere-expeditions.org
www.biosphere-expeditions.org

Desc.:	Worldwide wildlife conservation expeditions. The projects are not tours, or photographic excursions, but genuine expeditions with real conservation content. Adventure, remote locations, different cultures and people are part and parcel of these expeditions, but also the knowledge for paticipants to play an active role in conserving part of the planet's biosphere.
Spp.:	Large cats, primates, whales, dolphins, rainforest birds, etc.
Hab.:	Rainforest, desert, savannah, marine, mountains, etc.
Loc ·	Worldwide
Travel:	Volunteers are met in-country and taken to the project area.
Dur.:	Min. 2 weeks up to 3 months.
Per.:	Year round.
L.term:	Volunteers can join an expedition for several months.
Age:	No age restrictions. Minors with parents' consent.
Qualif.:	No specific skills or fitness required. Disabled/minority expeditioners are encouraged.
Work:	Expect to work (e.g., surveying, tracking, identification) for several hours a day, often independently, but never alone. All necessary training is given and a Biosphere Expeditions leader is always present.
Lang.:	English.
Accom.:	Varies from B&B to research stations to tent camps.
Cost:	Variable and depending on project. Expedition contributions start from GB£ 990 (approx. EUR1,400/US$1900) for 2 weeks, for longer periods discounts are available.
Agents:	Offices in Germany, France, N.America, Australia. See website.
Applic.:	Contact organisation for more details and application forms.

LES BLONGIOS
La Nature en Chantiers
Maison de la Nature et de l'Environnement
23 rue Gosselet, 59000 Lille   France
Tel.: ++33 (3) 2053 98 85 – Fax: ++33 (3) 2086 15 56
E-mail: lesblongios@free.fr
http://lesblongios.free.fr

Desc.: Les "Blongios" (*Ixobrychus minutus*) is an NGO which organizes more than 30 workcamps in natural reserves in France and Northern Europe.

Loc.: Natural reserves with a management plan in France and in Northern Europe (The Netherlands, Great Britain, Ireland, Belgium).

Travel: Depends on the location, details on the website.

Dur.: From one week-end to one month.

Per.: Year round.

Age: Min. 18.

Qualif.: No qualifications required.

Work: Maintenance work in natural reserves: habitat restoration (cutting bushes to restore natural sites, digging ponds for amphibians), trail blazing and building board walks, bulding visitor centers.

Lang.: French, English.

Accom.: In huts, lodges or hostels near naturals reserves. Cooking and dish-washing is in the group's responsibility.

Cost: Just travel to the site. Room, accommodation and meals are provided. Membership EUR20 (EUR15 for students or unemployed).

Applic.: Via e-mail or with the online application form available in various languages.

Notes: All the available workcamp locations are on the website.

BLUE VENTURES

52 Avenue
London N6 5DR   UK
Tel.: ++44 (208) 341 9819 — Fax: ++44 (208) 341 4821
E-mail:enquiries@blueventures.org
www.blueventures.org

Desc.: Blue Ventures co-ordinates expeditions of marine scientists and volunteers, working hand-in-hand with local biologists, marine institutes, NGOs, and communities whose livelihoods depend on coral reefs, to carry out research, environmental awareness and conservation programmes at threatened reef habitats around the world. Blue Ventures continues to offer opportunities and field experiences to people wanting to become actively involved in marine conservation, whether a beginner or an expert. The teams are made up of dynamic, enthusiastic and committed volunteers, coming from a wide range of backgrounds and cultures.

Spp.: Tropical marine (coral reef) species.

Hab.: Tropical coastal seas.

Loc.: Madagascar.

Dur.: Min. 3 weeks.

Per.: Year round.

L.term: Enquire with organisation.

Age: Min. 18.

Qualif.: Blue Ventures offers: Scuba training up to PADI Advanced Open Water (or up to Divemaster on site if required).

Work: Comprehensive marine science training course, learning from international team of marine biologists. Relaxed learning environment, maximum number of 18 volunteers per expedition. Staff to volunteer ratio of 1:2.

Lang.: English.

Accom.: Comfortable eco-cabins plus excellent food provided.

Cost: GB£1,050 - 1,950 (approx. US$1,800 - 3,200), including food, accommodation, equipment and training. Flights not included.

Applic.: Call or write to Blue Ventures for an application form.

27

BRATHAY EXPLORATION GROUP

Brathay Hall
Ambleside, Cumbria LA22 OHP   UK
Tel./Fax: ++44 (15394) 33 942
E-mail: admin@brathayexploration.org.uk
www.brathayexploration.org.uk

Desc.: The Brathay Exploration Group, a non-profit organisation founded in 1947, runs 10–15 expeditions each year in remote areas all over the world. Projects concern field sciences from glaciology to ornithology. They are lead by former experienced volunteers.

Hab.: Mountain, tropical rainforest, desert.

Loc.: Europe, Africa, India.

Dur.: 2–4 weeks.

Per.: July to August.

L.term: Inquire with organisation.

Age: Min.15, max. 25.

Qualif.: No special qualification or prior field experience is required, but self-motivation and a sense of humour are needed.

Lang.: English.

Cost: GB£395–1,170 (approx.EUR600–1,700) for European expeditions, GB£1,000–1,600 (approx. EUR1,500–2,500) for worldwide expeditions.

Applic.: Ask for application form and medical questionnaire, to be sent in with a deposit.

Notes: Each expedition can be joined by 20 or less volunteers. Members of the Brathay Exploration Group join a club with benefits such as the use of a mountain hut, an information magazine, discounts. The Brathay Exploration Group also offers courses in Mountain First Aid and Leader Training. Further information is available from the website.

BTCV

Sedum House
Mallard Way
Potteric Carr, Doncaster, DN4 8DB UK
Tel.: +44 (1302) 388 883 Fax: +44 (1302) 311 531
E-mail: information@btcv.org.uk International@btcv.org.uk
www.btcv.org.uk

Desc.: BTCV, formerly know as the 'British Trust for Conservation Volunteers' was founded in 1959 under the name Conservation Corps and is now the largest practical conservation organisation in the UK. BTCV provides information and advice on urban and rural projects, organises conservation holidays, weekend and weekday projects and supports around 2,500 community groups.

Spp.: Colobus monkeys, crocodiles, sea turtles, vultures, otters.

Hab.: Wetlands, woodlands, grasslands, rainforests, desert, mountains, islands, coastline.

Loc.: UK, USA, Albania, Bulgaria, Cameroon, China, Estonia, Germany, Iceland, Italy, Japan, Kenya, Lesotho, Nepal, New Zealand, Portugal, South Africa.

Dur.: 1 day to 3 weeks.

Per.: Year round.

L.term: Volunteer Officer positions available (min. 3 months).

Age: Under 18 with parental consent for UK projects; min. 18 for international projects.

Qualif.: Some international expeditions require reasonable fitness.

Work: Diverse, e.g. UK: variety including restoring paths and dry stone walls or hedgelaying. International: revegetation, construction, sustainable development, habitat management or animal research.

Lang.: English. Other languages encountered with various projects.

Cost: From GB£60 (approx. US$90) for UK projects; GB£375–1,450 (approx. US$730–2,800) for overseas expeditions.

Applic.: GB£50-100 deposit required (approx. US$100-200).

Notes: Conservation Holidays Brochure available on request.

Selected projects:

Mysterious Japan and its Wondrous Wetlands, Hokkaido, Japan
Wild Bird Rehabilitation, Bulgaria
Skaftafell National Park, Iceland

CARAPAX – European Center for Conservation of Chelonians

International RANA Foundation
C.P. 34 – Località Le Venelle
58024 Massa Marittima (Grosseto) Italy
Tel.: ++39 (0566) 940 083 – Fax: ++39 (0566) 902 387
E-mail: volunteers@carapax.org – carapax@cometanet.it
www.carapax.org

Desc.:	The Carapax Center conducts research and works towards the recovery and reintroduction of tortoises. Carapax reintroduces animals saved from captivity (private donations to the centre) and from illegal sale (confiscated by the authorities) back to nature. Once set free in natural reserves, the tortoises are marked and followed using radio-tracking techniques or by local environmental organisations or responsible authorities.
Spp.:	Mediterranean tortoises and fresh water turtles or terrapins. *Testudo hermanni spp., T. marginata, T. graeca.*
Loc.:	Central Italy, in the Tuscany region, 18 km from the west coast.
Travel:	Airplane to Rome, train to Grosseto and Follonica, then bus to Massa Marittima where Carapax staff will pick up volunteers.
Dur.:	Min. 2 weeks.
Per.:	Mid-April to mid-October.
Age:	Min. 18.
Qualif.:	Experience is not required; motivation and interest is important.
Work:	5 days a week.Management of infrastructure (upkeep, build or repair); care of animals (feed, sometimes help with veterinary care, scrupulously respecting hygiene standards); provide information to the public (receive and guide visitors); scientific research inside and outside the centre.
Lang.:	English, Italian, German, French, Dutch.
Accom.:	In wooden chalets (1 room; 6 beds) with electricity. There are outdoor showers, toilets and a kitchen protected by a roof.
Cost:	Cost for participation EUR189 + EUR30 membership; to pay at least 10 days before arrival (for the assicuration).
Applic.:	Contact Carapax directly for an application form.
Notes:	Volunteers must carry health and accident insurance.

CENTRE FOR ALTERNATIVE TECHNOLOGY

Machynlleth, Powys
SY20 9AZ Wales UK
Tel.: ++44 (1654) 705 950
Fax: ++44 (1654) 702 782
E-mail: info@cat.org.uk
www.cat.org.uk

Desc.: The Centre for Alternative Technology, open to the public since 1975, has working displays of wind, water and solar power, low energy buildings, organic farming and alternative sewage systems. It offers residential courses on topics such as water power, bird watching, organic gardening and rustic furniture making. The Centre also hosts an information service and a bookshop (with mail-order service). The Centre receives 80,000 visitors per year.

Loc.: Wales, Great Britain.

Dur.: Short-term volunteer programme of 1–2 weeks.

Per.: Specified weeks between March and September inclusive.

L.term: A limited number of long-term volunteers work in specific departments such as engineering, building, gardening and information for 6 months. Prospective long-term volunteers must stay for a 'trial' week before any offer of a placement can be made.

Age.: Min. 18.

Qualif.: Particular skills are not needed for short-term volunteers. Certain skills and previous experience may be criteria for the selection of long-term volunteers, as places are limited.

Lang.: English.

Cost: Volunteers contribute GB£10 (EUR15) per day for the cost of room and board. Accommodation and food are provided.

Agents: Contact the Centre directly.

Applic.: Application forms for the short-term volunteer programme are published in January. Early booking is necessary. Contact the Centre for details on the long-term volunteer programme.

CHANTIERS DE JEUNES PROVENCE CôTE D'AZUR

La Maison des Chantiers La Ferme Giaume
7 Avenue Pierre de Coubertin
06150 Cannes la Bocca France
Tel.: ++33 (4) 93 478969 – Fax: ++33 (4) 93 481201
E-mail: cjpca@club-internet.fr
www.cjpca.fr.st

Desc.:   This organisation offers programmes for teenagers who want to experience community life, work for heritage protection, and spend an unusual summer holiday.

Loc.:   St. Marguerite Island, Cannes, in the Region of Provence, France, and in the region of Piedmont, Italy.

Dur.:   2 weeks.

Per.:   Summer, but also year round during school holidays.

Age: Min. 13, max. 17.

Qualif.:   No qualifications necessary.

Lang.:   French.

Cost: Approx. EUR 350 (approx. GB£ 220).

Agents: Contact the organisation directly.

Work: Different for each project, from simple construction to trail maintenance.

Applic.:   Call or e-mail the organisation to receive an application form.

CORAL CAY CONSERVATION (CCC)

40-42 Osnaburgh Street
London NW1 3ND   UK
Tel.: ++44 (870) 750 0668 – Fax: ++44 (870) 750 0667
E-mail: info@coralcay.org
www.coralcay.org

Desc.: CCC is an organisation that sends teams of Volunteers to survey some of the world's most endangered coral reefs and tropical forests. Since 1986, thousands of Volunteers of all ages have participated on CCC expeditions throughout the Asia-Pacific and Caribbean. Volunteers play a crucial role in the conservation of threatened tropical environments through the collection of scientific data, which is used to help formulate sustainable management recommendations. To date, CCC has helped to establish numerous marine reserves and wildlife sanctuaries. Volunteers can be doing anything from recording butterflies in the Philippines rainforest to surveying spectacular corals in Fiji.

Spp.: Terrestrial and marine organisms.

Hab.: Coral reefs and tropical rainforests.

Loc.: Papua New Guinea, Philippines, Fiji and Tobago.

Dur.: Min. 3 weeks.

Per.: Year round.

L term: Inquire with organisation.

Age: Min. 16.

Qualif.: CCC offers: 1 Scuba Training week, 2 Skills Development weeks and numerous Conservation weeks. PADI Open Water divers are trained up to Advanced Open Water (AOW). PADI AOW divers are accepted directly onto the Skills development Programme.

Work: Training in marine and/or terrestrial ecology and survey techniques. Reef and forest data collection.

Lang.: English.

Accom.: Basic on-site accommodation provided.

Cost: Start at GB£600 (US$1,000). Prices include food, accommodation, equipment and training. Flights not included.

Applic.: Visit www.coralcay.org or call for an application form.

Notes: Monthly presentations are organised throughout the UK.

COTRAVAUX

11 Rue de Clichy
75009 Paris
France
Tel.: ++33 (1) 4874 7920 – Fax: ++33 (1) 4874 1401
E-mail: informations@cotravaux.org
www.cotravaux.org - www.cotravaux.free.fr

Desc.:	Cotravaux coordinates 12 French workcamps. Its role is to promote voluntary work and community projects concerning environmental protection, monument restoration and social projects. The organisation offers many workcamps in different regions of France. Many of the organisations members of Cotravaux work with foreign partners.
Loc.:	France and worldwide.
Dur.:	2–3 weeks.
Per.:	Year round; most projects run between June and October.
L.term:	Certain projects offer 3-12 months volunteering.
Age.:	Min. 18.
Qualif.:	No specific skills needed.
Lang.:	A few projects require French.
Cost:	Volunteers must pay for their own transportation to the camps. Room and board provided (some camps require a daily contribution).
Agents:	Some partner organisations (inquire with Cotravaux).
Applic.:	Contact Cotravaux by fax or mail to obtain the list of partner workcamps in France or other specific countries.
Notes:	A list of Cotravaux member organisations can be obtained by the website of Jeunesse et Réconstruction, one of the largest French volunteering organisations. Their website is www.volontariat.org, while the list of Cotravaux members is in the website www.cotravaux.org.

CTS – Centro Turistico Studentesco e Giovanile
Sezione Ambiente
Via Albalonga 3
00183 Roma Italy
Tel.: ++39 (06) 6496 0306 – Fax: ++39 (06) 6496 0335
E-mail: ambiente@cts.it
www.ctsambiente.it

Desc.: Founded in1974, CTS is now the largest youth association in Italy. Its Environmental Department organises research activities, ecotourism and environmental education programmes, training courses and workshops. It also publishes books and produces videos on environmental subjects. Projects concern endangered species, animal behaviour, habitat protection, and wildlife management.

Spp.: Bears, dolphins, whales, sea turtles, wolves, chamois.

Hab.: Alpine, Mediterranean Sea and coast, temperate forest, lagoons.

Loc.: Italian Alps, Appennines, Mediterranean coasts and islands, often inside protected areas.

Dur.: Depends on the project; average period is 6–15 days.

Per.: Year round.

L.term: Inquire with organisation.

Age: Min.18. Younger members with parental and CTS consent.

Qualif.: Physically fit, flexible, cooperative. Able to swim for marine projects.

Cost: EUR250–700 (approx. GB£170–450), excluding food and transportation.

Lang.: Italian, English.

Agents: CTS offices are throughout Italy and in London, Paris, Madrid, Barcelona and New York.

Applic.: Membership is required to join the expeditions (EUR 28).

Notes: CTS cooperates with organisations such as the Ecovolunteer Network (see organisation list).

(CVA) Conservation Volunteers Australia / Conservation Volunteers New Zealand

Booking Office   P.O. Box 423, Ballarat 3353
Victoria Australia
Tel.: ++61 (3) 5330 2600 – Fax: ++61 (3) 5330 2922 (2655)
E-mail: bookings@conservationvolunteers.com.au
www.conservationvolunteers.com.au – www.conservationvolunteers.co.nz

---

Desc.:	Founded in 1982, CVA is a non-profit organisation dedicated to practical conservation. CVA's activities concern environmental topics such as salinity, soil erosion, biodiversity and endangered species. Volunteers must be aged 18 – 70. Each team is supervised by a Conservation Volunteers Team Leader with a vehicle, first-aid equipment, hand tools and cooking equipment. CVA projects offer the opportunity to see parts of Australia, off the regular track, as well as to make international friendships through team activities. In 2006, Conservation Volunteers opened a new branch – Conservation Volunteers New Zealand.
Spp.:	Turtles, penguins, birds, koalas, wallabies, vegetation.
Hab.:	Rivers, coasts, dryland, swamps.
Loc.:	Various locations in Australia and New Zealand.
Dur.:	4 – 6 weeks.
Per.:	Year round.
L.term:	Inquire with organisation.
Age:	Min. 18.
Qualif.:	Experience and qualifications related to the environment are welcome but not essential.
Lang.:	English.
Cost:	AUS$1,400 (approx. EUR 840/US$1070) for 6 weeks, including food, accommodation and project-related transportation within Australia or New Zealand.
Applic.:	Call, write or e-mail Conservation Volunteers Bookings Office for information. Applications are accepted on-line.

CVG – Conservation Volunteers Greece

Veranzerou 15,
10677 Athens   Greece
Tel.: ++30 (210) 3825 506
Fax: ++30 (210) 3814 682
E-mail: 1987@cvgpeep.gr / marina@cvgpeep.gr
www.cvgpeep.gr

Desc.:	Summer work camps in Greece. These projects usually take place in remote areas of Greece in co-operation with Forestry Departments, local authorities, cultural associations, etc. Intercultural exchanges and conservation work allow young people to contribute to a hosting community. CVG is also involved in European Voluntary Service (EVS) projects.
Spp.:	Various: birds of prey, forest flora and fauna.
Hab.:	Mediterranean ecosystems, forests and wetlands.
Loc.:	Greece, usually remote areas.
Travel:	Contact the organisations for specific projects.
Dur.:	2–3 weeks; fixed dates are provided for every project.
Per.:	Summer.
Age:	Min. 18.
Work:	Nature conservation (forest-fire protection, tree-planting, footpath maintenance, construction and placement of signs), cultural heritage (restoration of traditional buildings, ancient cobbled-stone footpaths and help in archaeological digs) or social benefit (restoration of school buildings, construction of playgrounds). Work is 5 – 6 hours/day, 6 days/week.
Lang.:	English.
Accom.:	Facilities are modest. Hosting is usually in schools and community or youth centres. Volunteers should bring along a sleeping bag and sleeping mat. Household chores involved.
Cost:	Approx. EUR120 (approx. GB£80).
Agents:	The Alliance of European Voluntary Service Organisations (www.alliance-network.org).
Applic.:	A Volunteer Exchange Form to apply is provided by Alliance partner organisations or CVG web site.

EARTHWATCH

3 Clock Tower Place – Suite 100, Box 75
Maynard, MA 01754   USA
Tel.: ++1 (978) 461 0081 – 1 (800) 776 0188 (toll free in US/Canada)
Fax: ++1 (978) 461 2332
E-mail: info@earthwatch.org
www.earthwatch.org

Desc.:   Earthwatch is an international charity that supports around 130 scientific field research projects in 50 countries. All projects are open to paying volunteers who work alongside leading scientists. Volunteers work as part of a team of people from all corners of the world with one thing in common — a commitment to doing something to protect the environment. From tracking crocodiles in the Zambesi river valley, to studying dynamic glaciers in Iceland or to observing dolphin behaviour in New Zealand, Earthwatch has a wide range of projects around the globe.

Spp.:   Jaguars, chimpanzees, mountain lions, dolphins, birds, snakes, rhinos, crocodiles, and many others.

Hab.:   Rainforest, desert, savannah, tropical and temperate seas and coasts, arctic, antarctic, sub-arctic, alpine.

Loc.:   The Americas, Europe, Africa, Asia, Australia, Antarctica.

Dur.:   3 days to 3 weeks.

Per.:   Year round.

Age: Min. 18. Although there are special teams for teenagers and families.

Qualif.:   No specific qualifications.

Lang.:   English.

Cost: Approx. UK£150—1,995 (US$280—3,500), inc. accomodation, food, training, medical evacuation and the offsetting of greenhouse gas emissions.

Agents: Earthwatch Europe(UK), Australia and Japan (see website).

Applic.:   E-mail or call the nearest office for more information.

Notes: Grants are available for students and teachers.

Selected Projects:

Blach Rhino, Kenya
Spanish Dolphins, Spain

THE ECOVOLUNTEER NETWORK

Central Office
Meyersweg 29, 7553 AX Hengelo The Netherlands
Tel.: ++31 (74) 250 8250
Fax: ++31 (74) 250 6572
E-mail: info@ecovolunteer.org
www.ecovolunteer.org

Desc.:	About 30 projects offer hands-on experience in wildlife conservation and research, assisting in fieldwork, monitoring research and in wildlife rescue and rehabilitation centres. Volunteers work with local conservationists, researchers and rangers and are expected to adapt to local culture and food. Minimum 77-80% of the price goes to projects.
Spp.:	African wild dogs, wolves, bears, rhinos, elephants, gibbons, orang-utans, beavers, otters, dolphins, whales, seals, turtles, birds, rare breeds of dogs, horses and sheep, various species in wildlife rescue centres.
Hab.:	Ranging from subarctic to tropical rainforest.
Loc.:	Worldwide.
Dur.:	Min. 1, 2, 3 or 4 weeks, depending on projects.
Per.:	Some projects are seasonal, others are year round.
L.term:	Possible with many projects, especially for academic research.
Age:	Most projects min. 18; some projects min. 20. Some projects allow a parent with a minor.
Qualif.:	Variable. Physically fit and able to work independently.
Lang.:	English; some projects admit people who don't speak English, but French, Spanish or Portuguese.
Cost:	Variable Starting from EUR115 per week (approx. GB£80). See Ecovolunteer website .
Agents:	Agents in various countries are listed in the website.
Applic.:	Mail or fax the application form on www.ecovolunteer.org to the nearest agency, or ask the agency for a form in the preferred language.
Notes:	For projects and new agencies that would like to be included in the Ecovolunteer Network, contact the central office.

Selected Projects:

Brown Bear Project, Russia
Rhino Rescue Project, Swaziland
River Otter Project, Brazil

EUROPARC DEUTSCHLAND

Bundesgeschaftsstelle
Friedrichstrasse 60
D–10117 Berlin Germany
Tel.: ++49 (30) 2887 8820 – Fax: ++49 (30) 288 7882–16
E-mail: info@europarc-deutschland.de
freiwillige@europarc-deutschland.de (for VIP)
www.europarc-deutschland.de www.freiwillige-in-parks.de (for VIP)

Desc.: The German section of the EUROPARC was founded in 1991 to support protected areas in Germany. Europarc Deutschland works towards the promotion of environmental education as well as a system's plan of protected areas in Germany to preserve the natural heritage for future generations. Each year, there are about 40/60 volunteer placements in protected areas, most of them National Parks, through the project "Praktikum fuer Die Umwelt". The project is addressed to students who would like to contribute their knowledge and skills to the Parks. The Volunteers in Parks Programme (VIP) offers people of every age and qualification a variety of volunteer activities. The volunteers participate and enrich the work of the employees with their engagement and are important partners within the team in order to maintain the reserves.

Hab.: Temperate forest, coastal habitats, lakes, etc.

Loc.: Germany.

Dur.: 3–6 months for Praktikum; from a few hours to a few months for VIP.

Per.: April to October for Praktikum; year round for VIP.

L.term: Up to 6 months.

Age: Min. 18 for Praktikum; min. 14 for VIP.

Qualif.: Education, geography and biology backgrounds are advantageous. Sometimes field experience and a valid driver license are required. Interest in wildlife, nature conservation, environmental education.

Work: Environmental education, public relations, protection and monitoring of species and plants, environmental education, public relations.

Lang.: German.

Accom.: Always provided for Praktikum; provided in some parks for VIP.

Cost: No contributions; most of the positions are paid (for Praktikum).

Applic.: Deadline January for Praktikum. For information see: www.praktikum-fuer-die-umwelt.de. No deadline for VIP; for information contact the volunteer co-ordinators on www.freiwillige-in-parks.de

Notes: Mandatory work visa requirements for non-EU residents.

FRONTIER
50–52 Rivington Street
London EC2A 3QP UK
Tel.: ++44 (20) 7613 2422
Fax: ++44 (20) 7613 2992
E–mail: info@frontier.ac.uk
www.frontier.ac.uk

Desc.:	Frontier is an international non-profit organisation that carries out sustainable conservation and development projects in partnership with host-country institutions. Current projects are located in Cambodia, Ecuador, Fiji, India, Madagascar, Nepal, Nicaragua, Peru, and Tanzania. Volunteers can track lions and elephants across the savanna, dive with dolphins, sharks, and rays, teach English in a rural school, or learn to lead their own expedition. Full training is offered and volunteers can gain unique BTEC qualifications in Tropical Habitat Conservation or Expedition Management (biodiversity research). Participants on marine projects get free dive training to PADI Advanced Open Water and we offer teachers free TEFL training.
Hab.:	Rainforests, tropical forests, savannah, mangroves, coral reefs.
Loc.:	Cambodia, Ecuador, Fiji, India, Madagascar, Nepal, Nicaragua, Peru, Tanzania.
Dur.:	4 weeks and longer.
Per.:	Year round.
L.term:	Inquire with organisation.
Age:	Min. 17.
Qualif.:	Applicants must be enthusiastic and have a commitment to conservation and development issues in developing countries.
Work:	Biodiversity surveys, habitat mapping, socio-economic work with local communities.
Lang.:	English.
Cost:	Costs start from GB£695 (approx US$1,200), excluding flights and visa; contact Frontier for details.
Applic.:	Contact Frontier for an application form.

GEOGRAPHY OUTDOORS: THE CENTRE SUPPORTING FIELD RESEARCH, EXPLORATION AND OUTDOOR LEARNING

Royal Geographical Society with Institute of British Geographers
1 Kensington Gore, London SW7 2AR UK
Tel.: +44 (20) 7591 3030
Fax: +44 (20) 7591 3031
E-mail: go@rgs.org – www.rgs.org/je

Desc.:   Geography Outdoors: the Centre supporting fieldresearch, explroation and outdoor learning is an office oftheRoyal Geographical Society with IBG (Institute of British Geographers). It is primarily concerned with advising those who are planning their own expeditions, with an emphasis on field research projects overseas. The Centre provides information on all aspects of expedition planning and organises Explore: the annual RGS-IBG Expedition and Fieldwork Planning Seminar each November. A wide variety of resources are available on the website, including a directory listing over 100 organisations that regularly arrange expeditions from environmental research and conservation work to community projects and adventurous training. Guidelines are given on fund-raising to support participation in these ventures.

Notes: People who are thinking of organising their own field research project should e-mail: go@rgs.org.

GLOBAL SERVICE CORPS
Earth Island Institute
300 Broadway, Suite 28
San Francisco, California 94133–3312 USA
Tel.: ++1 (415) 788 3666 ext.128 – Fax: ++1 (415) 788 7324
E-mail: gsc@globalservicecorps.org
www.globalservicecorps.org

Desc.: Global Service Corps provides opportunities for adult volunteers to live and work on projects in developing nations. Volunteers do village-based community work in Africa and Southeast Asia.

Loc.: Tanzania, Thailand.

Dur.: Mini-projects 2 weeks; short term projects 3–4 weeks; long-term projects 5-8 weeks; internships 9 weeks.

Per.: Monthly, year round.

L.term: Most long-term volunteers participate on a short-term GSC trip and continue afterwards in their placement. The short-term project provides a good orientation to the country, area, organisations and people. Long-term volunteers pay an additional daily fee that covers room, board and supervision.

Age: Min. 18.

Qualif.: No specific skills needed beyond good English speaking skills.

Work: In Tanzania, volunteers help in implementing an organic farming project and in training local farmers in the methods of sustainable agriculture; other projects involve educating local students and community in HIV awareness and prevention. In Thailand, the work includes teaching English, healthcare in hospitals and rural clinics, and Buddhist immersion.

Lang.: English.

Cost: For Thailand 2-week project cost US$2,325 up to US$4,040 for 9 weeks. Tanzania 2-9 weeks project cost range from US$2,325 to US$4,040. Project fee covers all in-country expenses, except for personal items. Volunteers are required to provide round-trip international airfares for themselves as well as travel and medical insurance.

Applic.: Download and complete an application form from the GSC website. A CV and a 2–3 paragraph statement must be included with application as well as a US$150 refundable deposit.

GLOBAL VISION INTERNATIONAL

3 High Street, St Albans AL3 4ED UK
Tel.: ++44 (870) 608 8898 (UK) – ++1 (888) 653 6028 (toll free from N.America)
Fax: ++44 (1582) 834 002
E-mail: info@gvi.co.uk – info@gviusa.com
www.gvi.co.uk – www.gviusa.com

Desc.: Critical conservation and humanitarian projects in over 30 countries rely on GVI for volunteers, promotion and direct funding. GVI works locally with its partners to promote sustainable development through environment research, conservation and education. GVI volunteers benefit from exceptional support, training and a Careers Abroad job placement scheme. Projects include: marine research in Mexico and Seychelles; Amazonian and Costa Rican rainforest expeditions; research and exploration in Patagonia; predator research and marine studies in South Africa or Kenya; TEFL worldwide and in the UK; training as a safari field guide in South Africa; work in a primate sanctuary in Africa or Thailand; teaching in Guatemala, Peru, Honduras, Costa Rica.

Hab.: Rainforests, savannah, tropical coasts, coral reefs, glacial areas.

Loc.: 30 countries worldwide.

Dur.: 2 weeks - 2 years.

Per.: Year round.

L.term: Opportunities are available for who has completed a 10 week expedition, ranging from internships on an expedition or placements in National Parks and protected areas.

Age: Min. 18.

Qualif.: No qualifications are necessary as full training in the field is provided. Applicants must display an understanding of the aims of the project and cultural sensitivities.

Work: Data collection, biodiversity surveys, wildlife research, scuba diving surveys, teaching, construction, community volunteering.

Lang.: English.

Cost: From GB£595 (US$1,100), including food and accomodation, international flights are excluded.

Applic. Apply online.

GO XPLORE

Suite 7a Cowell Park, 47 Old Main Road, Hillcrest
Kwa-Zulu Natal South Africa
Tel.: ++27 (31) 765 1818
Fax: ++27 (31) 765 4781
E-mail: louise@goxploreafrica.com
www.goxploreafrica.com

Desc.: An opportunity to experience a real African adventure in the beautiful setting of Southern Africa in "big five" game farms, as well as working with people in rural communities.The opportunities suit the individual needs of each volunteer.

Spp.: Various species of African Mammals.

Hab.: Bushveld and savannah.

Loc.: Various areas around Africa, from the coastline to Kruger National Park.

Travel: Volunteers fly to the nearest local airport to the project.

Dur.: Varies from project to project; the main duration is 4 weeks.

Per.: Year round.

Age: Min.18.

Qualif.: No qualifications necessary, just a willingness to help and the desire to make a difference.

Work: The Wildlife volunteer work covers many broad spectrums which includes preparing the food and feeding the wild animals, hand rearing and bottle feeding the young animals (the lions and baboons in particular), cleaning the enclosures, general game farm management (alien plant eradication and bush clearing, etc.), working with the veterinarians to aid the sick, ill and injured animals. Some of the volunteers spend time learning about various conservation related topics. The humanitarian volunteer work offers volunteers a variety of local projects to participate in. From working at local AIDS Drop In Centres and hospices, to rural clinics and building projects.

Lang.: A minimum knowledge of basic English is required.

Accom.: Varies from project to project, always clean and comfortable!

Cost: Prices start from US$200 per week, which includes food accommodation, transfers to and from the local airport.

Agents: Volunteers must contact Go Xplore directly.

Applic.: On-line application form.

GREENFORCE

11–15 Betterton St. Covent Garden
London WC2H 9BP UK
Tel.: ++44 (20) 7470 8888
Fax: ++44 (20) 7379 0801
E-mail: info@greenforce.org
www.greenforce.org

Desc.: Greenforce works in fourteen countries around the globe on conservation and community projects. At the invitation of host country partners such as the WWF and the Wildlife Conservation Society mammal, plant and coral surveys are carried out as well as community restoration and sports work.

Hab.: Coastal, African Savannah, Amazon, tropical.

Loc.: Tanzania, Ecuador, Fiji, Bahamas, Brazil, Thailand, Egypt, Malta, Nepal/Tibet, India, Indonesia, Australia, Spain, South Africa.

Dur.: Two weeks to one year.

Per.: Year round.

L.term: Traineeships are available.

Age: Min. 17.

Qualif.: No scientific knowledge required; full training (including diving training to PADI EFR for marine projects) is provided.

Work: Conservation (land and marine) and community work.

Lang.: English.

Accom.: Varied from tents to grass huts (bures) to mud huts (bomas) to houses.

Cost: From GB£550 (approx.US$900).

Applic.: Online application form.

HELLENIC ORNITHOLOGICAL SOCIETY

Vas. Irakleiou 24
GR – 106 82 Athens Greece
Tel.: ++30 (1) 822 8704/822 7937
Fax: ++30 (1) 822 8704
E-mail: birdlife-gr@ath.forthnet.gr
www.ornithologiki.gr

Desc.: Protecting bird fauna and important bird areas of Greece.

Spp.: All endangered species of Greek bird fauna.

Hab.: All habitats of Greece (forests, lagoons, rivers, sea).

Loc.: Greece.

Travel: Bus, train or plane to the project area.

Dur.: Min. 3 weeks for foreign volunteers; 2 weeks for Greek volunteers.

Per.: May to October (mostly in the summer); some projects year round.

L.term: With project leaders approval.

Age: Min. 18.

Qualif.: Ability to work sometimes in difficult conditions, to do manual work, and to be reliable. Ability to live and work with people from different countries and cultures and to cooperate with the local communities. Experience in similar projects or studies in biology, environment, ornithology are more than welcome.

Work: Work in the field (constructing & monitoring nests, counting birds, feeding, monitoring of the habitats, etc.) and in public awareness.

Lang.: English, French, German.

Accom.: According to project, either provided by HOS in organized campsites, in rooms rented for the project (tents, sleeping bags, sheets and towels required) or different accomodation at special low-cost rates.

Cost: A EUR 60 (approx. GB£40) membership fee is required. Travel, food and personal expenses are not covered. Expenses needed for work during the project are covered by the HOS.

Applic.: Application form on HOS website, sent by mail, fax or e-mail.

Selected Project:

Management Plan for Pilos Lagoon, Greece

47

ICELAND CONSERVATION VOLUNTEERS
Umhverfisstofnun, Environment and Food Agency of Iceland
Sudurlandsbraut 24, 108 Reykjavik   Iceland
Tel.: ++35 4591 2000
Fax: ++35 4591 2020
E-mail: volunteer@ust.is
http://ust.is/

Desc.: Umhverfisstofnun (UST) is responsible for the management of Iceland's national parks and nature reserves. International volunteers are involved in all aspects of the practical management of these areas including trail construction and maintenance, heritage management and wilderness management projects. Volunteer teams work in some of the most beautiful parts of the country alongside local staff on these conservation projects. The focus of our work is the management of the hiking trails. The maintenance of good quality trails helps to protect ecologically fragile areas from tourism pressure and also improves safety for visitors.

Hab.: Remote upland areas with little vegetation.

Loc.: Based in Skaftafell National Park, includes projects in other national parks and nature reserves throughout Iceland.

Travel: The meeting place for all volunteers is Skaftafell National Park. There is a daily bus service to the Park from Reykjavik.

Dur.: 10 days - 4 weeks.

Per.: June - September.

L.term: Volunteers may be able to stay for up to 6 months.

Age: Min 18.

Qualif.: No previous experience is necessary as full training is offered. Nature conservation skills including trail construction skills are extremely useful.

Work: Volunteers work in teams and are guided by experienced leaders. Trail work includes constructing stone drains, steps, timber boardwalks and bridges. Wilderness management also include the removal of an invasive plant species (Lupinus nootkatensis).

Lang.: English is the working language of our international programme.

Accom.: Various - includes camping and shared rooms in bunkhouses. Personal good quality tents and sleeping bags are a must.

Cost: Volunteers pay for their own travel to Skaftafell National Park. Food, accommodation (often campsites) and trsfer to project site are covered.

Applic.: Apply online: http://english.ust.is/of-interest/ConservationVolunteers/

i to i
Woodside House
261 Low Lane
Horsforth, Leeds LS18 5NY UK
Tel.: ++44 (870) 333 2332 – Fax: ++44 (113) 205 4619
E-mail: info@i-to-i.com
www.i-to-i.com

Desc.:	i-to-i is an organisation specialized in ethical volunteer travel and TEFL/ TESOL training. The organisation sends 5,000 people a year to work with 500 vitally important community development, teaching, sports coaching and conservation projects in 28 countries across Africa, Asia, Latin America and Australia. i to i has a wide of recognised and respected TEFL/TESOL courses available and arranges well paid teaching placements in Thailand, South Korea, Turkey, Poland, Hungary and China. It also support projects across the world through the i-to-i foundation. ABTA bonded and internationally recognised, i-to-i gives the chance to get in touch, get inspired and help make the world a better place.
Hab.:	Forest areas, mountain regions, coastal areas, villages and towns.
Loc.:	28 countries across five continents, including South America, Africa, Asia, Europe and Australia.
Dur.:	One week to 12 months and over.
Per.:	Year round.
Age:	Min. 18, although some trips are available to school students.
Work:	Teaching English as a Foreign Language (TEFL), community development projects (working with underprivileged communities), animal and nature conservation, building, media placements, meaningful tours and working holidays programs.
Lang.:	English.
Accom.:	Hostels, basic hotels or with local families.
Cost:	Volunteer projects: from GB£495 (approx.US$800), TEFL courses from GB£195. Flights not Included.
Applic.:	Request brochures and application form by phone or online.

INTERNATIONAL OTTER SURVIVAL FUND
Skye Environmental Centre
Broadford, Isle of Skye
Scotland, IV49 9AQ UK
Tel./Fax: ++44 (1471) 822 487
E-mail: iosf@otter.org
www.otter.org

Desc.: IOSF works to conserve otters by safeguarding areas of good habitat and supporting people working in research and rehabilitation worldwide. The Fund's mission is to protect 13 species of otter worldwide.

Spp.: Eurasian otter (*Lutra lutra*).

Hab.: Coastal and rivers.

Loc.: Hebridean Islands, Scotland.

Dur.: 1 week.

Per.: April to October.

L.term: Inquire with organisation.

Age: Min. 19, no maximum age provided fit.

Qualif.: No specific skills needed but must be physically fit.

Work: Volunteers learn skills in otter surveying, such as identifying droppings (spraint), footprints, etc. They may also take part in surveying particular islands. Since the otters are not nocturnal the chances to observe them are very high (although it is not possible to guarantee).

Lang.: English.

Accom.: Volunteers stay in local guesthouses.

Cost: GB£240–495 (approx. US$400-800) depending on the project. Cost includes Bed & Breakfast, but volunteers pay for the other meals. Transport and equipment (except for personal camera, binoculars, etc.) are provided.

Applic.: Call or write IOSF for application form.

Notes: IOSF supports several otter conservation projects overseas (for example in Belarus or Vietnam). Inquire with IOSF for details.

INVOLVEMENT VOLUNTEERS ASSOCIATION INC.

P.O. Box 218, Port Melbourne
Victoria 3207 Australia
Tel.: ++61 (3) 9646 9392
Fax: ++61 (3) 9646 5504
E-mail: ivworldwide@volunteering.org.au
www.volunteering.org.au

Desc.: Involvement Volunteers Association Inc. (IVI) is a non-profit, NGO providing individual programmes for volunteering in 1 or more countries.

Loc.: Over 50 countries worldwide.

Dur.: 2, 6 or 12 weeks, up to 12 months.

Per.: Some projects are seasonal, others all year round.

Age: Min.18.

Qualif.: Suitable qualifications, determination, enthusiasm or experience.

Work: Various conservation related activities.

Lang.: English or Spanish in some countries.

Accom.: Various, depending on the project and the location.

Cost: Minimum AU$810 (approx. US$620/EUR490).

Applic.: Contact IVI by e-mail, airmail, fax or telephone.

Note: IV volunteering is organised to best suit the individual volunteer's needs or the group of individuals taking part.

IUCN – The World Conservation Union

28, rue Mauvernay
1196 Gland Switzerland
Tel.: ++41 (22) 999 0000
Fax: ++41 (22) 999 0002
E-mail: mail@iucn.org
www.iucn.org

Desc.: Founded in 1948, IUCN – The World Conservation Union brings together more than 1,000 governmental and non-governmental members and 10,000 technical and scientific experts in its six Commissions. IUCN's mission is to influence, encourage and assist societies throughout the world to conserve the integrity and diversity of nature and ensure that any use of natural resources is equitable and ecologically sustainable.

Loc.: Refer to www.iucn.org – About IUCN – Offices.

Dur.: Min. 3 months to 1 year.

Per.: Inquire to the appropriate IUCN Regional/Country Office in the preferred location.

L.term: Long-term assignments are preferred.

Age: Min. 21.

Qualif.: Vary according to specific assignments.

Work: Assist in collecting information, desk research and report writing. Organise and facilitate meetings and workshops. Develop project proposals and communication materials. Maintain databases and web-pages.

Lang.: Depends on the location of work (English, French and Spanish are also commonly used).

Cost: Conditions vary according to location and assignment.

Agents: Refer to www.iucn.org - About IUCN – Vacancies – Offices and Members – Directory. Contact the IUCN Regional/Country Office and/or IUCN members in the preferred location.

Applic.: Send CV and information on availability of time to preferred IUCN Regional/Country Office in the preferred location.

LEGAMBIENTE

Via Salaria 403 – 00199 Rome Italy
Tel.: ++39 (06) 862 681 – Volunteer office: ++39 (06) 8626 8323
For SCUBA activities: ++39 (06) 8626 8400
Fax: ++39 (06) 2332 5776
E-mail: volontariato@mail.legambiente.com
www.legambiente.com/volontariato

Desc.: Founded in 1980, Legambiente is a non-profit organisation involved primarily with public awareness and environmental campaigning activities. Volunteer opportunities include work camps and events such as the 'Clean up the World' day. Current projects include restoration and protection camps in small islands near Sicily, underwater archaeology and ecology camps in Sicily, ecological research in the Italian Alps, archeological study in Southern Italy and many others.

Spp.: Various species of the different habitats.

Hab.: Mediterranean seas, islands and coasts, temperate forest, lagoons, Alps.

Loc.: National Parks and Reserves, Mediterranean islands, Italian Alps, Germany, Brazil, Japan, France, Wales, Czech Republic, Mexico, Belarus, Turkey, Spain, Denmark, Poland, Belgium, Cuba, South Africa, Swaziland.

Dur.: 10–20 days.

Per.: Year round.

L.term: EU citizens can join the EVS (European Voluntary Service) programme from 3 months to 1 year. See Notes below.

Age: Min.18. Special programmes available for those under 18 and under 14.

Qualif.: No specific qualifications are required.

Lang.: Italian, English.

Cost: Min. EUR120, max. EUR270 (approx.GB£80–180).

Applic.: Contact Legambiente for information and application forms.

Notes: Legambiente is entitled to offer the EVS programme open to young EU citizens. The programme covers all the expenses of the volunteers for training in languages or in professional skills. For more information contact Paolo Maddonni Tel.:++39 (06) 8626 8326, e-mail: p..maddonni@mail.legambiente.com.

LIPU – Lega Italiana Protezione Uccelli, Birdlife Italy
Italian League for the Protection of Birds
Via Trento 49 – 43100 Parma   Italy
Tel.: ++39 (0521) 273 043
Fax: ++39 (0521) 273419
E-mail: info@lipu.it
www.lipu.it

Desc.: LIPU, founded in 1965, is the Italian representative of BirdLife International. The aim of the organisation is the protection of nature and in particular of birds. It supports bird rescue centres, research programmes for the conservation of endangered species, awareness campaigns and environmental education programmes.

Spp.: Birds.

Hab.: Mediterranean coasts and islands, temperate forest, Alps.

Loc.: Various locations in Italy.

Dur.: 7–10 days or more.

Per.: April to October.

L.term: Inquire with organisation.

Age: Inquire with organisation. Junior and adult camps.

Qualif.: Previous experience and qualifications are not required. Some camps need expert ornithologists.

Work: Birdwatching, counts, ringing, data collection, fire prevention, trail maintenance and restoration.

Lang.: Italian, English.

Cost: Min. EUR300, max. EUR700 (GB£200–450).

Applic.: Contact LIPU for information on international application.

MINGAN ISLAND CETACEAN RESEARCH EXPEDITIONS

Mingan Island Cetacean Study, Inc.
378 Rue Bord de la Mer
Longue-Pointe-de-Mingan, Québec, GOG 1V0 Canada
Tel./Fax: ++1 (418) 949 2845
E-mail: mics@globetrotter.net
www.rorqual.com

Desc.: Volunteers join a team of marine biologists conducting cetacean research in Northeastern Quebec (Canada), and in Baja California (Mexico). During research projects, participants spend most of their time on the water; there is a field station/museum building at the Quebec site.

Spp.: Blue, fin, humpback and minke whales.

Hab.: Gulf of the St. Lawrence River, Sea of Cortez.

Loc.: Northeast Quebec; Gaspé Peninsula and St. Lawrence Estuary. During winter in Loreto, Baja California, for blue whale studies.

Travel: Airplane to Sept-Iles. For Loreto fly to LA and then to Loreto.

Dur.: 7–14-day sessions.

Per.: June to October in Quebec; February to March in Loreto.

L.term: Possible to stay up to 1 month.

Age: Min. 12.

Qualif.: Be prepared to spend long periods on the water—sometimes up to 12 hours. Recommended a good physical condition.

Work: Help collect field data: take notes, observe researchers do biopsies and some photographic work. Assist with organizing daily logistics such as gas, food and boat preparation.

Lang.: English, French, German. Spanish useful in Mexico.

Accom.: B&B, inn or hotel.

Cost: Mingan CAD$1895 (approx. US$1,600), while Gaspe' estuary blue whale session CAD$2,090 (approx. US$1925); including transportation, accommodation, food and 7-day session with the biologists. US$1,590 in Loreto; including all activities on the water, hotel and meals; does not include air transportation and transfers to and from the airport.

Applic.: Request from the organisation registration and medical forms.

THE NATIONAL TRUST

Working Holidays Booking office

Sapphire House, Roundtree Way, Norwich NR7 8SQ   UK

Tel.:   ++44 (870) 4292429

fax: ++44 (870) 4292427

E-mail: working.holidays@nationaltrust.org.uk

www.nationaltrust.org.uk/volunteering/

Desc.:   The National Trust offers 400 working holidays every year. This includes activities from carrying out a conservation survey and herding goats to painting a lighthouse or planting trees and many more.

Loc.:   England, Wales, Northern Ireland.

Dur.:   3-14 days.

Per.:   Year round.

L.term: Inquire with the organisation. Many opportunities are listed on the website.

Age: Min. 18 (some working holidays 16).

Qualif.: No specific skills required. Some projects need botanists, archaeologists or builders.

Work: Work involves outdoor countryside conservation. On some holidays there are opportunities to learn specific skills such as dry-stone walling, hedge laying etc.

Lang.:   English.

Accom.: Basic. Volunteers stay in various types of accommodation; mostly dormitory.

Cost: From GB£37. Food and accommodation are included.

Agents: Contact the organisation directly.

Applic: On-line application form or to receive an application form call ++44 (870) 429 2429.

Notes: The National Trust has special programmes for young people.

THE NATURE CORPS

3600 Ridge Road
Templeton, California 93465 USA
Tel.: ++1 (805) 434 0299
Fax: ++1 (805) 434 3444
E-mail: info@thenaturecorps.org
www.thenaturecorps.org

Desc.: The Nature Corps recruits volunteers to work on projects in National Parks in California and Hawaii, such as Yosemite, Sequoia, Channel Islands and Hawaii Volcanoes National Park. Projects vary from revegetation and tree planting to species preservation.

Hab.: Rainforest, high sierra.

Loc.: California and Hawaii, USA.

Dur.: 6–8 day excursions.

Per.: May to October.

L.term: Nature Corps will help volunteers make arrangements to stay after the 8–day period.

Age: Min. 18 (12–17 with parents' permission).

Qualif.: No particular skills needed, photography and carpentry skills welcome.

Lang.: English.

Cost: Adults fees start from US$595, including food and camping arrangements. Transportation provided on most excursions. A portion of the adults' contribution goes to supporting the 6–day Youth Expeditions. Youth and students fees are about US$370.

Agents: Contact The Nature Corps directly.

Applic.: Apply on-line at www.thenaturecorps.org or ask for an application form.

Notes: Half of the excursion is devoted to the project and half to guided recreation and education. Further information available from The Nature Corps.

NZTCV – The New Zealand Trust for Conservation Volunteers

Three Streams; 343 S.H.17, R.D.3 Albany
Auckland, New Zealand
Tel.: ++64 (9) 415 9336
Fax: ++64 (9) 415 9336
E-mail: conservol@clear.net.nz
www.conservationvolunteers.org.nz

Desc.: NZTCV is a member of the International Conservation Volunteers Alliance. Projects offer opportunities to visit scenic locations in both the North and South Islands of New Zealand. NZTCV allows overseas visitors to share New Zealand's unique environment and culture. Patrons: Dr. David Bellamy, Stephen King, Sir Paul Reeves & Lady Beverley Reeves.

Spp.: Various species of New Zealand's flora and fauna.

Hab.: Coasts, dryland, National Parks and Reserves, forests, wetlands, natural bush.

Loc.: Throughout New Zealand.

Dur.: 1 – 3 weeks (varies).

Per.: Year round.

L.term: Inquire with organisation.

Age: Min. 18.

Qualif.: Experience and qualifications related to the environment are welcome but not essential.

Work: Species monitoring, general maintenance, planting, island revegetation, forest restoration.

Lang.: English.

Cost: Air travel to and from New Zealand. Free accommodation offered with some projects. Food costs for duration of stay and cost of transportation to and from project location are paid by the volunteer. See website for more information.

Applic.: Applications are accepted on-line or via e-mail.

OCEANIC SOCIETY EXPEDITIONS

Fort Mason Center, Building E
San Francisco, CA 94123   USA
Tel.: ++1 (415) 441 1106 – 1 (800) 326 7491 (toll free in North America)
Fax: ++1 (415) 474 3395
E-mail: info@oceanic-society.org
www.oceanic-society.org

Desc.:   Founded in 1972, Oceanic Society Expeditions (OSE) is a non-profit organisation that conducts research to protect aquatic environments and promote environmental education. OSE organises over 30 projects classified as 'Natural History Expeditions' (NHE) and 'Research Expeditions' (RE); the latter are designed to accomplish specific scientific objectives. For these projects volunteers work with field biologists, collecting data and logging information.

Spp.:   Dolphins, manatees, corals, seabirds, giant otters, seaturtles.

Hab.:   Tropical seas, temperate seas, rainforest, rivers.

Loc.:   Baja California, Caribbean, Belize, Micronesia and various locations in Central, South and North America.

Dur.:   4 – 10 days for NHE; 1 - 2 week for RE.

Per.:   Year round.

L.term: Inquire with organisation.

Age: Min. 18. Anyone under 18 must be accompanied by a guardian.

Qualif.:   Enthusiasm and willingness to take directions are necessary.

Lang.:   English.

Cost: Approx. US$1,000–3,000 for NHE, US$1,000–2,000 for RE.

Applic.:   Request application form to be returned with a deposit of US$300/ person/trip.

Notes: OSE also raises contributions through adopt-a-dolphin, adopt-a-whale and adopt-an-atoll programs.

Selected Projects:

Bottlenose Dolphin Project, Belize
Manatee Research Project, Belize

OCEANUS ONLUS

Via Nomentana, 175
00161, Roma
Italy
E-mail: oceanus@oceanus.it
www.oceanus.it

Desc.: Oceanus is a non-profit organization focused on promoting and developing several research projects aiming at the preservation of the marine ecosystems and environments, as well as the protection of the marine species under increasing threat due to an excessive interaction with human activities.

Spp.: All relevant marine species: whales and dolphins, sharks, seaturtles, etc.

Hab.: Pelagic and coastal waters.

Loc.: Mediterranean sea, Atlantic ocean and Caribbean sea.

Dur.: 10 - 15 days.

Per.: October to May.

L.term: Inquire with organisation.

Age: Min. 21.

Qualif.: Volunteers must be enthusiastic and flexible; ability to swim, willingness to take directions are necessary.

Work: Navigation and sailing (taking shifts with the trained crew and acquiring experience). Research (visual scan, use of the hydrophone, filling in forms, preliminary analysis of effort/distribution and Photo-id data, maintenance of equipment). Support activities (maintenance and cleaning of the vessel, cooking etc).

Lang.: English, Italian.

Accom.: The research takes place on board a 14.5 m research sailing catamaran equipped with all necessary navigation safety and research instrument (GPSs, plotters, echo-sounders, underwater digital video and still cameras, binoculars etc) as well as a dual frequency hydrophone and DAT recorder.

Cost: Approx. EUR 600-1200 for 10 days (Mediterranean sea) or 15 days (Atlantic ocean and Caribbean sea) .

Applic.: Contact the organisation for more information and application forms.

OPERATION WALLACEA

Hope House
Old Bolingbroke, Spilsby, LincolnshirePE23 4EX   UK
Tel.: ++44 (1790) 763 194
Fax: ++44 (1790) 763 825
E-mail: info@opwall.com
www.opwall.com

Desc.: Operation Wallacea (OW) is a series of biological and social science expeditions designed to achieve wildlife conservation aims. The expeditions have been running for the last 9 years in remote corners of the globe. OW volunteers join marine, rainforests and desert projects organized by a 150 strong team of scientist from UK, US and other academic institutions.

Spp.: Corals, sponges, fish, birds, bats, butterflies, mammals, macaques, reptiles and amphibians.

Hab.: Coral reefs, rainforest, deserts.

Loc.: Indonesia, Honduras, Egypt, South Africa, Peru an Cuba.

Travel: Airplane to nearest interanational airport (see website).

Dur.: 2, 4, 6 or 8 weeks.

Per.: June to September.

L.term: Inquire with organisation.

Age: Min. 16.

Qualif.: Enthusiasm and a positive attitude towards the environment. Full training for diving, jungle survival and field skills are given.

Work: Volunteers work alongside scientists to complete surveys of the endemic species. Both flora and fauna in the marine and rainforest habitats are surveyed. Education and Anthropology.

Lang.: English.

Accom.: From hammocks under bashas in the rainforest to huts on the beach in Indonesia.

Cost: From GB£950 (US$1,750) toGB£2,800 (approx.US$5,150) depending on length of stay. Prices include food, accommodation, dive training to PADI OW and internal transfers. Prices do not include flights and insurance.

Applic.: Contact UK office.University presentations take place in the UK.

Notes: Dive equipment, excluding wetsuit, may be hired on site.

RALEIGH INTERNATIONAL

27 Parsons Green Lane
London, SW6 4HZ   UK
Tel.: ++44 (20) 7371 8585 – Fax: ++44 (20) 7371 5852
E-mail: info@raleigh.org.uk
www.raleighinternational.org

Desc.: Raleigh International, is a charity committed to the personal development of young people from all backgrounds and nationalities, through its UK and overseas programmes. International programmes consist of three projects: community, environmental and adventure. All projects are supported by the host country government and development organizations to ensure they are both worthwhile and sustainable. Projects may include scientific research, wildlife surveys, infrastructure work such as building schools, installing water systems etc. and improving facilities for tourists and scientists in national parks. Participants work in groups of 10-15 people (diverse mix of nationalities and backgrounds) supported by staff volunteers. A variety of roles is available for staff volunteers eg. project managers, medics, bookkeepers, mountain leaders, administrators, photographers, drivers etc.

Hab.: Various.

Loc.: Namibia, Costa Rica & Nicaragua, Malaysia (Borneo).

Dur.: 5 and 10 weeks for young people aged 17-24; 7 and 13 weeks for staff volunteers aged 25 or older.

Per.: Year round.

L.term: Volunteers may continue their involvement with Raleigh at home after the programme. Volunteers may also continue travelling independently.

Age: 17-24 (participants); 25 or over (staff volunteers).

Qualif.: Volunteers must be physically fit, able to swim 200 metres and speak basic English. An introduction weekend that includes physical and mental challenges is required.

Accom.: Tents. Living conditions during the programme are very basic.

Cost: From GB£1,500 to GB£ 2,995 for participants and from GB£1,350 to GB£1,950 for staff volunteers excluding airfare from the UK. Volunteers raise funds through sponsorship, rotary clubs, trusts etc. With support from the head office, 1,000 young people and staff volunteers join a Raleigh programme annually.

Applic.: Online application form.

RSPB – THE ROYAL SOCIETY FOR THE PROTECTION OF BIRDS

The Lodge, Sandy
Bedfordshire SG19 2DL   UK
Tel.: ++44 (1767) 680 551
Fax: ++44 (1767) 692 365
www.rspb.org/helprspb/volunteering/

Desc.:   RSPB Residential Volunteering Scheme operates in 40 reserves around the UK, providing an opportunity for those interested in ornithology and conservation to gain practical experience of the day-to-day running of a RSPB reserve.

Spp.:   Birds.

Hab.:   Woodland, swamps, ponds, lakes, moorland, coastal lagoons.

Loc.:   England, Scotland, Wales, Northern Ireland.

Dur.:   Min. 1 week (Saturday to Saturday); max. 1 month.

Per.:   Year round.

L.term: Negotiable by arrangement.

Age: Min.16 (18 for international volunteers and in some reserves).

Qualif.:   Good physical health.

Work: Duties vary and may include: habitat and estate management, tourist assistance, reception work, survey/research assistance, car park duties, working with stock, grass cutting, bird counts, animal population monitoring. Duties allocated according to volunteer knowledge and experience.

Lang.:   English.

Accom.:   Chalets, cottages, houses, cabins, caravans or bungalows. May have to share a room with at least 1 other person of same sex. Bedding is provided (except sleeping bag). Cooking facilities available (volunteers must provide and cook their own food).

Cost: Free accommodation. Food and travel expenses not included.

Applic.:   The web address above features an on-line brochure and an application form.

Selected Project:

Operation Osprey, Scotland

63

SANCCOB – The Southern African Foundation for the Conservation of Coastal Birds

P.O. Box: 1111 6 Bloubergrant, 7443 Cape Town South Africa
Tel.: ++27 (21) 557 61 55
Fax: ++27 (21) 557 88 04
E-mail: penguininfo@sanccob.co.za
www.sanccob.co.za

Desc.:	SANCCOB rehabilitates sea birds, mostly from oil pollution, some injured or ill. The species most affected is the African penguin, a bird only found along the southern African coast and classified as 'vulnerable.' The South African route is a popular ship-faring route and is very polluted.
Spp:	African penguin (*Spheniscus demersus*), Cape gannet, Cape, crowned and whitebreasted cormorants, kelp and hartlaub gulls, petrel, tern, albatross.
Hab.:	Coastal.
Loc.:	20 km north of Cape Town, South Africa.
Travel:	Airplane to Cape Town.
Dur.:	Min. 6 weeks.
Per.:	May to October is busy but oil spills can happen any time.
L.term:	Possible, with project leaders approval.
Age:	Min. 16.
Qualif.:	Willingness to work hard with wild, difficult birds.
Work:	Keeping the centre clean, scrubbing pools and pens daily (cleaning after 30–200 birds), feeding and stabilizing birds and assisting veterinary staff.
Lang.:	English.
Accom.:	Bed & Breakfast or contact the organisation for other possibilities.
Cost:	Volunteers are responsible for food, transport and accommodation costs, approx. US$30–40/day.
Agents:	Contact the organisation directly.
Applic.:	Fill out application form from the web page.
Notes:	Winters can be cold and wet in Cape Town. Old clothes to work in should be brought.

SCA – Student Conservation Association, Inc.

P.O. Box 550
Charlestown, New Hampshire 03603 USA
Tel.: ++1 (603) 543 1700
Fax: ++1 (603) 543 1828
E-mail: admissions@thesca.org
www.thesca.org

Desc.: SCA is an educational organisation operating volunteer and internship programmes in conservation and natural resource management. The Conservation Internship Programs (CIP) are for anyone 18 or older to serve alongside seasonal staff for public and private natural resource management agencies. The Conservation Crew Program (CCP) allows high school students aged 15–19 to join summer conservation projects.

Loc.: USA: opportunities exist in all 50 states

Dur.: Usually 12–52 weeks for CIP; 3–5 weeks for CCP.

Per.: CIP are available year round, CCP from June to August only.

L.term: Max. 12 months, depending upon project.

Age: Min. 18 for CIP, no upper age limit; 15–19 for CCP.

Qualif.: Good health, enthusiasm, flexibility, fluent English.

Work: Interns work with widlife, in back country patrol, trail building, hydrology and resource management, visitor services and interpretation, environmental education with youth, research, public outreach, and in museum curator positions to name a few.

Lang.: English.

Cost: No cost: CIP Interns receive paid travel (within the US), free housing and related expenses, weekly living allowance of US$60-160 and free accident insurance. CCP volunteers receive free room and board and equipment but no travel.

Applic.: An application must be submitted with a medical form and at least 2 references. Request by mail or phone or download from SCA's website. Applicants can apply directly on-line. No deadline for CIP; deadline for CCP is March 1, or until all positions are filled. Application fee of US$10–40.

Notes: Listings of positions on website. Searchable database updated weekly; applications can also be filled out on website directly.

SCI – Service Civil International

International Secretariat
St-Jacobsmarkt 82, B-2000 Antwerpen Belgium
Tel.: ++32 (3) 226 5727
Fax: ++32 (3) 232 0344
E-mail: info@sciint.org
www.sciint.org (to find all the national contacts)

Desc.:	SCI is a voluntary NGO founded in 1920 that aims to promote international understanding and peace. It provides volunteers for projects in communities that cannot afford labour. Every year more than 20,000 volunteers of all nationalities work in over 100 camps.
Loc.:	Western and Eastern Europe, United States, Australia.
Dur.:	2–3 weeks.
Per.:	Year round, mainly June to September.
L.term:	People with workcamp experience can join projects for 3–6 months; short-term volunteers need approval of host in order to stay longer.
Age:	Min. 18 for Europe; min. 16 for the United States.
Qualif.:	Ability to work as part of a team and live simply.
Lang.:	English. For other languages, inquire with local SCI office.
Cost:	Volunteers must provide transportation; contributions are US$65 in the United States, EUR120 in Europe, EUR250 in Eastern Europe. Accommodation, food and insurance are provided.
Agents:	Local SCI offices listed in the above website. SCI has many branches in the world and cooperates with many organisations: contact the nearest office for information.
Applic.:	Standard application; no need to be a member.
Notes:	Smallest projects could be for 6 volunteers and largest for 20 volunteers. Usually only 2 volunteers from the same country can join the same project in order to form international teams.

SCI Germany: www.sci-d.de

SCI-IVS USA: www.sci-ivs.org

IVS UK: www.ivsgbn.demon.co.uk

IVP Australia: www.ivp.org.au

TETHYS RESEARCH INSTITUTE
Civic Aquarium
Viale G.B. Gadio 2
20121 Milano Italy
Tel.: ++39 (02))7260 1446 – (02) 7200 1947
Fax: ++39 (02)8699 5011
E-mail: tethys@tethys.org – www.tethys.org

Desc.: This private non-profit organisation is dedicated to the study and protection of marine habitats, focusing on Mediterranean cetaceans. Founded in 1986, TRI is formed by a team of researchers conducting research with the help of volunteers.

Spp.: Cetaceans.

Hab.: Mediterranean Sea.

Loc.: Mediterranean (France, Greece, Italy).

Dur.: 1–2 weeks.

Per.: May to October.

L.term: Biology students or researchers may assist TRI biologists for the duration of projects with the leader's approval.

Age: Min.18. Minors may be accepted if accompanied by an adult.

Qualif.: Volunteers must be enthusiastic and flexible; ability to swim is necessary. Photography and computer skills are helpful.

Work: Assist the researchers with observations, cetacean photo-identification, data entry, operation of hydrophones and recording instruments. Share boat or household duties (shopping, cleaning, cooking).

Lang.: English, Italian.

Accom.: Aboard the 21–metre ketch *Pelagos* for research cruises. In house along the coast for dolphin project in Greece.

Cost: Approx. EUR 500–830 (approx. GB£350–580) for 6 days. Food, membership and insurance included. Travel to and from project not included.

Applic.: Contact TRI for information and application forms.

Selected projects:

Cetacean Sanctuary Research, Ligurian Sea
Ionian Dolphin Project, Greece

TREKFORCE WORLDWIDE

Community & Conservation Projects, C/O Naldred Farm Offices
Borde Hill Lane, Haywards Heath
West Sussex, RH16 1XR, UK
Tel.: ++44 (845) 241 3085
Fax: ++44 (0845) 241 3086
E-mail: info@trekforceworldwide.com
www.trekforceworldwide.com

Desc.: Trekforce Worldwide is the new expedition company to evolve out of UK-based charity Trekforce Expeditions. Keen to continue the charity's legacy of running conservation expeditions to remote and challenging destinations, Trekforce Worldwide has taken 20 years worth of experience and developed it into an expedition consultancy service. Working with remote communities in far flung corners of the globe, TFW combines the challenge of expedition life with sustainable conservation projects. As well as working on such worthwhile ventures, individuals can enhance their overseas experience and develop their own skills with language training, remote trekking, teaching placements and diving courses. TFW has a series of established gap year expeditions at the start of every year. TFW organises in the UK several informal Open Days.

Hab.: Rainforest.

Loc.: Central America (Belize, Guatemala), South America (Guyana, Peru).

Dur.: 2 – 5 months.

Per.: January-June.

L.term: Many 'trekkers' return for more expeditions at discounted rates.

Age: Min. 18.

Qualif.: No specific skills needed.

Lang.: English. Longer programmes involve learning local languages.

Accom.: Deep in the jungle in Hammocks under mosquito nets and waterproof shelters.

Cost: Between GB£2,800 and GB£4,050 depending on expedition length.

Applic.: Apply online for a brochure or a place on an Open Day.

Notes: Prospective volunteers join Open Days where they are offered help and advice on fund-raising and can discuss projects and placements and meet ex-volunteers.

UNITED NATIONS VOLUNTEERS (UNV)

P.O. Box 260–111,
D–53153 Bonn Germany
Tel.: ++49 (228) 815 2000
Fax: ++49 (228) 815 2001
E-mail: information@unvolunteers.org
www.unv.org

Desc.: The United Nations Volunteers programme is open to specialists in various fields. Since 1971 over 30,000 volunteers have joined the programme in about 140 countries (particularly in developing ones), co-operating with local organisations and communities for teaching or offering their professional skills. UNV programmes include: education, environment, peace operations and democracy, humanitarian relief and rehabilitation, technical co-operation and refugee assistance. Today, some 10% of the serving UNVs work with environmental or conservation issues in specific areas such as plant protection, forestry conservation, sanitation/waste disposal, energy engineering, meteorology, coastal erosion, preservation of cultural heritage and tourism. UN Volunteers have been assigned to projects on pandas in a reserve in China or on global warming policy planning in the Maldives.

Loc.: Developing countries throughout the world such as India, Brazil, Mali and Burkina Faso (for the environmental programme).

Dur.: Assignments last from a few months to 1-2 years.

Per.: Year round.

L.term: Some assignments can be extended beyond the 2-year period.

Age: Min. 25, but UNV volunteers are usually older than 35, as a professional working experience is necessary.

Qualif.: Volunteers must be professionals or technicians with at least 2 years of experience. Teachers, medical doctors, nurses, mechanical or electrical engineers, geologists, automotive mechanics, librarians, midwives, etc.

Work: Varies depending on programme and location.

Lang.: English, French, Spanish, Arabic, Portuguese. Language ability of selected volunteers will be tested.

Accom.: Simple accommodation provided for volunteer and dependent relatives (spouse and up to 2 children under 21 years of age). Furniture and utilities are normally provided. If these arrangements cannot be made, the paid rent will be reimbursed.

Cost: UNV volunteers receive a monthly living allowance that ranges from US$600–1,400 for single specialists and from US$800–1,900 for specialists with direct dependents. Upon completion of an assignment, a resettlement allowance will also be paid. Life, health and permanent disability insurance is provided free of charge. Return travel to duty station is also provided (includes direct dependents).

Applic.: Write or call for the PHS (Personal History Statement) form (either in French or English), which must be completed and sent in together with 2 photos and reference forms completed by both professional and personal referees. If the PHS is approved by UNV headquarters, the application is added to the roster of candidates. If a volunteer is selected for a particular post, the PHS is submitted for clearance by a UN agency and for approval by the Government requesting the services of a UNV specialist. Submission and selection of candidates may take several months. Candidates who are accepted must begin the assignment within 8 weeks of being notified of final selection.

U.S. DEPARTMENT OF AGRICULTURE - FOREST SERVICE
Volunteering in the National Forests
P.O. Box 96090, Washington, DC 20090 – 6090 USA
or Sidney R. Yates Federal Building
201, 14 Street, SW at Independence Ave., SW Washington, DC
www.fs.fed.us (then search for 'employment')

- Region 1–Northern Region, Federal Bldg., P.O. Box 7669, Missoula, Montan 59807, tel. ++1 (406) 329 3511 / 329 3510

- Region 2–Rocky Mountain, P.O. Box 25127, Golden, Colorado 80401, tel. ++1 (303) 275 5350

- Region 3–Southwestern, 333 Broadway, SE, Albuquerque, New Mexico 87102, tel. ++1 (505) 842 3292

- Region 4–Intermountain, Federal Bldg. 324, 25th St., Ogden, Utah 84401, tel. ++1 (801) 625 5306

- Region 5–Pacific Southwest, 1323 Club Drive, Vallejo, California 94592, tel. ++1 (707) 562 9130

- Region 6–Pacific Northwest, 333 SW First Avenue, P.O. Box 3623 Portland, Oregon 97208–3623, tel. ++1 (503) 808 2468

- Region 8–Southern, 1720 Peachtree Rd., NW, Atlanta, Georgia 30309, tel. ++1 (404) 347 4191

- Region 9–Eastern, 626 W. Wisconsin Ave., Milwaukee, Wisconsin 53202, tel. ++1 (414) 297 3600

- Region 10–Alaska, Federal Office Bldg., P.O. Box 21628 Juneau, Alaska 99802–1628, tel. ++1 (907) 586 7847

- Pacific Northwest Research Station, 333 SW 1st Avenue, P.O. Box 3890, Portland, Oregon 97208-3623, tel. ++1 (503) 808 2468

- North Central Research Station, 1992 Folwell Avenue, St. Paul Minnesota 55108, tel. ++1 (651) 649 5272

- Rocky Mountain Research Station, 240 W. Prospect Road, Fort Collins, Colorado 80526–2098, tel. ++1 (970) 498 1392

- Northeastern Area State and Private Forestry, 11 Campus Drive, Newtown Square, Pennsylvania 19073, tel. ++1 (612) 713 7300

- International Institute of Tropical Forestry, P.O. Box 25000, UPR Experimental Station, 1201 Calle Leiba, Puerto Rico 00928, tel. ++1 (787) 766 5335

Desc.: The Forest Service manages and protects the National Forest System and cooperates with private forest and woodland owners, State and local government agencies and private organisations. It performs research for improving the quality of the forest and forest products. Volunteer service is needed in US National Forests because the Forest Service has a limited budget. The programme goal is to provide fulfilling work experience to volunteers while accomplishing necessary tasks.

Spp.: Various in the United States.

Hab.: Various in the United States.

Loc.: National Forests throughout the United States.

Dur.: Inquire with the National Forest of choice.

Per.: Inquire with the National Forest of choice.

L.term: Inquire with the National Forest of choice.

Age: No age limit. Those under 18 must have the written consent of a parent or guardian.

Qualif.: No specific skills required. Volunteers must be in good health to allow them to perform their duties without risk to themselves or others. A medical examination may be required for some tasks. Persons with disabilities are encouraged to volunteer.

Work: Maintaining and hosting campgrounds, working at visitor centres and ranger stations, planting trees, presenting environmental education programmes, building and repairing structures, taking photographs. Training provided if necessary.

Lang.: English.

Accom.: Housing may be available. Inquire with National Forest of choice.

Cost: Some expenses such as transportation, lodging, subsistence and uniforms may be reimbursed on a case-by-case basis.

Applic.: Write or call the volunteer coordinator of the region of interest. See list in the previous page or from the directory on the website: www.fs.fed.us/intro/directory/orgdir.shtml (or search for 'directory').

Notes: Non-U.S. citizens are eligible to work for a U.S. Federal Agency only if permanent residents of the U.S. or if non-immigrant aliens with F-1 visa status or if bona fide students residing in the U.S. Enquire with your nearest U.S. Consular Office.

U.S. FISH AND WILDLIFE SERVICE

1849 C Street, NW
Washington DC 20240   USA
Tel.: ++1 (800) 344 WILD (toll free in the USA)
E-mail: volunteers@fws.gov
www.fws.gov/volunteers/

Desc.: The United States Fish and Wildlife Service mission is to conserve, protect and enhance fish, wildlife and plants and their habitats. Volunteers work at national wildlife refuges, fish hatcheries, wetland management districts, regional offices or ecological service offices.

Spp.: Migratory birds, fish and all endangered species.

Hab.: Various in the United States.

Loc.: Throughout the United States.

Dur.: From a few days to several months.

Per.: Year round.

Age: Min. 18.

Qualif.: No special skills are required. Experience with the life sciences is preferable. Some positions require teaching, public speaking or other specialized skills. Training provided if necessary.

Lang.: English.

Cost: Volunteers must pay their way to the United States. Assistance is available at times for travel within the US, for US applicants. Travel, food and lodging are usually covered while on duty .

Applic.: Contact the service directly by e-mail, or contact the regional office of your choice. For the list of Regional Offices see menu on top USFWS home page: www.fws.gov

Notes: Non-US citizens must plan well ahead and secure a proper visa or entry papers to enter the US and work as a volunteer. The USFWS does not work with whales and dolphins.

U.S. NATIONAL PARK SERVICE
VIP (Volunteers-In-Parks) Program
National Capital Region
1100 Ohio Dr., SW, Washington, DC 20242 USA
Tel.: ++1 (202) 619 7256
www.nps.gov/volunteer/

Desc.:	The United States National Park Service is officially entrusted with preserving more than 350 national parks in the US Through the VIP (Volunteers-In-Parks) Program, anyone can help conserving the parks' natural and historical resources.
Spp.:	Various of North America.
Hab.:	Various of North America.
Loc.:	National parks throughout the United States.
Dur.:	Inquire with the park or the field area of choice.
Per.:	Inquire with the park or the field area of choice.
L.term:	Inquire with the park of choice.
Age:	Min. 18. Persons under 18 years of age must have permission of their parents or guardian or be accompanied by adults in a family or group.
Qualif.:	Various skills and talents desired. Reasonably good health is expected. A medical examination may be required for some jobs. Disabled individuals are encouraged to volunteer.
Work:	Providing information at a visitor centre, accessioning artifacts into a park's archaeological or historic collection, conducting surveys of plant and animal species in the park or doing construction and repair work on hiking trails. Accepted volunteers receive appropriate training and orientation at the beginning of the service.
Lang.:	English.
Accom.:	Some of the larger parks may provide free housing for VIPs. Arrangements made between the volunteer and the park.
Cost:	Some parks reimburse volunteers for some expenses, such as local travel costs, meals and uniforms. Volunteers must cover the cost of travel to and from the park.
Agents:	**Alaska Area Region**, 240 West 5th Avenue, Anchorage, Alaska 99501, tel. ++1 (907) 644 3347.
	Intermountain Region, 12795 West Alameda Parkway, Denver,

Colorado 80225–0287, tel. ++1 (303) 969 2020.

Midwest Region, 1709 Jackson St., Omaha, Nebraska 68102, tel. ++1 (402) 221 3456.

Northeast Region, U.S. Customs House, 200 Chestnut St. Fifth Floor, Philadelphia, Pennsylvania 19106, tel. ++1 (215) 597 4971.

Pacific West Region, One Jackson Center, 1111 Jackson Street, Suite 700, Oakland, California 94607, tel. ++1 (510) 817 1300.

Southeast Region, 75 Spring St., SW, Suite 1130. Atlanta, Georgia 30303, tel. ++1 (404) 331 5711.

Applic.: The website lists hundred of opportunities (click on opportunities) and gives detailed application contacts for each position. Addresses of parks can be obtained from the Regional offices listed above. Ask for a VIP application form. Prospective volunteers can apply to more than 1 park. Selection for summer positions are usually made between February and April.

Notes: Non-U.S. citizens are eligible to work for a U.S. Federal Agency only if permanent residents of the U.S. or if non-immigrant aliens with F-1 visa status or if bona fide students residing in the U.S. Enquire with your nearest U.S. Consular Office.

VOLUNTEER FOR NATURE

Nature Conservancy of Canada and Ontario Nature
Orchard Park Office Centre
RR#5, 5420 Highway 6 North
Guelph, Ontario N1H 6J2 Canada
Tel.: ++1 (519) 826 0068 (ext.222) – Fax: ++1 (519) 826 9206
E-mail: visit www.vfn.ca – www.ontarionature.org

Desc.: Volunteer for Nature is a conservation volunteer program created in partnership by the Nature Conservancy of Canada and Ontario Nature. The goal of the program is to engage people in the protection of Canada's biodiversity while providing a meaningful and educational experience in ecologically significant natural areas.

Hab.: Habitats protected through Volunteer for Nature include Ontario's limestone alvar, oak savannah, tall grass prairie, Great Lakes shoreline, Carolinian forest and Alberta's Rocky Mountain foothills, parklands and grasslands.

Loc.: Ontario and Alberta, Canada.

Dur.: Min. 1 day, max. 16 days.

Per.: April to October.

Age: Min.16.

Qualif.: No specific qualifications required. Must be reasonably fit.

Lang.: English.

Cost: Fees vary per event and are designed to cover direct expenses, including food and the transit of leaders and tools to the work sites.

Accom.: Accommodations range from basic camping to dormitory style to Park staff houses, lodges, field study centres or bed and breakfasts. All volunteers are responsible for contributing to cooking and general duties at the accommodation.

Applic.: Visit the VfN website to learn more about our events and registering.

Notes: See website for full Volunteer for Nature Schedule of Events.

VOLUNTEERS FOR OUTDOOR COLORADO (VOC)

600 South Marion Parkway
Denver, Colorado 80209–2597   USA
Tel.: ++1 (303) 715 1010
Fax: ++1 (303) 715 1212
E-mail: voc@voc.org
www.voc.org

Desc.: This non-profit organisation, founded in 1984, promotes and fosters citizen and visitor responsibility for Colorado's public lands. VOC organises 1-day to week-long conservation projects and provides volunteer resources to land management agencies, non-profits and user groups. VOC also manages V Outdoors (www.voutdoors.org), a state-wide clearinghouse for public lands volunteer opportunities. Land managers and non-profits post hundreds of opportunities to volunteer in Colorado's public lands.

Hab.: Urban gardens and parks, streams, lakes, mountains.

Loc.: Urban and natural areas, National Parks, National Forests, State Parks, public lands, Colorado, USA.

Dur.: 1 day to 4 months.

Per.: Year round.

L.term: No.

Age: Min. 8 for VOC projects; under16 must be accompanied by an adult.

Qualif.: Desired experience varies from none to skilled.

Lang.: English.

Cost: No cost.

Applic.: Sign up online.

Notes: The VOC website has an excellent list of links to other volunteering organisations in the US and in Colorado.

THE WILDERNESS FOUNDATION

47-49 Main Road, Broomfield,
Chelmsford, Essex, CM1 7BU   UK
Tel.: ++44 (1245) 443 073
Fax: ++44 (1245) 445 075
E-mail: info@wildernessfoundation.org.uk
www.wildernessfoundation.org.uk

Desc.:   The Wilderness Foundation charity promotes self-financed adventurous journeys on foot, horseback and by canoe into the last remaining wilderness areas across the world. Additional volunteer and guide training programmes focus on rural communities, conservation, teach wilderness skills for groups of young people and adults. Groups size is from 6 to 8 people.

Loc.:   Trails are held in Wales, Scotland, Tanzania, South Africa and USA.

Dur.:   Min. 7 days, max. 30 days for adults and students.

Age: Min. 15.

Qualif.:   No specific qualifications required. Must be reasonably fit.

Lang.:   English.

Cost: Costs on average are GB£68 (approx.US$120) per person per day. This excludes travel to and from destination but includes food, guides and equipment. Apart from travel to and from the destination this is all inclusive.

Accom.:   Normally in the open or in remote bush camps for journeys in Africa and USA. Basic bunkhouse accommodation is provided in Wales and Scotland.

Notes: Trails focus on the ethics and values of wilderness experience – tailor made programmes can be put together for groups of four or more.

WWF Italy

Ecotourism Division
Via Orseolo 12
20144 Milano Italy
Tel.: ++39 (02) 831 33245 – Fax: ++39 (02) 831 33222
E-mail: turismo@wwf.it
www.wwf.it/vacanze

Desc.: WWF Italy is the largest national environmental association, managing about 130 wildlife refuges. Volunteers are recruited for field study projects, restoration activities and conservation workcamps.

Spp.: Birds, wolves, sea turtles, whales, dolphins, bears.

Hab.: Sea, mountains, wetlands, lakes.

Loc.: All over the world.

Dur.: Min. 5 days; max. 2 weeks.

Per.: Year round.

L.term: Inquire with organisation.

Age: Min. 18.

Qualif.: Previous experience and specific qualifications maybe required according to chosen field.

Lang.: According to country of destination.

Cost: Inquire qwith organisation.

Agents: WWF has offices in many countries. Contact your national WWF office for information on workcamps in your country or on international volunteering opportunities. For a complete list of national offices see: www.panda.org/how_you_can_help/volunteer/index.cfm

Applic.: Request an application form. Volunteers must be WWF members to participate.

YCI – Youth Challenge International

20 Maud Street, Suite 305
Toronto, Ontario M5V 2M5 Canada
Tel.: ++1 (416) 504 3370
Fax: ++1 (416) 504 3376
E-mail: generalinfo@yci.org
www.yci.org

Desc.:	Youth Challenge International combines community development, health promotion and environmental work in adventurous projects carried out by teams of volunteers aged 18–30. Volunteers are accepted from across the world and represent different backgrounds. Conditions are basic and work schedules are demanding. Experienced staff teams ensures projects are dynamic and results oriented. Self-discovery, personal growth and community development are key elements.
Spp.:	Rainforest and riverine/coastal fauna.
Hab.:	Rainforest, coast, mountains.
Loc.:	Costa Rica, Guyana, Vanuatu, Benin, Ghana, Ethiopia, Kenia, Tanzania.
Dur.:	5, 6, 8, and 10 week projects.
L.term:	Placements for field staff are for 4–6 months at a time. Upon review, volunteers can work for another placement period.
Age:	Min. 18, max. 30.
Qualif.:	No specific qualifications are needed.
Lang.:	English.
Cost:	Cost range from CDN$2,900 to CDN $3,800 plus airfare. Volunteers must pay for inoculations and personal equipment.
Applic.:	Participants and field staff can apply at any time; applications can be submitted on-line.
Notes:	Due to insurance limitations YCI is able to accept applications only from Canadian citizens, residents or landed immigrants.

PROJECT LIST

AMERICAN CONSERVATION EXPERIENCE (ACE), USA

123 South San Francisco Street, Suite 7
Flagstaff, Arizona 86001 USA
Tel.: ++1 (928) 814 8225
E-mail: annis@conservationvolunteersusa.org
www.conservationvolunteersusa.org

Desc.: ACE organises volunteer work adventures in America's most stunning National Parks and allows to experience a different range of conservation opportunities throughout the Southwest U.S. Typical projects include trail reconstruction, habitat surveys and planting, revegetation in remote sections of the Grand Canyon, Zion and other National Parks. Work is physically demanding and production oriented in a supportive multi-cultural atmosphere.

Spp.: Work with flora and fauna ecosystems ranging from low desert to 3,500 ft (1,200 m) mountains.

Hab.: Grand Canyon desert, high elevation mountain forests, and everything in between.

Loc.: Grand Canyon, Zion and other National Parks and Forests. Home base in Flagstaff, Arizona

Dur.: 8-12 weeks (longer terms possible).

Per.: Year round.

L.term: Inquire with organisation.

Age: 18-35.

Qualif.: Physically capable of hiking and camping in remote areas. Sense of adventure. Enthusiastic work ethic.

Work: Trail construction and restoration, planting/revegetation, forest restoration, habitat survey.

Lang.: English.

Cost: Air travel to and from Phoenix. Booking fees through our international partners apply, typically US$300-500 (approx.EUR 250-400) for 12 week program. Visit the registration page of the website for details.

Applic.: Register on line at www.usaconservation.org Accepting applications year round.

ADRIATIC DOLPHIN PROJECT, Croatia
Blue World – Plavi Svjet
Kastel 24 – 51551 Veli Losinj   Croatia
Tel./Fax: ++385 (51) 604 666/8
E-mail: adp@blue-world.org
www.adp.hr or www.blue-world.org

Desc: The Adriatic Dolphin Project is the longest ongoing study of a Bottlenose dolphin population in the Mediterranean. Since 2000 the research has been carried out by a local NGO, Blue World, in cooperation with international researchers. In 2003 Blue World constructed an educational centre in Veli Losinj which provides a professional environment to study cetaceans. The size of this community has been estimated at around 100–150 individuals, the majority of whom are identifiable. The standard research procedure includes photo-ID, acoustic and behavioural sampling. Dolphin habitat use, association patterns and reproductive rate are also recorded.

Spp.: Bottlenose dolphin (*Tursiops truncatus*). Other marine species occasionally observed include: marine turtles, blue sharks, tuna, cormorants, seagulls, terns and other marine birds.

Hab.: Coastal waters.

Loc: Cres–Losinj archipelago, Northern Adriatic Sea (Croatia).

Travel: The island of Losinj can be easily reached by bus, via Rijeka, from Trieste (Italy), Zagreb (Croatia) and Ljubljana (Slovenia), or (during the summer) by ferry from Venice or hydrofoil from Trieste (Italy); all these cities have major train and flight connections.

Dur.: 12 days. Up to 4 volunteers can participate in each shift.

Per.: May to September.

L.term: Extra days beyond the initial 12 can be arranged.

Age: Min.18.

Qualif.: Interest in the research and positive motivation is required. Volunteers must be physically fit and able to endure long hours, possibly in hot sun or in harsh sea conditions on a small boat. The team cooperates in data handling and analysis. Film projections and lectures are organised and volunteers are also free to visit the island and enjoy its sights.

Work: Behavioural observations, acoustics and photo-ID of the dolphins from the inflatable boat. With good weather researchers and volunteers

83

conduct boat surveys. With bad weather volunteers may work in the centre, entering and analysing data and matching the catalogued dolphins. Lectures on the dolphin biology are also carried out by the researchers.

Lang.: English, Croatian, Italian and German are spoken by researchers.

Accom.: Shared rooms in a house in Veli Losinj. Volunteers take part in cooking and housekeeping.

Cost: Min. EUR700, max. EU830 (approx. GB£ 470–560), depending on the season. Volunteers must confirm that they have personal insurance. The contributions of volunteers are used to defray part of the research costs and food. Fees do not include travel expenses. All tourists coming to Losinj are required to pay the local tourist fee (about EUR1/day for the duration of the programme).

Applic.: Write, e-mail, phone or refer to the website for further information. A downloadable application form is available on the website. Given the limited availability of places and the high number of applications, early booking is suggested.

Notes: From 2–3 researchers reside at the field station with the volunteers. Safety gear for on the boat is provided. Volunteers must be aware that they are participating in scientific research rather than a vacation programme.

AFRICAN CONSERVATION TRUST, South Africa

P.O.Box 310, 3652 Linkhills South Africa
Tel.: ++27 (31) 767 5044
Fax: ++27 (31) 767 5044
E-mail: info@projectafrica.com
www.projectafrica.com

Desc.: The African Conservation Trust has initiated a urban greening project on the north coast of KwaZulu-Natal.

Spp.: Indigenous trees.

Hab.: Coastal forest.

Loc.: Dukuduku Forest, St Lucia, KwaZulu-Natal, South Africa.

Travel: Flight to Durban International Airport where volunteers are met.

Dur.: From 2 weeks up to 1 year.

Per.: Year round, this is a permanent project.

L.term: Long-term volunteers are welcome.

Age: Min. 18.

Qualif.: Volunteers must have good physical health, a very flexible attitude, be able to withstand long working hours on various tasks.

Work: Assisting with various construction projects at the nursery as well as propagation of trees and community work.

Lang.: English.

Accom.: Volunteers must pay for their own accommodation at nearby backpackers.

Cost: GB£400 per month.

Applic.: Request application form.

Notes: The trust has other projects in South Africa.

AFRICAN IMPACT LION REHABILITATION PROGRAMMES, Zimbabwe

African Impact
P.O.Box 1218, Gweru, Zimbabwe
Tel ++263 488 2721 – 0871 720 5439 (from within the UK).
E-mail: impact@africanencounter.org
www.africanimpact.com

Desc.: African Impact supports with the help of volunteers 2 lion rehabilitation Centres in Zimbabwe: Antelope Park and Victoria Falls. In Antelope Park, volunteers walk and work with lions in an exclusive private game reserve, where they get involved in the research on lions behaviour and work on the world's only programme for their release into the wild. They also assist with orphaned Elephants and in the vital wildlife management and boundary patrols of the reserve. The programme at Victoria Falls is a combination of work on lion breeding and rehabilitation and an extension of the Antelope Park programme.

Spp.: Lions, elephants and free roaming wildlife.

Hab.: In the heart of the Zimbabwe Midlands at Antelope Park, and just outside the Victoria Falls in a Big 5 conservancy area

Loc.: Two locations in Zimbabwe: Antelope Park, 10km from Gweru town centre; Victoria Falls in NW Zimbabwe.

Travel: Antelope Park: fly into Harare where volunteers are met. Victoria Falls: fly to Victoria Falls from Johannesburg, where volunteers are met.

Dur.: 1-2 months.

Per.: Year round.

Age: Min 17, max dependent on participants health.

Qualif.: No previous experience necessary, training will be given.

Work: Data gathering and observation of lions behaviour, meat preparation and bottle feeding of cubs, boundary patrols and snare sweeps in the reserve. Supervision of cubs and adolescent lions out in the bush as they learn about their natural environment and practice their hunting skills on small game within the reserve.

Lang.: English.

Accom.: Comfortable twin thatched rooms with adjacent clean ablutions.

Cost: US$3,230 for one month, US$4850 for two months. This includes food, comfortable board and transports as well as project donation.

Applic.: Green Volunteers Standard Applictation Form (see page 255) welcome.

AFRICAN WILD DOG CONSERVATION (AWDC), Zambia

C/O PO Box 80, Mfuwe,
Eastern Province, Zambia.
Tel.: ++26 (099) 593 27
E-mail: martynb@awdczambia.org
www.awdczambia.org

Desc.: AWDC has been studying the eastern Zambia population of African wild dogs since 1999. Wild dogs are one of the most highly endangered carnivore species in Africa with a population estimate of 3,000 to 5,000. Zambia is one of only 6 countries with a large population left.

Spp.: African Wild Dog (Lycaon pictus).

Hab.: Riverine Valley.

Loc.: South Luangwa National Park, Zambia.

Travel: Plane to Lusaka where volunteers are met for flight or drive into camp. Pick up in Lusaka must be previously arranged.

Dur.: Usually 30 days due to visa requirements.

Per.: Dry season only, March to end of November.

L.term: Enquire with the organisation after initial month trial.

Age: Min. 20.

Qualif.: Biological or Environmental Sciences or related degree graduates only.

Work: Radio tracking wild dogs, prey surveys, hyena surveys, data entry, camp maintenance.

Lang.: English.

Accom.: Shared safari tent, shared bathroom. Need own sleeping bag and mosquito net.

Cost: US$2,000 for 30 days. This includes food, board and transport to and from Lusaka.

Applic.: Send application and CV to the above email address. Green Volunteers Standard Applictation Form welcome.

Notes: Max 2 volunteers at a time. 100% of fees go directly to project. Volunteers need to arrange insurance and visas.

AMIGOS DE LAS AVES, Costa Rica

Flor de Mayo, 600m norte Super Santiago, Rio Segundo, Costa Rica
Apdo 2306 - 4050 , Alajuela, Costa Rica.
Tel./Fax: ++ (506) 441 2658
E-mail: richmar@racsa.co.cr
www.hatchedtoflyfree.org

Desc.: Amigos de las Aves is a Costa Rican non profit organization dedicated to the conservation of the two endangered species of macaws found in Costa Rica. Activity is concentrated on breeding and re-introduction into their native habitat at designated release sites. Recently, for the first time, a pair of captive bred macaws have produced two youngsters in the wild. The Organisation also runs a refuge with various endemic birds and an education program for schools in the local areas.

Spp: Scarlet macaw (*ara macao*), Great Green macaw (*Ara ambigua*), 4 species of Amazon parrot, 2 of Toucan, 2 of Aracari and various small parakeets.

Loc.: Central Valley: 10 minutes from San Jose airport, 40 minutes from San Jose city, 5 minutes from Alajuela town.

Dur.: Minimum of a month at the Breeding Centre - two or more in the 'field'.

Per.: Year round.

L.term: No long term limits.

Age: Min.18.

Qualif.: No qualifications necessary - but 'bird' experience would be a help. Students in the field of biology preferably for 'field' work.

Work: Breeding Centre: feeding, aviary maintenance, perching, cleaning, making toys, playing with babies. In the field: working with biologist in our field research program.

Lang: English, Spanish helpful in the field.

Accom.: Homestays: shared facilites or private room and shower in a family home.

Cost: Breeding Centre: US$12-15 per day for accommodation, 3 meals and laundry. In the field: basic facilities and meals.

Applic.: Via email or by telephone.

Notes: Field research opportunities are available, as are gardening, educational and fund raising opportunities upon application.

ANDEAN BEAR RESEARCH PROJECT, Ecuador

Fundación Espíritu del Bosque
Barcelona 3-11 y Tolosa, La Floresta, Quito Ecuador
Tel.: ++593 (2) 239 703
E-mail: volunteer@andeanbear.org
www.andeanbear.org

Desc.: The only project in the world that radiotracks Andean bears in the wild. The research is conducted as part of ongoing efforts to expand protected areas and prevent the extinction of the species. The primary purpose of this study is to determine the use of the habitat, activity patterns and size of home range and core area of the Andean bear.

Spp.: Andean Spectacled Bear (*Tremarctos ornatus*).

Loc.: Intag region, north western Ecuador.

Travel: Airplane to Quito. Transportation to project area provided.

Dur.: Min. 4 weeks.

Per.: Year round.

L.term: Volunteers can stay for as long as they want.

Age: Min. 18 years.

Qualif.: There are no special qualifications to participate in the project. However, volunteers should have a good level of fitness as the work can be strenuous.

Work: Volunteers follow roads or trails, listening for signals from the bears by means of radio-telemetry equipment. Volunteers may also be required to clear trails to be used for tracking, help collect samples and record marking behaviour.

Lang.: English or Spanish.

Accom.: Traditional Andean house with electricity, running water. Volunteers sleep in a large dormitory room.

Cost: Approx. US$420 for the first month, US$380 per month thereafter. Includes three meals per day, accommodation, transportation to project site. Transport costs at project site not included (approx. $15-20 per month).

Appl.: A simple application via e-mail. Include possible dates.

ARFA – ASOCIACION DE RESCATE DE FAUNA, Venezuela

Calle La Vista, Edif. La Vista, Apto. 11–B,
Colinas de Los Caobos, Caracas 1050   Venezuela
Tel.: ++58 (212) 782 4182
Fax: ++58 (212) 793 4421
E-mail: lucyalio@cantv.net
www.geocities.com/arfavenezuela/index.html

Desc.: ARFA is an NGO devoted to the conservation of wildlife in Venezuela, through educational programmes and its centre where animals of the central plains are rescued and rehabilitated.

Spp.: Capuchin and howler monkeys (*Cebus olivacea,Allouata sealicus*), aquatic turtles and terrapins, parrots, macaw (*Ara spp.*). Occasionaly deer, ant eating bear, iguana, alligator, some birds of prey and many other bird species from the area.

Hab.: Plains or flatlands, 'llanos' (similar to savannah), rainforest.

Loc.: Flatlands of the Edo.Cojedes, between the towns of Las Vegas and Tirado, Central Venezuela.

Travel: Airplane to Caracas, car or bus from Caracas to project area. Transportation from Caracas to project area will be provided.

Dur.: 3 months.

Per.: Year round.

L.term: 3 months limited by visa requirements.

Age: Min. 22.

Qualif.: Veterinary, biologist or related careers and good physical condition.

Work: Feeding the animals, facility maintenance, assistance with the ecological educational programmes, wildlife record keeping and observation, assistance on wildlife rehabilitation.

Lang.: Spanish.

Accom.: Private room in a house with indoor bathroom and shower.

Cost: Room, accommodation and simple meals are provided. There is a fee of US$450.

Applic.: Via e-mail with the subject heading: 'Volunteer program'. In the text, include CV, letter of intentions, 2 references and possible dates.

Notes: Web page has other volunteers' experiences. Health insurance and vaccinations (yellow fever, tetanus and rabies) mandatory.

ASOCIACION SALVEMOS LAS TORTUGAS DE PARISMINA (ASTOP), Costa Rica

Barra de Parismina
Siquirres, Limon 7200 Costa Rica
Tel.: ++504 (710) 77 03
E-mail: parisminaturtles@gmail.com
www.parisminaturtles.org

Desc.:	ASTOP is a Costa Rican grass roots conservation project whose primary goal is to save Leatherback, Green, and Hawksbill sea turtles from local poachers who take the turtles and their eggs to sell for profit. Through night beach patrol and hatchery monitoring, ASTOP has decreased poaching by 60% in the past 3 years.
Spp.:	Leatherback, Green, and Hawksbill turtles.
Hab.:	Tropical Coasts and Oceans.
Loc.:	Barra de Parismina, Caribbean Coast of Costa Rica.
Travel:	Fly to San José, 2 hour bus to Siquirres, 2 hour bus to Cabo Blanco, 20 minute boat to Parismina.
Dur.:	Preferably 1 week or more.
Per.:	Peak season March - October.
L.term:	Preferably 1 week or more.
Age:	Min.18, no upper limit. Under 18 with adult supervision or approval letter.
Qualif.:	Physically able to walk on beach in all types of weather in the dark. Commitment to turtle conservation.
Work:	Assist local guides with beach patrol, nest relocation and monitoring hatchery. Office assistance if needed.
Lang.:	English or Spanish. Spanish encouraged but not compulsory.
Accom.:	Private rooms with local families with 3 meals, laundry. Hotels and camping also.
Cost:	Varies from $15-25/day, depending on accommodation and length of stay.
Applic.:	Send e-mail to parisminaturtles@gmail.com describing availablity, age, special qualifications and restrictions, etc.

BDRI-Bottlenose Dolphin Research Institute: Dolphins, Education and Research, Italy

Via Diaz 4, 07020 Golfo Aranci (Sassari) Italy
Tel.: ++39 (346) 081541
E-mail: info@thebdri.com
www.thebdri.com

Desc.: BDRI carries on scientific research and education programmes to contribute to the conservation of bottlenose dolphins and of the marine environment. Motivated volunteers can participate with BDRI in comprehensive and intensive periods of training in the study of wild bottlenose dolphins.

Spp.: Bottlenose dolphin (Tursiops truncates).

Hab.: Mediterranean coast.

Loc.: Golfo Aranci, Emerald coast, Sardinia, Italy.

Travel: Plane to Olbia Airport or Ferry from mainland Italy directly to Golfo Aranci or to Olbia (large town 15 km near the project), bus or train to project area.

Dur.: 6 or 13 days or more.

Per.: Year round.

L. term: Volunteers can join a project for a longer period.

Age: Min. 18.

Qualif.: A strong interest and motivation to participate to dolphin research and conservation campaigns. No background knowledge of cetaceans is required.

Work: Boat-based research surveys investigating ecology and behaviour of bottlenose dolphins. Data collection and analyses as part of an ongoing research (bioacoustics analysis, photoidentification, behaviour).

Lang.: English, Spanish or Italian

Accom.: In an apartament in bunk beds. Space is limited in the field base. Bedding is not furnished, sleeping bags required.

Cost: From EUR375 to EUR450 for 6 days (approx.GB£220-300). From EUR700 to EUR900 for 13 days (approx.GB£440-600). Room and Board included. Volunteers must provide for their own transportation to Golfo Aranci.

Applic.: Download application form from website or request it via e-mail.

BIMINI LEMON SHARK PROJECT, Bahamas
Bimini Biological Field Station
c/o RSMAS University of Miami
9300 SW 99 Street, Miami, Florida 33176-2050 USA
Tel./Fax: ++1 (305) 274 0628
E-mail: sgruber@rsmas.miami.edu
www.miami.edu/sharklab/

Desc.:	Study of the feeding, predator-prey relations, growth, survival, movements and community relations of the lemon shark using field techniques and computer modelling/simulations. Disciplines of systems ecology, bioenergetics, life history studies, population genetics, ethology and sensory biology involved.
Spp.:	Lemon shark, (*Negaprion brevirostris*) and its prey organisms, primarily mojarra fish, (*Gerres spp.*).
Hab.:	Coastal reefs, mangrove forest, seagrass meadows.
Loc.:	Bimini Bahamas, 85 km east of Miami across the Florida straits.
Travel:	Flight to Fort Lauderdale International Airport; taxi to Fort Lauderdale Executive Airport for Bimini Island Air charter.
Dur.:	Min. 1 month.
Per.:	Year round.
L.term:	With project leader's approval.
Age:	Min.20, max. 38.
Qualif.:	Students or graduates with a biology background are given priority, preferably with an interest in graduate school. Also necessary some boating skills, swimming and computer literacy.
Work:	Field research on boats in shallow water all hours of the day; cooking, household and mechanical maintenance, etc.
Lang.:	English.
Accom.:	Wood frame, air-conditioned house with bunk beds for 4 persons in small dorm rooms.
Cost:	Room and board approx. US$625/month. Transportation not included. Return flight to Bimini approx. US$220.
Applic.:	Contact Dr. Samuel H. Gruber or Katie Grudecki.

BIRDS OF TORTUGUERO, Costa Rica

Caribbean Conservation Corporation
4424 NW 13th Street, Suite A–1
Gainesville, Florida 32609 USA
Tel.: ++1 (352) 373 6441 – Fax: ++1 (352) 375 2449
E-mail: resprog@cccturtle.org
www.cccturtle.org

Desc.: Tortuguero is the most important site in Costa Rica for resident and migratory neotropical birds. Caribbean Conservation Corporation (CCC) is working to gather information on the status of the bird populations and the number of species residing or migrating here (up to 300).

Spp.: Resident and migratory neotropical birds.

Hab.: Tropical coast.

Loc.: Tortuguero, Costa Rica.

Travel: Airplane to San José, where participants are met.

Dur.: 1, 2 or 3 weeks.

Per.: March to June and August to November.

L.term: Volunteers can stay longer than 3 weeks with prior approval.

Age: Min. 18.

Qualif.: Volunteers must be in good physical condition, able to live in a rustic setting and tolerant of harsh weather.

Work: Assist researchers in mist netting, point counts, identification and transects.

Lang.: English.

Accom.: Dormitory style with shared baths in research station.

Cost: US$1,399 for 1 week; US$1,849 for 2 weeks; US$2,299 for 3 weeks. Cost includes 2 nights in San José, transfers to Tortuguero, all room and board at CCC station in Tortuguero.

Agents: Contact the organisation directly.

Applic.: On-line application form to be submitted with a US$200 deposit.

BLACK RHINO, Kenya

Earthwatch Institute (Europe)
267 Banbury Road
Oxford OX2 7HT   UK
Tel.: ++44 (1865) 318 831 –   Fax: ++44 (1865) 311 383
E-mail: projects@earthwatch.org.uk
www.earthwatch.org/europe

Desc.: The number of Black Rhinos in Kenya has declined from an estimated 20,000 in 1970 to about 500 today. The principal reason for this decline is unrelenting poaching—the rhino is sought for the medicinal and decorative use of its prestigious horn. This project is in the enclosed 100 km² Sweetwaters Black Rhino Reserve, which has a healthy and well protected rhino population. But new concerns have arisen: competition with other large herbivores, predatation of calves by hyenas and lions and an excessive concentration of rhinos. Only an accurate study of these factors can help preserving the balance of the ecosystem.

Opp.: Black rhino (*Diceros bicornis*), zebra, impala, kudu, lion, leopard, hyena, wild dog, giraffe, elephant, wildebeest, buffalo.

Hab.: Savannah with acacias.

Loc.: Sweetwaters Black Rhino Reserve, Nanyuki, Kenya.

Travel: Airplane to Nairobi then bus to Nanyuki.

Dur.: 12 days.

Per.: January, February, August, September.

L.term: No long-term volunteer opportunities available.

Age: Min. 18.

Qualif.: No special skills required.

Work: Volunteers observe rhinos and other large mammals and gather data on vegetation and feeding preferences of the competing species. Acacia trees damage is also assessed.

Lang.: English.

Accom.: Comfortable single rooms in the Reserve Research Centre.

Cost: Approx. GB£1,500 (US$1,900).

Agents: Earthwatch Institute (Europe, see organisation list).

Applic.: Apply online at www.earthwatch.org/europe.

BLACK SHEEP INN, Ecuador

Andres Hammerman & Michelle Kirby
P.O. Box 05–01–240 Latacunga, Cotopaxi Ecuador
Tel.: ++593 (3) 2814 587
Fax: ++593 (3) 2814 588 (call ahead)
E-mail: info@blacksheepinn.com
www.blacksheepinn.com

Desc.: A small Ecological Lodge in the Ecuadorian Sierra. It grows its organic vegetables, uses composting toilets, gray water systems and a recycling programme. Volunteers learn how low impact sustainable tourism works. A small reforestation programme is also carried out with native tree species. Lodge managers also help the local community and in conservation work.

Spp.: The Illiniza Ecological Reserve has over 172 species of birds; it also may host the endangered Andean spectacled bear (*tremarctos ornatus*).

Hab.: High Andean Sierra and Andean Cloud Forest.

Loc.: Western Cordillera of Central Ecaudor, Cotopaxi.

Travel: Flight to Quito, bus Quito to Chugchilan and to the Inn.

Dur.: Min. 6 weeks.

Per.: Year round.

L.term: Long term welcome after initial period.

Age: Min. 25, no max.

Qualif.: Volunteers must be fit and physically active. No allergies, to animals: dogs, llamas, sheep, chickens and ducks. Useful skills are: small business administration, farm work, trip leading, hotel service, computer skills and construction.

Work: Volunteers help in the lodge and in taking care of guests needs (hiking and travel information, etc.) general maintenance, gardening, cooking and cleaning, animal care and participating in all the hikes, horseback rides and excursions.

Lang.: English and Spanish are essential.

Accom.: Comfortable room at the Inn with full bedding.

Cost: First 2 weeks are a trial period; volunteers pay US$10/day for room and board. After trial week, room and board are usually free.

Applic.: Send e-mail or visit website for more information.

BLUE-FRONTED PARROT PROJECT, Argentina

D.pto Vertebrados Museo de Ciencias Naturales de La Plata

Fac. de Ciencias Naturales y Museo - Universidad Nacional de La Plata

La Plata Argentina

E-mail: igorberkunsky@yahoo.com.ar

www.loreros.com.ar

Desc.: The objective of this long-term project is to obtain information on the reproductive ecology of the blue-fronted parrot in order to conserve and sustainably manage the species in the Gran Chaco, Argentina. Volunteers have the opportunity to visit a remote part of Argentina while gaining experience in a variety of field ornithology methodologies and learning about the local relevant issues, such as poaching and the pet trade.

Spp.: Blue-fronted parrot or loro hablador (*Amazona aestiva*).

Hab.: The Dry Chaco, a thick thorny forest known as the "Impenetrable", with over 000 species of birds and mammals such as jaguar, anteaters, brocket deer and armadillo.

Loc.: Blue-fronted Parrot Natural Park, Chaco Province, Argentina.

Travel: By bus from Buenos Aires to Castelli, Chaco Province.

Dur.: 2–3 months.

Per.: October to March.

L.term: Volunteer periods are specific terms as required for the project.

Age: Min. 18.

Qualif.: Responsible, self-disciplined, tolerant to extreme weather and insects, willing to work in group and able to stay at a remote place without long distance communication such as telephone or internet. Bird handling experience preferred but not required.

Work: Daily nest-checking assistance (tree-climbing), territory spot mapping, banding, blood and diet sampling, parrot point counts, behavioral observations, fruit censuses and data entry.

Lang.: Spanish, English and French also spoken.

Accom.: Camping, conditions are very basic.

Cost: Approx. US$85/week. Lodging and equipment provided.

Applic.: Send cover letter and CV with references to Igor Berkunsky.

BOHOROK ENVIRONMENTAL CENTRE, Indonesia

Jl. Wahid Hasyim No 51, Medan 20154
Sumatera Utara Indonesia
Tel./Fax: ++62 (61) 451 4363/451 4360
E-mail: lawang@indosat.net.id or mail@paneco.ch
www.sumatranorangutan.org
www.paneco.ch

Desc.: The Centre originates from a programme started in 1995 to help control the environmental impact of tourism on the Orangutan Rehabilitation Station of Bohorok. The Centre has input in the town planning process and in environmental management programmes (such as water pollution control/waste water treatment). Other goals include environmental education in general and development of eco-tourism.

Spp.: Orangutan/environmental education.

Hab.: Tropical rainforest.

Loc.: Bukit Lawang, Bohorok, Langkat, North Sumatra, Indonesia.

Travel: Airplane to Medan, then bus to Bukit Lawang.

Dur.: Min. 2, max. 4 months.

Per.: Year round.

L.term: Inquire with the organisation.

Age: Min. 21.

Qualif.: Specific skills are required depending on the topic. Teamwork capacities and interest in Indonesian culture are important.

Work: Development of the Centre: environmental education (school programme), ecotourism, environmental management (waste, water bio-filtration). No work at the Orangutan Quarantine Station.

Lang.: English. Bahasa Indonesian would be helpful.

Accom.: Simple local accommodation. Free housing food not included.

Cost: US$500 for students, US$1,000 for persons with regular income, travel and insurance are covered by the volunteer.

Agents: PanEco Foundation, Ms. Cornelia Jenny, Chileweg 5, CH– 8415 Berg am Irchel, Switzerland, tel.: ++41 (52) 318 2323, fax: ++41 (52) 318 1906, e-mail: mail@paneco.ch

Applic.: Download and mail the application form, from www.paneco.ch.

BOTTLENOSE DOLPHIN PROJECT, Belize

Oceanic Society Expeditions
Fort Mason Center, Building E
San Francisco, CA 94123 USA
Tel.: ++1 (415) 441 1106 – (800) 326 7491 (toll free in N.America)
Fax: ++1 (415) 474 3395
E-mail: info@oceanic-society.org
www.oceanic-society.org

Desc.: The Oceanic Society has been studying the behavioural ecology of free-ranging bottlenose dolphins in Belize since 1992 at its Blackbird Caye research station in the pristine waters of coral reef-ringed Turneffe Atoll. This is the first long-term study of dolphins in such a diverse ecosystem. The objective is to examine foraging patterns and social behaviour, as well as continue long-term baseline monitoring of dolphin distribution. Participants work directly with researchers in small teams, from small boats inside the atoll. There will also be some free time for snorkeling and birdwatching.

Spp.: Bottlenose dolphin (*Tursiops truncatus*).

Hab.: Tropical coastal waters.

Loc.: Turneffe Atoll, Belize, Central America.

Travel: Airplane to Belize City.

Dur.: 8 days.

Per.: Year-round.

L.term: Inquire with organisation.

Age: Min. 18.

Qualif.: Volunteers must be able to swim.

Work: Assist researchers with fieldwork such as collecting environmental data, searching for dolphins, recording behaviour, and identifying dolphins individually through natural markings.

Lang.: English.

Accom.: Beachfront cabanas with porches, double rooms with private bath.

Cost: US$1,790, excluding flight.

Applic.: Request application form to be returned with a deposit of US$400.

BROWN BEAR PROJECT, Russia
The Ecovolunteer Network
Meyersweg 29, 7553 AX Hengelo The Netherlands
Tel.: ++31 (74) 250 8250
Fax: ++31 (74) 250 6572
E-mail: info@ecovolunteer.org
www.ecovolunteer.org

Desc.: Orphan bear cubs are rescued from hunters with the aim of raising them and returning them back into the wild. The cubs need to be fed for approximately 3 months. In the spring, one-year old bear cubs are released and some are equipped with radio-collars, and their dayly movements are recorded.

Spp.: Brown bear (*Ursus arctos*).

Hab.: Typical southern taiga.

Loc.: Isolated biological station approx. 400 km west of Moscow.

Travel: Airplane to Moscow then train to Staraya Toropa, meeting is at the train station. Private transportation by car from Moscow can be arranged for an extra cost of EUR110.

Dur.: Minimum one month commitment.

Per.: February – October.

L.term: Inquire with the organisation.

Age: Min. 18

Qualif.: February – April: some practice and experience of animal handling is preferred. May – October: be very fit, long and strenuous walking may be required.

Work: February – April: preparing food for and feeding of brown bear orphan cubs. May – October: radio-tracking dayly movements of released one-year old bear cubs.

Lang.: English or Russian.

Accom.: Simple rooms at a biological station.

Cost: Approx.US$1270 for the first month; US$170/week for the 5th, 6th, 7th and 8th week; US$80/week for the 9th and every extra week.

Agents: The Ecovolunteer Network at www.ecovolunteer.org.

Applic.: The Ecovolunteer Network (see Organisation list).

CALIFORNIA WILDLIFE CENTER, California USA

26026, Piuma Road, Calabasas, California 91302 USA
Tel.: ++1 (818) 222 2658 (administration)
E-mail: victoria@californiawildlifecenter.org
volunteer@californiawildlifecenter.org
www.californiawildlifecenter.org

Desc.:	California Wildlife Center is a non-profit organization dedicated to the rescue, rehabilitation and release of sick, injured and orphaned native wildlife. The Center provides expert medical care and community outreach and education. Since 1998 CWC has responded to over 10,000 wildlife emergencies in Los Angeles County for a wide variety of species: from raptors and songbirds to pelicans, sea lions, coyotes and deer. The Center works with a small staff, as trained interns, volunteers and a number of consulting veterinarians.
Spp.:	Birds (65%), native mammals (squirrels, opossum, coyotes and deer). Marine mammals are also rescued from the Malibu's coastline.
Hab.:	Southern California.
Loc.:	Southern California, Los Angeles County.
Travel:	Fly into either Burbank, CA or Los Angeles International, then by car.
Dur.:	Minimum of 3 months.
Per.:	Volunteers are accepted year round, but are needed most during the busy season: March through September.
Age:	Min. 18.
Qualif.:	Ability to work as part of a team, experience with animal care a plus.
Work:	Volunteers will go through mandatory training classes, including but not limited to basic training, dispatch (how to handle calls from the public), baby bird, squirrel and Marine Mammal Rescue training. Volunteers prepare food, feed animals, clean enclosures, wash dishes, do laundry, answer phones, and do administrative support as necessary. Shifts from from 8 to 10 hours per day depending on season.
Lang.:	English.
Accom.:	No accommodations available.
Cost:	Volunteers must provide accommodation, food and transportation. There is no public transportation to the site.

CANO PALMA BIOLOGICAL STATION, Costa Rica
COTERC, Canadian Organization for Tropical Education and Rainforest Conservation
Tortuguero SJO 1882 Costa Rica
Tel.: ++(506) 709 8052
P.O. Box 335, Pickering, Ontario L1V 2R6, Canada
Tel.:++1 (905) 831 8809 – Fax: ++1 (905) 831 4203
E-mail: info@coterc.org   www.coterc.org

Desc.:	The station serves as a facility for visiting biologists and student groups interested in studying various aspects of neotropical lowland forest biology. The station also supports a volunteer programme.
Spp.:	Over 300 bird species, 120 mammal species, 100 reptile and amphibians.
Hab.:	Lowland Atlantic tropical wet forest.
Loc.:	9 km north of the village of Tortuguero and Tortuguero National Park, in northeastern Costa Rica.
Travel:	Tortuguero is accessible only by bus then boat, or by small airplane from San José. There are no roads nearby. Contact station staff for travel details well in advance to ensure accommodation available
Dur.:	Min. 2 weeks.
Per.:	Year round.
L.term:	Applicants with useful skills will be taken into consideration.
Age:	Min. 18.
Qualif.:	Volunteers should be enthusiastic, self-starting, in good physical condition and able to fit in with remote field station conditions.
Work.:	Participation in the station's activities, including grounds and equipment maintenance, helping out in the kitchen, etc. Assisting visiting researchers.
Lang.:	English, Spanish.
Cost:	US$180 or colone equivalent per week, in cash. No travellers cheques or personal cheques. Tortuguero has no banks.
Accom.:	A dormitory with bunks capable of sleeping 30 persons. Bedding is provided, but volunteers should bring mosquito nets. Conditions are basic but clean and comfortable.
Applic.:	Contact COTERC in Canada.

CAPE TRIBULATION TROPICAL RESEARCH STATION, Australia

PMB 5, Cape Tribulation
Qld. 4873   Australia
Tel.- Fax: ++61 (7) 4098 00 63
E-mail: austrop@austrop.org.au
www.austrop.org.au

Desc.:   An independent field research station (in a World Heritage site) open to all researchers interested in working in the area, funded through the Australian Tropical Research Foundation. Station staff conduct research on a wide range of issues, from radio-tracking bats, rainforest rehabilitation to weed control, alternative technology and the design of GPS animal tracking systems.

Spp.:   About 12 microbats and 5 mega bats; figs: at least 12 species; angiosperm plant species, many rare and locally endemic. Captive colony of 9 flying foxes (*Pteropus* spp.) at the Station.

Hab.:   Lowland rainforest and tropical coastal communities.

Loc.:   Australia (far north Queensland).

Travel: Contact the station for travel details (hugh@austrop.org.au).

Dur.:   After initial 2 weeks volunteers can negotiate a longer stay.

Per.:   Year round.

L.term: Encouraged; duration is negotiable after the first stay.

Age: Over 23 preferred.

Qualif.:   Any skills; carpenters, botanists, computer programmers, etc. Researchers must provide a proposed research summary.

Work: From routine maintenance, forest regeneration to assisting with research projects.

Lang.:   English.

Accom.:   The station has bunkhouse accommodation and 2 air-con labs.

Cost: US$25/day for food and accommodation. Interns, students and researchers pay more. Rates are negotiable.

Applic.:   Applications should be sent via e-mail (be prepared to send reminders) to the Station director. Also send a brief CV with photo and a statement of experience. Faxes can only be received during working hours (recognise time differences).

Notes: The climate and conditions (Nov.-April) can be wet in this remote area.

CARDIGAN BAY MARINE WILDLIFE CENTRE, Wales UK

Patent Slip Building, Glanmor Terrace, New Quay
Ceredigion, West Wales SA45 9PS
Tel.: ++01 (54) 556 0032
E-mail: volunteer@cbmwc.org
www.cbmwc.org

Desc.:	A research and education project focusing on cetaceans and other marine life. An opportunity to gain valuable skills used in environmental and conservation fields. Assist with CBMWC's ongoing research and education programmes concerning the marine wildlife of Cardigan Bay, including photo-identification of bottlenose dolphins.
Spp.:	Bottlenose dolphins, harbour porpoise, Atlantic grey seals, sunfish, jellyfish and other marine fauna.
Hab.:	Temperate seas, coasts.
Loc.:	Wales, United Kingdom.
Travel:	Train to Aberystwyth or Carmarthen and then bus to New Quay (on the coast between Aberystwyth and Cardigan).
Dur.:	Volunteering opportunities from 2 days a week to 6 months.
Per.:	Year round (focus April - October).
L.term:	Limited long term positions up to 6 months (see notes).
Age:	Min. 15. There is no maximum age. Something for everyone.
Qualif.:	Willingness to work in a conscientious, responsible and reliable manner, Enthusiastic and hard working, interest in marine wildlife and conservation.
Work:	Boat based data collection surveys, educate passengers, day to day operation of visitor centre, photo-identification, advise public, data input.
Lang.:	English
Accom.:	Local accommodation can be arranged.
Cost:	GB£45-50 per week for accomodation. Volunteers are responsible for their own food, travel and accommodation costs.
Applic.:	Send CV and a covering letter detailing any relevant experience.
Notes:	Long term posts (6 months): photo-identification catalogue officer, Sightings officer and volunteer co-ordinator

CARETTA RESEARCH PROJECT, USA

Savannah Science Museum

P.O.Box 9841

Savannah, Georgia 31412 USA

Tel.: ++1 (912) 447 8655 – Fax: ++1 (912) 447 8656

E-mail: wassawCRP@aol.com

www.carettaresearchproject.org

Desc.:	Since 1973, the Savannah Science Museum, in co-operation with the U.S. Fish and Wildlife Service and the Wassaw Island Trust has been conducting a research and conservation programme on the endangered loggerhead sea turtle. The program's purpose is to learn more about population levels, trends, and nesting habits of loggerheads. It also hopes to enhance the survival of eggs and hatchlings and to involve the public in this effort.
Spp.:	Loggerhead sea turtle (*Caretta caretta*).
Hab.:	Coastal barrier island.
Loc.:	Wassaw Island, about 10 miles south of Savannah.
Travel:	Bus or airplane to Savannah, then boat to Wassaw. The island is accessible only by boat.
Dur.:	1 week.
Per.:	May to September.
L.term:	Inquire with organisation.
Age:	Min. 15.
Qualif.:	No previous experience required.
Work:	Volunteers patrol the beaches in search of female turtles, tag and measure the animals, record data, monitor the nests and escort hatchlings to the sea.
Lang.:	English.
Accom.:	Rustic cabins (dormitory style).
Cost:	The registration fee is US$650/week.Most of the fee is tax-deductible (for US citizens) and includes lodging, meals, leadership/instruction and transportation to and from the island.
Applic.:	Full payment must accompany the application (refund is granted if cancellation takes place at least 60 days prior to departure).

CATS OF ROME, Italy
Torre Argentina Cat Sanctuary
Largo Argentina - 00100 Rome Italy
Tel./Fax: ++39 (06) 45 425 240
E-mail: torreargentina@tiscali.it
www.romancats.com

Desc.: An international group of volunteers, working together to raise the quality of life of Rome's abandoned cats. Approximately 600 cats get abandoned annually at the Sanctuary, which shelters anywhere from 250 to 450 cats. The Sanctuary promotes spay/neuter, proper animal care, adoptions and education projects through public relations events. All funding comes from the 8,000 tourists who visit every year.

Spp.: Domestic cat.

Loc.: In the archaelogical ruins of Largo Argentina.

Dur.: Minimum one week with a full or part time schedule.

Per.: All year round.

L.term: Inquire with the sanctuary.

Age: No age limits.

Qualif.: No particular qualifications other than strong motivation, flexibility and love of animals, especially cats.

Work: Everyday jobs include cleaning cages, distributing food and treating sick cats, clerical work such as stuffing envelopes, making photocopies and various other administrative tasks. People who are able to speak to the many tourists who visit, give a tour of the sanctuary (mostly in English) and eventually ask for contributions.

Lang.: English, other languages useful but not necessary.

Accom.: Housing is available for approximately EUR 500-700 (approx. US$650-850) a month. This usually consists of a nice room in someone's apartment with private bath.

Cost: Volunteers are responsible for travel, housing, food and personal expenses.

Applic.: Prospective volunteers must send a resumè with a short letter about themselves.

CENTRE FOR DOLPHIN STUDIES (CDS), South Africa

P.O. Box 1856
6600 Plettenberg Bay South Africa
Tel.: ++27 (44) 533 6185
E-mail: info@dolphinstudies.co.za
www.dolphinstudies.co.za

Desc.: A non-profit marine research trust, which aims to promote responsible research and effective conservation of whales, dolphins, seals and other marine animals. Volunteers are encouraged to help with surveys, population analysis, dietary studies, identification and monitoring of individual whales and/or dolphins: observe and conserve.

Spp.: Bottlenose and humpback dolphins Southern right, humpback and Bryde's whales.

Hab.: Coastal beaches, temperate ocean.

Loc.: Plettenberg Bay, South Africa.

Travel: Plane to Cape Town; plane/bus to George/Plettenberg Bay; bus/taxi to Plettenberg Bay.

Dur.: Minimum stay 1 month; 2-3 months is ideal.

Per.: Year round.

L.term: Volunteers may stay for a longer period if they wish.

Age: Min.18. No max age but fitness and good health are required.

Qualif.: No particular skills needed other than enthusiasm and an interest in marine life.

Work: Marine mammal surveys (land and boat); dietary analysis; photo id of whales and dolphins.

Lang.: English.

Accom.: Room in bunk house (5 rooms with bunk beds) with lounge/dining/ kitchen area, showers and toilets. Outside deck area.

Cost: GB£175 per week (approx. US$300).

Applic.: Volunteers may use the Green Volunteers Standard Application form.

CENTRE FOR REHABILITATION OF WILDLIFE (CROW), South Africa

P. O. Box 53007, Yellowwood Park
4011Durban, Kwa-Zulu Natal   South Africa
Tel: ++27 (31) 462 127 – Fax:+ +27 (31) 462 9700
E-mail: info@crowkzn.co.za
www.crowkzn.co.za

Desc.: CROW is a non-profit organisation that takes care of South Africa's indigenous wildlife, both injured and orphaned. CROW is the only rehabilitation centre of its kind in KZN. It has approximately 400 animals under its care at any given time, all of which are wildlife indigenous to Natal, from birds and mammals to raptors and reptiles, and many primates. The main objective is to rescue, rehabilitate and release these animals either back into the wild, or into sanctuaries.

Spp.: All wildlife indigenous to Natal: from blue vervet monkeys, to tortoises, bushbuck, genet, garden birds, fish eagles, vultures, owls, crocodiles, zebra, lemurs, baboon, mongoose, etc.

Hab.: Tropical forest, tropical beach, mangrove coastal wetland.

Loc.: In the outskirts of Durban, about 10 minutes from the airport, next to the Kenith Stainbank nature reserve.

Travel: Airplane to Durban.

Dur.: Minimum of 5 day's (as training is involved).

Per.: Year round, peak is from November to March (baby season).

L.term: V olunteers can stay for as long as they want.

Age: Min. 18.

Qualif.: No specific skills required for volunteers.

Work: Volunteers help cleaning cages and feeding and caring for the animals. Special projects may include: observing animals in the rehabilitation area, building cages, animal releases, etc.

Lang.: English.

Accom.: The volunteer house is situated on the property, sleeps 8 people on a sharing basis and has a kitchen, diningroom and comfortable lounge

Cost: R160 (approx. US$25) per person/day. Includes 3 basic meals.

Applic.: Online application form. www.crowknz.co.za

CERCOPAN, Nigeria

4 Ishie Lane, Housing Estate
P.O. Box 826, Calabar, Cross River State Nigeria
Tel.:/Fax: ++234 (087) 234 670 – Mob.: ++234 (0802) 827 5428
E-mail: info@cercopan.org
www.cercopan.org

Desc.: An NGO dedicated to tropical rainforest conservation through primate rehabilitation, education and research.

Spp.: Red-capped mangabey (*Cercopithecus torquatus*) and forest guenons (*Cercopithecus spp.*).

Hab.: Tropical rainforest.

Loc.: Southeast Nigeria (close to Cameroon border).

Travel: Flight to Lagos; internal flight Lagos-Calabar.

Dur.: Short-term volunteers: min. 4 weeks, max. 3 months.

Per.: Any time of the year. Rainy season is June to September.

L.term: Min. 1 year with coordinator's permission (possible stipend).

Age: Short-term volunteers min. 21; long-term volunteers min. 25.

Qualif.: Short-term (paying) volunteers skills: field experience (ecology, primatology), building skills, biological surveying. Long-term volunteer skills: veterinary, building skills; environmental education, community development/communication skills, biological research (ecology, animal behaviour, botany).

Work: Varies with skills and needs of the project.

Lang.: English.

Accom.: At forest site: bush sheds with tent/mosquito net, solar power for evening lighting, fridge, outdoor showers and toilets. In Calabar: shared house/room, electricity and running water.

Cost: Short-term volunteers: room and board (approx. GB£ 100-150/week). Long-term volunteers: room and board provided. International travel, medical insurance and visa are responsibility of the volunteer.

Agents: Prospective volunteers may also contact the UK based trustee: Bob Baxter, 13 Prestbury Crescent, Banstead, Surrey ++44 (784) 102 1147, e-mail: bob.baxter1@ntlworld.com

Applic.: Send letter of interest with C.V. (including 3 referees with tel. no.) by snail mail or e-mail without attachments to Cercopan.

CETACEAN RESEARCH & RESCUE UNIT (CRRU) Scotland UK

P.O. Box 11307,
Banff AB45 3WB, Scotland UK
Tel: ++44 (1261) 851 696
E-mail: mailbox@crru.org.uk
www.crru.org.uk

Desc: The CRRU is a small charitable research organisation dedicated to the understanding, welfare, conservation and protection of cetaceans (whales, dolphins and porpoises) in Scottish waters through scientific investigation, environmental education and the provision of professional veterinary assistance to sick, stranded and injured individuals.

Spp.: Primarily the bottlenose dolphin (*Tursiops truncatus*) and minke whale (*Balaenoptera acutorostrata*).

Hab.: Marine, coastal.

Loc.: Moray Firth, Northeastern Scotland.

Travel: By plane, bus or train to Aberdeen, then bus to Banff.

Dur: 12 days.

Per.: May to October.

L.term: Possible for outstanding volunteers.

Age: Min. 18.

Qualif.: Commitment to wildlife conservation and positive attitude towards living and working in a small group of enthusiastic people from different backgrounds and cultures is essential.

Work: Counting animals, recording behaviour, determining geographical positions and taking photographs under scientific supervision from a 5.6 m inflatable boat. On shore, identifying animals, cataloguing slides, and inputting data into the computers (full training provided). Opportunities to train in marine mammal rescue techniques will also be available.

Lang.: English;

Accom.: Researchers and volunteers will be accommodated together in 1 of 2 furnished houses.

Cost: GB£695 (approx.EUR1,000) for 12 days including food.

Agents: Earthwatch Europe (See Organisation list).

Applic.: See website, "How you can help".

CETACEAN SANCTUARY RESEARCH, Italy and France

Tethys Research Institute
c/o Civic Aquarium, Viale G.B. Gadio 2
20121 Milano Italy
Tel.:++39 (02) 7200 1947 / 7201 3943 — Fax:++39 (02) 8699 5011
E-mail: tethys@tethys.org
www.tethys.org

Desc.: "Cetacean Sanctuary Research" is a long term project on the ecology and conservation of cetaceans in the western Ligurian Sea. Research is carried out in two main habitats: the continental slope zone and the pelagic environment. In the continental slope the focus is on odontocetes such as sperm whales, beaked whales and several dolphin species. In the pelagic environment the research focuses on fin whales. The study area includes the waters of the Pelagos Sanctuary for the Conservation of Mediterranean Cetaceans. Through a multidisciplinary approach, the researchers investigate different aspects of cetacean biology and ecology (distribution, abundance and population dynamics, stock discreteness, behaviour, social organisation) and the impact of human activities like unregulated whale watching, in order to suggest effective conservation measures.

Spp.: Fin whale (*Balaenoptera physalus*), striped dolphin (*Stenella coeruleoalba*), Risso's dolphin (*Grampus griseus*), sperm whale (*Physeter macrocephalus*), long-finned pilot whale (*Globicephala melas*), Cuvier's beaked whale (*Ziphius cavirostris*), short-beaked common dolphin (*Delphinus delphis*), common bottlenose dolphin (*Tursiops truncatus*).

Hab.: Pelagic and coastal waters.

Loc.: Ligurian Sea, Mediterranean Sea.

Travel: Departure and arrival is in San Remo (Portosole), Italy. Airplane to Nice, Genoa or Milan, then train to San Remo.

Dur.: 6 nights on board.

Per.: May to October.

L.term: Consecutive cruises can be booked. Discount granted to university students less than 26 years old.

Age: Min. 18 years.

Qualif.: No qualifications required. Volunteers should be able to swim. Flexibility, enthusiasm and willingness to help with all research and household activities are necessary.

111

Work: Volunteers will be trained at the beginning of the cruise and then will assist with research activities (data collection, observations, photo-ID, etc.). Lectures on cetacean biology and research methods are carried out by the researchers. In bad weather conditions the boat stays in a safe harbour; volunteers may decide to stay on board, helping researchers entering and analysing data and matching digital photos, or visit the area.

Lang.: Italian, English.

Accom.: On board the 21-metre ketch *Pelagos*, up to 12 participants will be hosted in a 6 bed room and 2 quadruple cabins, with bunk beds. Sleeping bags, bed sheets and pillow case required. There are 4 showers and 4 toilets.

Cost: Costs range between EUR 720—820 (approx. GB£ 500—570) for a 6—day cruise, depending on the season. Food (except for the first evening and alcoholic beverages), fuel, membership and insurance are included. Travel to San Remo is not included.

Agents: Tethys Research Institute (see Organisation list).

Applic.: Request a standard application form to be completed and returned to the Tethys Research Institute. Early booking is suggested.

Notes: Participants gain insight into research methods and the management of a field research project.

CHARLES DARWIN FOUNDATION, Galapagos

External Relations Unit Charles Darwin Research Station
P.O. Box 17–01–3891 Quito   Ecuador
Tel.: ++ (593) 5 2-526 146/147 (ext. 251)
Fax: ++ (593) 5 2-526 146/147 (ext.102)
E-mail: vol@fcdarwin.org.ec or volunteer@darwinfoundation.org
www.darwinfoundation.org

Desc.: In 1971 the Charles Darwin Foundation (CDF) began the National and International Volunteer Programme. Its purpose is to collaborate with the training of university and undergraduate students, who focus their careers in biology and conservation science and those who want to improve their skills through field experience in the Galapagos Islands.

Spp.: Terrestrial and marine flora and fauna of the Galapagos.

Hab.: Various marine and terrestrial habitats of the Galapagos.

Loc.: Galapagos Islands, Ecuador. Stations on 4 different Islands.

Travel: Flight to Quito or Guayaquil, then Puerto Ayora, Galapagos.

Dur.: Min. 6 months.

Per.: Year round.

L.term: Duration is set by the project: 6 months minimum.

Age: Min. 20.

Qualif.: Qualifications vary according to position available. Volunteers must be at least a second year undergraduate.

Work: There are 4 areas of investigation: vertebrate ecology monitoring, invertebrate research, botany and marine investigation and conservation. Non-scientific areas include communication, participation, education and institutional development. Volunteers can participate in any of these areas.

Lang.: English and Spanish. Fluency not essential.

Accom.: Dormitory in the Station or apartment or hotel in town.

Cost: International volunteers are responsible for their own travel costs to and from the Galapagos Islands and their room and board costs during their stay. Volunteers must provide their own accident and life insurance coverage for the travel to and from the Galapagos Islands and for the duration of their volunteer period in the islands.

Applic.: Application form to be downloaded and sent with specified documentation via regular mail at least 2 months in advance.

Notes: For information of available openings see website.

CHEETAH CONSERVATION FUND, Namibia

711, Quail Ridge Road
Aledo, Tx., 76008 2870 USA
Tel.: ++1 (817) 441 7205
Fax: ++1 (817) 441 9079 – (866) 909 3399 (toll free in North America)
E-mail: ccfinfo@iway.na
www.cheetah.org

Desc.:	CCF sponsors scientific research and education programmes in areas such as cheetah population biology, ecology, health and reproduction and human impacts; and works with stakeholders.
Spp.:	Cheetah *(Acynonix jubatus).*
Hab.:	Semi-arid, bush-encroached savannah.
Loc.:	Central Namibia, Southwest Africa.
Travel:	Flight to Windhoek International Airport; shuttle bus or taxis to city centre. Transport from Windhoek (at volunteer's cost) to Otjiwarongo (3 hours) can be arranged prior to arrival.
Dur.:	2 – 4 weeks.
Per.:	Year round.
L.term:	Depending on the needs of CCF, the volunteers qualifications and commitment and on the CCF Director's approval.
Age:	Min. 20.
Qualif.:	No particular skills required.
Work:	Cheetah collecting, feeding and care; habitat monitoring of game and vegetation; assisting with data input, mapping, radio tracking; assisting with goat, sheep and livestock guarding dog healthcare and education programmes.
Lang.:	English.
Accom.:	Two-person thatched huts with beds: detached latrine block. All bedding is provided.
Cost:	US$3,000 for 2 weeks, US$5,000 for 4 weeks.
Agents:	Earthwatch Institute or African Conservation Experience, for UK students, (see Organisation list).
Applic.:	Contact the organisation at the above address or the agents.

CHEETAH CONSERVATION, Botswana

Mokolodi Nature Reserve
Private Bag 0457
Gaborone, Botswana
Tel.: ++ (267) 3500613 — Fax: ++ (267) 3165488
E-mail: info@cheetahbotswana.com
www.cheetahbotswana.com

Desc.: CCB is a long term monitoring program, including research into behaviour and population status; with an essential focus on community participation/education, working with rural communities to encourage coexistence of these elegant, endangered cats. Botswana is one of the last hopes for this species' survival.

Spp.: Cheetah (*Acinonyx jubatus*).

Hab.: Savannah and bush lands.

Loc.: Jwaneng Game Reserve, Southern Botswana.

Travel: Airplane to Johannesburg, then plane to Gaborone, then by vehicle to Jwaneng.

Dur.: Min. 1 month, max. 3 months.

Per.: Year round Volunteer program can be temporarily on hold, check website for information as to current status.

L.term: Possible opportunities of longer term stays as research assistants, for keen volunteers who have already completed a term of volunteering with the project.

Age: Min. 18.

Qualif.: Wildlife background useful but not required. Strong passion for conservation essential. Desire to learn new skills. Ability to work long days, often in heat during summer, or cold during winter. Ability to live in the bush with a small group of people.

Work: Assisting with radiotracking cats, spoor surveys, camera trapping, possible capture and release, community visits, school presentations, data input, camp maintenance, etc.

Lang.: English, Setswanan.

Accom.: Small chalets for 2 people sharing. Electricity and lights. Separate kitchen and bathroom facilities.

Cost: Approx. US$2500/ month for room and board.

Applic.: By e-mail or by mail.

115

COCHRANE ECOLOGICAL INSTITUTE (CEI), Canada

P.O.Box 484, Cochrane, Alberta, T4C 1A7 Canada
Tel.: ++1 (403) 932 5632
Fax: ++1 (403) 932 6303
E-mail: cei@nucleus.com
www.ceinst.org

Desc.:	CEI is an NGO devoted to the conservation of wildlife in Alberta, Canada, through captive breeding for reintroduction of endangered species, habitat inventories, educational programmes, wildlife rescue, rehabilitation and release.
Spp.:	Swift fox (*Vulpes velox*) and other wildlife of the Great Plains.
Hab.:	Foothills of the Rockies, short, mixed grass, and fescue prairie.
Loc.:	Town of Cochrane, between Banff and Calgary, Alberta.
Travel:	Airplane or bus to Calgary. Transportation from Calgary to project area will be provided.
Dur.:	Min. 1 month.
Per.:	Year round.
L.term:	There is no limit of time for long-term stays.
Age:	Min. 20.
Qualif.:	High school diploma, veterinary or biology studies helpful but not necessary and good physical condition.
Work:	Feeding the animals, facility maintenance, assistance with the ecological educational programmes, wildlife record keeping and observation, assistance on wildlife rehabilitation.
Lang.:	English essential.
Accom.:	Rustic.
Cost:	Room, accommodation and simple meals are provided.
Applic.:	By e-mail with the subject heading: 'Volunteer program'. In the text, include CV, letter of intentions and possible dates.
Notes:	Webpage has other volunteers' experiences. Health insurance and clean international driving license mandatory.

COMUNIDAD INTI WARA YASSI, Bolivia

Parque Machia
Villa Tunari
Chapare, Cochabamba Bolivia
Tel.: ++ 591 (44) 136 572
E-mail: intiwarayassi@gmail.com
www.intiwarayassi.org

Desc.:	A sanctuary that rescues and rehabilitates native wild animals taken from unsuitable captive environments. Aims of the project include: confiscation of animals from illegal markets; rehabilitation where possible; education and awareness to prevent illegal trading of wildlife.
Spp.:	Wild cats, including pumas and ocelots. Monkeys, including Capuchins and black spiders, tropical birds and reptiles.
Hab.:	Tropical rainforest.
Loc.:	Two locations: Chapare and Santa Cruz regions of Bolivia.
Travel:	Plane to La Paz or Santa Cruz, then bus to project.
Dur.:	Minimum 2 weeks. Staying at least 1 month is encouraged.
Per.:	Year round.
L.Term.:	Long-term volunteers are encouraged.
Age:	Min.18, due to strenuous work and basic living conditions.
Qualif.:	No set qualifications required. Experience with animals is advantageous, as well as carpentry and building skills. Volunteers must be hard working and committed.
Work:	Work is physical and includes:maintenance, building cages and fences and clearing forest areas, care and supervision of animals and basic husbandry tasks such as preparing food and cleaning. Working days can be long and in a humid climate.
Lang.:	English, Spanish an advantage.
Accom.:	Basic shared rooms, with communal bathroom and kitchen areas. Personal sleeping bag and mosquito net required.
Cost:	Volunteers pay all transport expenses to and from the project. Accommodation is US$90 or US$100 (depending on the location) for the first 15 days, then US$3.5-5 daily thereafter. Food is approx. US $5 daily.
Applic.:	No official application required. Volunteers should verify the website for full details. Work is allocated on arrival.

COMMUNITY INTEGRATED CONSERVATION PROJECT AT TOFU BEACH, Mozambique

Questoverseas

The North-West Stables, Borde Hill Estate,
Balcombe Road, Haywards Heath, West Sussex, RH16 1XP UK
Tel.: ++44 (14) 44 47
E-mail: questunderseas@gmail.com
www.questoverseas.com

Desc.: Tofu beach in Mozambique is attracting increasing numbers of visitors to its shores to see Whale Sharks, Manta Rays and a variety of other amazing marine life. Working in partnership with Mozambican stakeholders and local community Quest Overseas is running a marine research and conservation project and wants you to be part of it.

Spp.: Whale sharks, manta rays, humpback whales, humpback dolphins, common dolphin, turtles.

Hab.: East African subtropical coastal zone.

Loc.: Tofo, Inhambane, Mozambique, East Africa.

Travel: Plane to Maputo, bus to Inhambane, truck to Tofo.

Dur.: Min 2 weeks for training and surveying but can last 2-3 months.

Per.: Mid february 2007-onwards.

L.term: Max. 2 months.

Age: 18 - 65. All ages, divers, students and marine enthusiasts very welcome.

Qualif.: Aiving cert AOW preferred- not neccessary, marine biology, oceanography, science background useful.

Work: Diving, snorkelling and surveying from boat, entering into data base and taking part in community days.

Lang.: English, Spanish, Portugese all spoken.

Accom.: Communal house with kitchen in Tofino, all included, all provided through the organisation.

Cost: From GB£1,195, including all dives, dive equipment, accommodation, food.

Applic.: Forms online. Contact via email info@questoverseas.com

Notes: See: www.myspace.com/underseas; www.questoverseas.com/marine_expeditions

CONSERVATION PROJECT UTILA IGUANA (CPUI), Honduras

Department of Herpetology
Senckenberganlage. 25, D-60325 Frankfurt am Main,   Germany
Iguana Station Utila, Iguana Road, Island Utila
Islas de la Bahia, Honduras
E-mail: volo@utila-iguana.de
www.utila-iguana.de

Desc.: CPUI runs a research and conservation center which includes an environmental education programme in local schools, ecological field work, public awareness work and practical conservation work aswell as nature reserve development.

Spp.: Various iguana species: Utila iguana (*Ctenosaura bakeri,* endemic), *Norops bicaorum, Norops utilensis* and others.

Hab.: Mangrove forest, Caribbean dry forest, sandy and rocky beachshores as breeding grounds.

Loc.: Utila Island, in the Caribbean coast of Honduras.The Iguana Station is located in the center of the island.

Travel: Airplane to La Ceiba via San Pedro Sula. Via Ferry or Airplane to the Utila island. Meeting at the dock or airport.

Dur.: Min. 3 Weeks.

Per.: Year round.

L.term: There is no limit of time for long-term stays.

Age: Min. 18.

Qualif.: Motivation and willingness to dedicate time and work.

Work: Feeding the animals, facility maintenance, assistance with the ecological educational programmes, wildlife record keeping and observation, assistance on wildlife rehabilitation.

Lang.: English (primary language on the Bay Islands), Spanish (additionally) for schoolwork or official communication.

Accom.: Double bedrooms at the first floor of the wooden station building.

Cost: EUR100/Month: room, accommodation, use of kitchen is provided. Food and beverages are not included.

Applic.: Via e-mail please refer to website.

Notes: Health insurance and vaccinations (hepatitis, tetanus) mandatory.

CONSERVATION VOLUNTEERING IN ST. LUCIA, Caribbean

Durrell Wildlife Conservation Trust
Les Augres Manor
Trinity Jersey Channel Islands JE3 5BP
Tel.: +44 (153) 486 0031
E-mail: charlotte.linney@durrell.org
www.durrellwildlife.org

Desc.: An ideal project for conservationists and field biologists. Volunteers can join for a 3 months period. Work can be hard but rewarding and it is a great way to make a vital difference to species conservation.

Spp.: Various Caribbean Islands species: birds, various mammals, bats, etc.

Hab.: Coastal tropical.

Loc.: St Lucia - Caribbean.

Travel: Airplane to Saint Lucia; further details provided on application.

Dur.: 3 month periods.

Per.: Year round.

L.term: Inquire with organisation.

Age: Min. 21.

Qualif.: Preference to candidates with previous experience in projects in the tropics, and/or with a background in the biological sciences.

Work: Ability to handle wild animals, and to work with local people. Many activities will be field-based and will involve habitat surveys, distribution mapping population monitoring.

Lang.: English.

Accom.: Must bring own tent.

Cost: GB£600 (approx. US$ 1000) to cover costs, plus flights, vaccinations, full insurance.

Applic.: For further information and details, contact Charlotte Linney by email or post.

CREES VOLUNTEER PROGRAMME, Peru
CREES - The Rainforest Education and Resource Centre
Calle San Miguel 250, Cusco Peru
Tel: ++51 (84) 262 433
E-mail: info@crees-manu.org
www.crees-manu.org

Desc.:	An opportunity to live, work and train in one of the most bio-diverse regions tropical rainforests on earth. Volunteers contribute to a variety of ongoing conservation, sustainability and educational projects at the MLC Research Facility in the Manu Biosphere Reserve.
Spp.:	Tropical rainforest species of birds, mammals, insects, amphibians, reptiles and plants.
Hab.:	Tropical rainforest.
Loc.:	Manu Biosphere Reserve (MBR), southeastern Peru.
Travel:	Airplane to Cusco, then by bus and river boat to the MBR.
Dur.:	Min. 4 weeks.
Per.:	Year round, although seasons affect what project work is being undertaken.
L.term:	Volunteers are welcome to participate for long periods of time. Undergrads and grads in natural sciences can also apply through a Resident Naturalist Programme to carry out their own research projects.
Age:	Min. 18.
Qualif.:	Volunteers should speak either fluent English or Spanish, be in good health and fit enough to participate in physical activity.
Work:	Volunteers will learn data collection techniques and will subsequently undertake wildlife monitoring of mammal, bird, plant and aquatic fauna populations. There are also opportunities for involvement in local educational programmes and as well as sustainability projects.
Lang.:	English and/or Spanish.
Accom.:	Comfortable, shared accommodation and facilities (catering provided).
Cost::	Around $1,500 for four weeks (prices subject to change) Price includes: lodging, 3 meals a day and transport, as well as a contribution towards the projects themselves
Applic.:	Online at: www.crees-manu.org

DOLPHIN OBSERVATION, Greece

Fiskardo's Nautical and Environmental Club (FNEC)
Museum of Fiskardo,
28084 Fiskardo, Kephalonia, Greece
Tel./Fax: ++30 (267) 404 1182
E-mail: info@fnec.gr
www.fnec.gr

Desc.: Volunteers take part in cetacean observation from boats and from the coast recording cetacean (dolphin and whale) presence, identifying species, recording behaviour and taking video/photographs. There is strictly no swimming or feeding of dolphins. Underwater research into local seahorse populations in collaboration with the National Aquarium, Plymouth, UK is also conducted using SCUBA diving, free diving and snorkelling. Data write up and boat and equipment cleaning are involved in both research projects. Distribution and collection of sightings forms for opportunistic sightings, leaflet production, sign making, presentations and questionnaires, article writing are also undertaken on this project.

Spp.: Cetaceans found in this region include Bottlenose dolphin (*Tursiops truncatus*) , Striped dolphin(*Stenella coeruleoalba*).

Hab.: Mediterranean Coastal.

Loc.: Most Northerly village on the Greek Island of Kefalonia.

Travel: Direct flights available from some European countries May to October. Otherwise plane to Athens and bus + ferry.

Dur.: Periods of 3 weeks (see web-site for details).

Per.: Year round.

L.term: See web site.

Age: Min 19.

Qualif.: No specific skills required. Instructions provided to aid cetacean identification. PADI Open water certification.

Work: No specific skills required. Instructions provided to aid cetacean identification. PADI Open water certification.

Lang.: English.

Accom.: Volunteers bring their own tent, sleeping mat and sleeping bag.

Cost: EUR550 for 3 weeks (excluding travel expenses and insurance). Includes the cost of a PADI Open Water Certification.

Applic.: E-mail a CV (max.2 pages) with a short cover letter of intents.

DOLPHIN RESEARCH CENTER, Florida USA
Volunteer and Internship Program
58901 Overseas Highway
Grassy Key, Florida 33050–6019 USA
Tel.: ++1 (305) 289 1121 ext. 230   Fax: ++1 (305) 743 7627
E-mail: drc-vr@dolphins.org
www.dolphins.org

Desc.: Dolphin Research Center (DRC) is a non-profit organisation dedicated to marine mammal research and education. It offers volunteers unique opportunities for learning about dolphins and various aspects of the daily operations of a marine mammal care facility. DRC also offers Internships involving concentration in a specific department. For individuals desiring a more interactive programme, see DolphinLab in Notes.

Spp.: Bottlenose dolphin, California sea lion.

Loc.: Grassy Key, Florida, USA.

Travel: Flights to Miami then by bus to Marathon.

Dur.: 1 – 4 months for volunteers; 3 – 4 months for internships.

Per.: Year round.

L.term: Available for local residents.

Age: Min. 18.

Qualif.: Good physical shape (able to lift 30 lbs/15 kg).

Work: Assist in animal food preparation, monitor visitors and answer questions, assist staff in conducting public interactive programmes, perform various facility maintenance tasks and provide administrative support. Interns duties vary depending upon the specific internship (animal care & training, dolphin-child therapy, research, education and visual communications.

Lang.: English fluency is a requirement.

Accom.: Not provided, DRC assists with house sharing information.

Cost: Living expenses can be as much as US$1,500/month.

Applic.: Application available on website or mailed upon request.

Notes: Individuals desiring a shorter, more interactive learning experience may be interested in the week-long DolphinLab class. See website or contact for info: drc-ed@dolphins.org.

DOLPHINS & SEA LIFE AROUND THE MALTESE ISLANDS, Malta

The Biological Conservation Research Foundation (BICREF)
P.O. Box 30, Hamrun Malta
Tel./Fax: ++(356) 2340 3049
E-mail: bicref@gmail.com
www.bicref.org

Desc.:	Boat and aerial research surveys undertaken in the region throughout the year to analyse the associations between environmental variables and observe different marine organisms. Boat surveys take 1 day, but 3-day research cruises are planned when weather permits.
Spp.:	Bottlenose dolphin (*Tursiops truncatus*), common dolphins (*Delphinus delphis*), sea turtles (*Caretta caretta*), sea birds, such as cory shearwaters, large fish, manta rays.
Hab.:	Mediterranean coastal and pelagic waters.
Loc.:	Maltese Islands.
Travel:	Fly to Luqa International Airport, Malta, or ferry from Sicily.
Dur.:	Negotiable, inquire with the organisation.
Per.:	Year round; summer is most intense.
L.term:	Possible, but ask more information to the project.
Age:	Min. 18, max. 45.
Qualif.:	A background in biology. Sea-faring stamina and interest or experience in marine research and conservation required. Training on basic survey techniques and applications of research is provided.
Work:	Observation and data recording during research surveys. Organise information and data after the surveys.
Lang.:	English or Italian.
Accom.:	Hotels, hostels, etc., are available in Malta. During 3-day trips, volunteers will sleep on board of the sailing or survey boat.
Cost:	Contact the organisation for information.
Applic.:	Send a brief CV, letter of interest and application form 6–4 months prior to the volunteering period.
Notes:	Any special needs should be stated in the application letter.

DONKEY SANCTUARY, Netherlands Antilles

P.O.Box 331
Bonaire Netherlands Antilles
Tel.: ++ (599) 9510 7607
E-mail: donkeyshelp@telbonet.an
www.Donkeysanctuary.org - www.donkeycam.com

Desc.:	Donkey Sanctuary Bonaire is a non-profit foundation taking care of the wild donkeys of the Island of Bonaire, particularly the abused and motherless donkeys who lost their mothers in car accidents. There are about 300 donkeys to care for at the sanctuary and they can not be released in the wild, because of the possible car accidents.
Spp.:	Donkeys.
Hab.:	Caribbean Island farmland.
Loc.:	The Sanctuary is 100ha estate, located in the middle of the island.
Travel:	Airplane to Bonaire, airport pick-up is available.
Dur.:	Min. 2 months.
Per.:	Year round.
L.term:	There is no limit of time for long-term stays.
Age:	Min. 20.
Qualif.:	No particular qualifications required, just a strong motivation and love for animals. Veterinary medicine students are welcome. Good physical condition is important.
Work:	Feeding the animals, facility maintenance, assistance with the educational programmes for school kids, record keeping and observation of the donkeys, cleaning stables, care of injured animals.
Lang.:	English or Dutch.
Accom.:	Private small house on the compound, with kitchen, shower and toilet.
Cost:	Accommodation and lunch is provided at no cost.
Applic.:	Via e-mail with the subject heading: 'Volunteer program'. In the text, include CV, letter of intentions and possible dates.
Notes:	Personal medical insurance required.

EAST AFRICAN WHALE SHARK TRUST, Kenya

PO Box 933 Ukunda
South Coast 80400 Kenya
Tel.: ++ 254 (0) 720 293
E-mail: info@giantsharks.org
www.giantsharks.org

Desc.: An education and research project dedicated to whale shark conservation along the Kenya coast giving the opportunity to monitor and study the local whale shark population and raise awareness in local schools. The project works alongside stakeholders with the emphasis being on the value of the whale shark alive.

Spp.: Whale shark (*Rhincodon typus*).

Hab.: Tropical oceans.

Loc.: Diani beach, South Coast of Kenya, East Africa.

Travel: Airplane to Nairobi and/or direct to Mombasa then a 2 hour drive south to Diani beach.

Dur.: Shorter terms possible. Longer terms welcome upon application.

Per.: Year round, whale shark season is Oct-March.

L.term: Longer periods welcome upon application.

Age: Min. 18. No maximum age if fit, healthy and motivated.

Qualif.: Volunteers should be fit, physically active. Useful skills are experience in marine biology and SCUBA diving.

Work: Volunteers gather whale shark data, give presentations and work with local fishermen.

Lang.: English. Swahili helpful.

Accom.: Comfortable double rooms in the EAWST accomodation centre on the beach, a short drive from the research base.

Cost: US$750 per month includes food and board. Travel expenses not included.

Applic.: Contact info@giantsharks.org or fill out the Green Volunteers Standard Application Form.

Notes: Vaccinations, anti-malaria tablets and insurance required. Most visitors to Kenya also require a visa.

ECOLOGY & CONSERVATION OF DEER IN PATAGONIA, Argentina

Deerlab

JoAnne Smith-Flueck, PhD

C.C. 176 (8400) S.C. de Bariloche Argentina

Tel./Fax: ++54 (944) 467 345

E-mail: *j.smith@deerlab.org*

www.deerlab.org

Desc.: The project objectives are to estimate population density and determine the reproductive status, health condition, predation by puma and habitat use of red deer in southern Patagonia. Population surveys of endangered deer are conducted as well.

Spp.: Andean huemul deer (*Hippocamelus bisulcus*), exotic red deer (*Cervus elaphus*).

Hab.: Mountainous temperate rainforest and edge of steppe.

Loc.: Southwest Argentina.

Travel: Airplane to Buenos Aires or Santiago, Chile, then airplane or bus to Bariloche.

Dur: 2–5 weeks.

Per.: November to March.

L.term: Only with project leader's approval after regular period.

Age: Min. 18.

Qualif.: Good backpacking and camping experience in mountainous wilderness.

Work: Research includes: herd counts, radio-telemetry work of red deer, habitat surveys, morphometric analysis, use of topographic maps and GPS units. Direct observations with binoculars and scopes. A telemetry study on predation by puma is pending funding.

Lang.: English or Spanish (German also spoken).

Accom.: Sleeping bags and tents during field work. Hostel in town.

Cost: Contact leader for information. Room and board in Bariloche is approx. US$20/day.

Agents: Contact project leader directly.

Applic.: A short CV with a letter of introduction is required.

Notes: The climate is harsh and unpredictable even in summer. Expect windy, rainy and even snowy conditions. Supportive hiking boots, warm clothing, rain gear, sleeping bag and tent are required.

ECUADORIAN REPTILE AND AMPHIBIAN RESEARCH EXPEDITIONS
Reptile Research
PO Box 1348, Arizona 85702 USA
Tel.: ++1 (602) 363 033
E-mail: paul@reptileresearch.org
www.ReptileResearch.org

Desc.:	The project offers opportunities for students and volunteers to work in the rain forests of Ecuador, focused on the Conservation Ecology of reptiles and amphibians. Participants receive training, guidance, and the experience to last a lifetime.
Spp.:	Entire communities of reptiles and amphibians.
Hab.:	Tropical rain forest and dry forest.
Loc.:	Western Ecuador, Manabi Province.
Travel:	Participants fly into the international airport in Quito. All in-country transportation is provided.
Dur.:	Two or three week durations.
Per.:	January and May-September.
L.term:	Independent volunteering and internship are available.
Age:	Min. 18, no max. Less than 18 accepted if accompanied by and adult.
Qualif.:	No set prerequisites, except maturity and motivation. Previous ecology experience and knowledge of Spanish helps.
Work:	Running transects and identifying, measuring and photographing animals.
Lang.:	English. Spanish useful but not required.
Accom.:	Field stations with shared accommodations with three hot meals a day.
Cost:	US$1,000-1,500, for 2 or 3 weeks, plus international flight.
Applic.:	See website for complete application.

EL EDEN FLORA Y FAUNA: ANIMAL RESCUE AND REHABILITATION, Argentina

Villa Rumipal, Cordoba Argentina
Tel.: ++54 (351) 457 636
E-mail: marianacarrascosa@yahoo.com.ar
www.eledenflorayfauna.org

Desc.:	A Center in the mountains, 25 hectareas, with almost 500 animals of 60 species. Volunteers are able to do: feeding, vet help, interaction, help and care of new members or baby animals, observation, general duties (cleaning cages, construction of new places for animals)riding horses. Volunteers can also have cultural interactions.
Spp.:	Over 60 spp.: pumas, howler monkeys, cervants, capybaras, parrots, farm animals, flamingos, buffalo, llamas, horses.
Hab.:	Mountain.
Loc.:	Villa Rumipal, Cordoba, Argentina.
Travel:	Airplane to Buenos Aires, then plane or bus to Cordoba, where volunteers are met.
Per.:	Volunteers can stay up to one year.
Age:	Min.18 or 17 with parents' permission. No maximum age.
Qualif.:	No particular skills needed, just a strong motivation and love for animals.
Work:	Feeding, vet help, interaction, help and care of newcomers or babies, cleaning, general maintenance, rescue.
Lang.:	Spanish or English.
Accom.:	Typical rancho lodging, with beds, bathroom with hot/cold water, heat in winter, kitchen.
Cost:	EUR380 (about GB£250) per month (includes all food, accomodation, internet, rides to town).
Applic.:	No application form, just direct contact with Mariana.

ELEPHANT NATURE PARK, Thailand

209/2 Sridornchai Road
Chiang Mai 50100 Thailand
Tel.: ++66(53) 818 932/818 754/818 7442
Fax: ++66 (53) 818 755
E-mail: info@elephantnaturepark.org
www.elephantnaturepark.org

Desc.: Thailands Elephant population is struggling for its very survival with existing numbers down to some 3,000. Land encroachment as the population grows is the main problem facing both wild and domesticated elephants. This majestic gentle giant is finding it harder to find places to live without exploitation by humans. The Park, founded in 1966, provides a home for 31 elephants. The location, in a valley surrounded by jungle mountains and bordered by a river, is the ideal setting and natural habitat for elephants.

Spp.: Asian elephant (*Elephus maximus*), dogs and cats.

Hab.: Tropical rainforest.

Loc.: Northern Thailand, 60km from the city of Chiang Mai.

Travel: About one hour from Chiang Mai. Transport from Chiang Mai is provided. No public transportation available.

Dur.: Min. 1 week, max. 1 month (12 volunteers at a time).

Per.: Year round.

L.term: Only after initial period and approval by project manager.

Age: Min. 18 in good physical health. Children may participate if accompanied by their legal guardian.

Qualif.: No particular skills needed. Constant instruction and supervision by park staff is provided.

Work: Volunteers help with a variety of tasks including basic elephant health care and park duties.

Lang.: English.

Accom.: Simple bamboo tree huts, with toilet and shower, in the center.

Cost: US$275/week (includes lodging, food, local transport).

Applic.: See 'volunteer' section of website.

Notes: Health insurance is required.

FLAT HOLM ISLAND, Wales UK
Flat Holm Project
Pierhead Barry Docks
Vale of Glamorgan CF62 5QS UK
Tel.: ++01 (446) 747 661
E-mail: flatholmproject@cardiff.gov.uk
www.cardiff.gov.uk/flatholm

Desc.: Flat Holm Island is a Site of Special Scientif Interest, Geological Conservation review Site and Local Nature Reserve. Education, conservation and buildings management go hand in hand. Home to one of the largest Lesser Black Backed Gull colonies in Wales and home to the rare Wild Leek.

Spp.: Shelduck, lesser lack-backed gulls, butterflies, moths.

Hab.: Limestone Grassland, rocky shore, scrub habitats.

Loc.: Bristol Channel, Wales, UK.

Travel· Plane to Cardiff, train to Barry Island Station, 10 minute walk.

Dur.: Minimum 2 weeks preferably committment of 6 months to 1 year.

Per.: Year Round.

L.term: Up to 1 year.

Age: Min. 18.

Qualif.: No specific qualifications required. Keen interest in conservation, education and a general level of practical ability.

Work: Species monitoring, habitat management, buildings maintenance, livestock husbandry, environmental education, guided tours.

Lang.: English.

Accom.: House with bunkbeds. May need to share room. Sleeping bags required.

Cost: GB£10 per day food and accommodation for short stay (2 weeks). Free for long term volunteers of 6 months.

Applic.: Cover letter stating interest and abilities to flatholmproject@cardiff.gov.uk

FOREST RESTORATION, USA

National Park Service, Center for Urban Ecology
4598 Mac Arthur Blvd., NW
Washington, DC 20008 USA
Tel.: ++1 (342) 144 3217 – Fax: ++1 (202) 282 1031
E-mail: sue_salmons@nps.gov
www.nps.gov/rocr/

Desc.:	This project focuses on exotic plant management, vegetation surveys and mapping. Projects depend upon the season and take place in 14 National Parks in Mid Atlantic Region. Researchers may also write grant proposals and use Global Positioning software.
Spp.:	*Celastrus orbiculatus, Ampelopsis brevipedunculata, Winsteria Sinensis*, etc.
Hab.:	Eastern deciduous forest.
Loc.:	Mid-Atlantic of North America.
Travel:	Airplane to Washington DC, USA.
Dur.:	Variable.
Per.:	Year round.
L.term:	Inquire with organisation.
Age:	Min. 18.
Qualif.:	Familiarity with botany and computer knowledge is welcome. Must be in good shape and fluent in English. Participation or completion in a college level programme required.
Work:	Integrated pest management may include vine cutting and work with herbicides, monitoring rare, threatened and endangered species, as well as vegetation plot monitoring and data entry.
Lang.:	English.
Accom.:	Group housing may be available. Bring sheets or sleeping bag. A small stipend for lunch may be available.
Cost:	If a room cannot be provided, the cost will vary, depending on the type of accommodation. Hostels range from US$20-50/day. Volunteers must pay for transportation.
Agents:	Contact Sue Salmons at the above address directly.
Applic.:	Send CV, 3 references and copy of school transcript.
Notes:	For non-U.S. citizens see Note at the end of Page 74.

GIBBON REHABILITATION PROJECT, Thailand
The Wild Animal Rescue Foundation of Thailand (WAR)
65/1 Sukhumvit 55, Wattana
Bangkok 10110 Thailand
Tel. ++ 66 (2) 712 9515 – Fax. ++ 66 (2) 712 9778
Email: volunteer@warthai.org
www.warthai.org

Desc.: "The first gibbon project in the world." The sanctuary is located on the remote area of Phuket which currently houses over seventy gibbons. The aim of this project is the rehabilitation of gibbons back to their natural habitat additionally providing ongoing care to those unsuitable for repatriation.

Spp.: White-handed gibbon (*Hylobates lar*).

Hab.: Tropical rainforest.

Loc.: Bang Pae Waterfall, Khao Phra Thaew non hunting area, Phuket, Thailand.

Travel: Airplane to Bangkok, then bus or plane to Phuket..

Dur.: Min. 3 weeks.

Per.: Year round.

L.term: Students and graduates in biology, anthropology and veterinary medicine are especially welcome to stay for long periods.

Age: Min. 18.

Qualif.: Good physical condition, enthusiastic and able to work without assistance. Experience with animals or skills in construction, tourist assistance, public relations, etc.,

Work: Quarantine and Rehabilitation, reintroduction, conservation, education and fund-raising. Volunteers work 6 days a week.

Lang.: English.

Accom.: Bungalows for 2 or more persons located close to the sanctuary, with toilet, shower and cooking facilities.

Cost: $US 1,020 for the first 3 weeks and $US 105 for each additional week. Or $US 945 for the first 8 weeks and $US 105 foe each additional week. Or $US 2,500 for 6-month stay.

Applic.: Through www.warthai.org or www.ecovolunteer.org.

Agents: The Wild Animal Rescue Foundation of Thailand at www.warthai.org or the Ecovolunteer Network at www.ecovolunteer.org.

GOECO, Israel

Rozanis 13,
Tel Aviv Israel
Tel.: ++972 (036) 499 146-1 / (050) 576 2797 / (054) 734 5643
E-mail: goeco@goeco.org ecounity@yahoo.com
www.goeco.org www.goeco.co.il

Desc.: GoEco currently offers two projects. The first one is the Sea turtle Conservation with the Israel Nature and Parks Authority (STC). It focuses on the treatment and rehabilitation of loggerhead and green turtles, the protection of sea turtle nests on secluded beaches, and the general maintenance of the rescue center. The other project is the Migratory Bird Conservation with the Society for the Protection of Nature in Israel (MBC). It focuses on the protection of migratory birds that cross through Israel, one of the major migratory routes on the planet.

Spp.: Loggerhead, green turtle, nile soft shell turtle and red eared turtle (STC). A variety of migratory birds, barn owls and other birds of prey (MBC).

Hab.: Mediterranean beaches and the Jordan Valley (MBC).

Loc.: Michmoret Marine College, 40km north of Tel Aviv (STC). Maagan Michael, Hahula Valley and other locations in Israel (MBC).

Travel: Airplane to Tel Aviv. Further details upon application.

Dur.: Min 4 weeks for STC. Min 2 weeks for MBC.

Per.: July – September for STC, all year for MBC.

L.term.: Long term positions may be available, see website.

Age: Min. 18

Qualif.: Strong motivation, good health and fitness, keen interest in sea turtles and marine environment (STC), in bird and nature conservation (MBC).

Work: Treatment of turtles, general maintenance, night nest protection on beaches, data collection and input (STC). Construction of bird houses and water rafts to facilitate nesting and biological pesticides, environmental education, data collection (MBC).

Lang.: A good level of English is required.

Accom.: Comfortable shared rooms with shower, bed and air-conditioning at Beit Yannai village (STC). Shared rooms in Kibbutz style at MBC.

Cost: EUR200/week (US$250). Includes: room, food and a 3 day trip in Israel.

Applic.: Through the project page on the website.

134

GREAT WHALES IN THEIR NATURAL ENVIRONMENT, Canada

ORES – Foundation for Marine Environment Research
Postfach 1252, 4502 Solothurn, Switzerland
Tel./Fax.: ++41 (32) 623 6354
E-mail: utscherter@ores.org
www.ores.org

Desc.: The coastal ecosystem in the St. Lawrence River estuary in Eastern Canada is known for the near-shore abundance and diversity of its marine life forms, especially of baleen whales. ORES marine biologists, with the help of volunteers, study their feeding behaviour, distribution, abundance and habitat utilisation applying minimally intrusive research methods. During the course, volunteers not only will have daily encounters with different species and are actively involved in data collecting, they also will learn what the whales are doing and why. Research results, conservation issues and general knowledge on whales are shared on the water and during several slide and film presentations.

Spp.: Harbour porpoise, beluga, sperm whale, minke, humpback, finback and blue whale, several seal species.

Hab.: Ocean-river estuary in protected marine waters.

Loc.: Province of Québec, Canada, Les Bergeronnes (220 km east of Québec City), St. Lawrence and Saguenay River confluence.

Travel: Airplane to Toronto, Montreal or Québec City, then by bus (or car) to Les Bergeronnes.

Per.: July to September.

Dur.: Two programmes are offered: the General Interest Course (GIC) of 2 weeks to broaden knowledge of the ocean generally and of whales in particular (students-degree or diploma credit available); the Internship Course (ISC; medium-term 6 weeks, long-term 12 weeks) is open to anybody who has completed the introductory course and who would like to gain deeper insight into the ongoing studies.

L.term: See previous section.

Age.: Min. 18.

Qualif.: No particular skills or knowledge are needed. ORES volunteers should show strong interest in field work, team work, outdoor activities and must be able to spend 4–6 hours on an open boat.

Work: Observation and data gathering daily (weather permitting) by small research teams from open inflatable boats. Protected waters offer encounters with whales without any seasickness. Studies carried out among others: feeding strategies and techniques, ventilation recording, spatial and temporal distribution, photo-identification. Volunteers help collect data on the water and quickly learn to distinguish species and to identify individual animals.

Lang.: English. The language in the province of Québec is French. ORES personnel also speak French and German.

Accom.: At the research station overlooking the St.Lawrence Estuary well-equipped with kitchen, sanitary infrastructure, lecture hall, and internet. Three to four participants share spacious cabins.

Cost: Fee for GIC (incl. accommodation, exposure suits, on-water and land transportation, lectures and excursions; excl. travel and food) is US$1,300 (approx. EUR1050/GB£700). Fees for ISC on request. Volunteers individually organise their travel to and from the Centre.

Agents: The Ecovolunteer Network at www.ecovolunteer.org.

Applic.: Apply directly via e-mail to receive detailed information and an application form. Due to the high demand, it is recommended to contact ORES early in the year. After enrolment, participants will receive a comprehensive booklet on the project.

GREY WHALES RESEARCH EXPEDITIONS, Canada and Mexico

Coastal Ecosystems Research Foundation
43 Park Hill Dr, Frome BA11 2LQ   UK
Tel.: ++44 (7745) 730 873   –   Fax: ++1(815) 327 0183
E-mail: info@cerf.bc.ca
www.cerf.bc.ca

Desc.: The Coastal Ecosystem Research Foundation conducts research on the behavioural ecology of whales, dolphins, sea-turtles and their environment in British Columbia and Baja California. Projects include: population census, home-range determination, micro-habitat use, prey dynamics, social behaviour and impacts of feeding behaviour on the benthic ecosystem. Graduate student research currently includes work on the migration of grey whales between summering and wintering grounds and a study of the underwater behaviour of the whales, dolphins and turtles in relation to the bottom topography and distribution of their prey. Studies on other marine mammal species include abundance, distribution and association patterns of humpback whales, river otters, harbour seals and killer whales. In some years, depending on funding and staffing, research is also conducted on the biodiversity of the intertidal, subtidal and coastal forest ecosystems.

Spp.: Marine mammals: grey whales (*Eschrichtius robustus*), humpback whales (*Megaptera novaeangliae*), river otters (*Lutra canadensis*), black sea-turtles (*Chelonia agassizi*).

Hab.: Northern Pacific coastal waters, temperate rainforest coast in BC, desert coast in Baja.

Loc.: Central coast of British Columbia, Canada, and west coast of Baja California, Mexico.

Travel: BC. Participants will be met in Port Hardy, BC, for the day-long boat trip to CERF's research base at Xusela, near Allison Harbour. Baja: participants will be met in Loreto, where they will be met by project staff, for the 6-hour road trip to San Ignacio.

Dur.: 7 days (Sunday to Saturday or Saturday to Friday).

Per.: Year round.

L.term: Possible with approval. Subject mostly to space and funding.

Age: Min. 15.

Qualif.: No particular skills required. Volunteers must be willing to spend long

137

hours at shore stations or on boats. Previous experience with boat handling and photography is an asset, but not necessary.

Work: Volunteers are incorporated into the research team for the duration of their stay, and will participate in all of the research, including: boat handling (training provided), photo-ID (taking photos of the animals and identifying individuals by pigmentation patterns), data collection (behaviour, distribution, micro-habitat use, and movements) and ROV (mini-submarine) operations. Short talks are given every morning on research methods and evening lectures provide a background for the work.

Lang.: English, French, German, Spanish, Swedish on some trips.

Accom.: BC: double cabins (bunks) at Xusela. Baja: camping.

Cost: Canada: US$1,849; all food and accommodation provided. Baja: US$2,149. Participants must provide their own transportation to Port Hardy or Loreto. The organisation can help arrange details at time of booking.

Applic.: Deposit of CAD$250 (approx. US$200) is due at time of booking, balance is due 60 days before trip date.

Notes: Max. group size is 12.

GREY WOLF PROJECT, Idaho USA
Wolf Education and Research Center (WERC)
517 Joseph Ave, P.O. Box 217, Winchester, Idaho 83555 USA
Tel.: ++1 (208) 924 6960
Fax: ++1 (208) 924 6959
E-mail: werced@camasnet.com
www.wolfcenter.org

Desc.: Public information, education and research concerning endangered species, with an emphasis on the grey wolf, its habitat and ecosystem in the northern Rocky Mountain region. WERC cares for a captive pack of wolves: "The Sawtooth Pack: Wolves of the Nez Perce". WERC is in partnership with the Nez Perce Tribe, which currently handles the wolf management and reintroduction for Idaho.

Spp.: Grey timber wolf (*Canis lupus*).

Hab.: Camas prairie, timber.

Loc.: North-central region of Idaho; near the borders of Idaho, Washington and Oregon, USA.

Travel: From Lewiston, ID take Highway 95 south to Winchester, ID. Follow signs for the Winchester Lake State Park. The centre is approximately 1 mile past the State Park.

Dur.: Varies with prior agreement between individual and WERC.

Per.: Year round; the need is greater from June to September.

L. term: Possible: inquire with the project.

Age: Min.18.

Work: Volunteers are involved in maintenance and/or construction, building, staffing the visitor centre; providing educational programmes, assisting with membership documentation and generally helping where needed.

Lang.: English.

Accom.: Local off-site lodging facilities can be recommended.

Cost: Max. US$20/day; excluding meals and transportation to/from Winchester.

Applic.: Request information and application form via e-mail or mail.

GRIFFON VULTURE CONSERVATION PROJECT, Croatia
Eco-center Caput Insulae – Beli
E Beli 4, 51559 Beli Croatia
Tel./Fax: ++385 (51) 840 525
E-mail: info@caput-insulae.com caput.insulae@ri.t-com.hr
www.caput-insulae.com

Desc.: The griffon vulture has disappeared from many European countries and is declining in its southeastern European range. The Croatian population includes approximately 100 breeding pairs. The objective of this project is to study griffon vulture biology and ecology to determine the critical factors for their survival on the islands and to develop new conservation strategies in order to maintain the present breeding population.

Spp.: Griffon vultures (*Gyps fulvus*), golden eagle (*Aquila chrysaetos*), short-toed eagle (*Circaetus gallicus*), peregrine falcon (*Falco peregrinus*), eagle owl (*Bubo bubo*), shag (*Phalacrocorax aristotelis*).

Hab: Mediterrannean sea-cliffs, oak forests and grasslands.

Loc.: Kvarner Archipelago, Northeast Adriatic, Croatia.

Travel: Airplane to Zagreb or Trieste (Italy); then bus or train to Rijeka; then bus or catamaran to Cres.

Dur.: Min. 1 week.

Per.: Year round.

L.term: Possible, for extremely motivated volunteers.

Age: Min. 18 years (16 with parent's permission).

Qualif.: Good physical conditions and strong motiviation.

Work: Recording griffons at colonies, noting all sightings at feeding station, taking care of ill or exhausted birds in the Rehabilitation Center.

Lang.: English.

Accom.: Eco-center: 26 beds, 4 bathrooms, hot showers, fully-equipped kitchen

Cost: From EUR80–125 (approx.GB£55–85) for 1 week. Food not included (approx. EUR5/day). Volunteers help cook and housekeep.

Agents: The Ecovolunteer Network at www.ecovolunteer.org.

Applic.: Application form on website.

Notes: Volunteers can also participate in other activities: interpretation for tourists and locals, dry stone wall or trail reconstruction, etc.

GRUPO LOBO, Portugal

Fac. Ciências de Lisboa
Dept. Bio. Animal, Bloco C2 – 3° Piso, 1749-016 Lisboa   Portugal
IWRC - Quinta da Murta. Gradil. Amartado 61, 2669 - 909 Malveira Portugal
Tel: ++351 (261) 785 037 (IWRC)
Fax:++351 (261) 788 047 (IWRC)
Email: globo@fc.ul.pt
http://lobo.fc.ul.pt/

Desc.: Grupo Lobo is a non-profit association, founded in 1985, to work on wolf conservation and its habitat in Portugal, where the wolf is in danger of extinction. One of the aims is to spread accurate information about this misunderstood and persecuted predator. The Iberian Wolf Recovery Center (IWRC) was created by GL with the aim of providing a suitable environment in captivity for wolves that can no longer live in the wild, allowing the public to understand the species' biology and conservation problems.

Spp.: Wolf (*Canis lupus*).

Hab.: Atlantic ecosystem.

Loc.: Malveira, 25 km north of Lisbon, Portugal

Travel: Airplane to Lisbon and then by bus or car to Vale de Guardia-Malveira.

Dur.: Minimum 15 days.

Per.: Volunteers are accepted year round.

L.term: Volunteers can stay up to 1 month.

Age: Min. 18.

Qualif.: Ability to work as part of a team. Anyone is welcome to join and apply their skills and interests.

Work: Several tasks can be performed by volunteers: monitor and feeding the wolves; take part in the daily activities of the Center; take part in the reforestation project; during the summer assist in pratolling the area for fire control.

Lang.: English or Portuguese.

Accom.: In volunteer house is fully equiped. Own sleeping bag needed.

Cost: Volunteering costs depend on the lodging availability at the IWRC. Contact IWRC for information.

Applic.: Online application form.

Notes: Accident and health insurances is mandatory.

HAWAIIAN FOREST PRESERVATION PROJECT, Hawaii USA

Kokee Resource Conservation Program c/o Natural History Museum
P.O. Box 100, Kekaha, Hawaii, 96752 USA
Tel.: ++1 (808) 335 0045
Fax: ++1 (808) 335 0304
E-mail: rcp@aloha.net
www.krcp.org

Desc.: In the isolated Hawaiian Islands over 1,000 flowering plant species evolved, and the forests of Kokee State Park contain many species found nowhere else in the world. However, because of invasive weed species introduced to the islands in the last 2 centuries, Hawaii also contains over 50% of the US Federally listed endangered plant species. This programme removes invasive weeds from selected areas of the mountain state park in order to restore those forested areas to their native state.

Spp.: Weed species: strawberry guava, blackberry, kahili ginger.

Hab.: Mesic montane Koa-dominated forests, wet montane Ohia-dominated forests, mixed-bog communities.

Loc.: Kokee State Park, Kauai, Hawaii.

Travel: Airplane to Kauai.

Dur.: 1 week to 1 month.

Per.: Year round.

L.term: Possible, inquire with organisation.

Age: Min. 21, or enrolled in an environmentally oriented degree.

Qualif.: Must be physically fit. Volunteers are trained and supervised. Priority is given to volunteers with a degree and/or experience in ecology, conservation or botany.

Work: Supervised by programme staff, volunteers use herbicides and hand weed to maintain the nearly native state containing unique, rare and endangered plant species. Volunteers work 8-hour days, often involving strenuous hiking in mountainous areas.

Lang.: English.

Accom.: Rustic housing in historic camp (bunk beds).

Cost: Volunteers pay for their own food and must rent a car.

Applic.: Request application form via e-mail.

Notes: Groups are welcome but space is limited to parties of 14.

HELLENIC WILDLIFE HOSPITAL, Greece
Hellenic Wildlife Hospital
PO. Box 57
18010 Aegina Greece
Tel.: ++30 (229) 703 1338/++30 (697) 925 2277
ekpaz@ekpazp.gr
www.ekpazp.gr

Desc.:	Founded in 1990, is the oldest and largest wildlife rehabilitation center in Greece dedicated to rehabilitation of wildlife, education and information of the public on wildlife protection issues, protection of endangered species, research on threats to wildlife and wildlife rehabilitation (illegal shooting, trapping, poisoning and pollution, habitat degradation and destruction) and taking preventative action, cooperation with public authorities, national and international NGO's with similar goals.
Spp.:	Indigenous and exotic species (may be rare or threatened).
Hab.:	All the animals are found in Greece, but can be migrating birds or illegally transported animals from all over the world.
Loc.:	Island of Aegina, 10km from Aegina near Pachia Rachi.
Travel:	Fly to Athens, then by ferry to Aegina from Piraeus.
Dur.:	Min. 10 days, max. one year.
Per.:	All year around.
Age:	Minimum 18.
Qualif.:	No special skills required. Team work. All skills are welcome, especially veterinarian, wildlife expertise.
Work:	Cleaning of outdoor and indoor (also where the animals are treated), food preparation, feeding and watering, maintenance and construction work, help in treatments, work in the information booth of the Aegina Island and other special duties depending on experience. Training opportunities for veterinarian, biology or administration students or graduates.
Lang.:	English.
Acc.::	There is a house for volunteers in the center.
Cost:	No fees, volunteers pay own living costs and travel expenses.
L.term:	Long-term is welcome with a maximum duration of one year.
Applic.:	Application and agreement forms can be found in the website.

HOEDSPRUIT ENDANGERED SPECIES CENTRE, South Africa

P.O. Box 1278
Hoedspruit, 1380 South-Africa
Limpopo Province
Tel.: +27 (15) 793 1633
E-mail: accounts.students@campjabulani.org.za
www.wildlifecentre.co.za

Desc.: A research and breeding project on feline species especially cheetah. Based in South-Africa Limpopo province, 40km from Kruger Park. Educational programme with hands on veterinary experiences. Cultural and tourism activities included with accomodation and all meals provided. Lectures on S.A. wildlife followed by practical sessions.

Spp.: Cheetah, wild dog, African wild cat, lion, rhino, buffalo, black footed cat, caracal, serval, ground hornbill.

Hab.: African savannah.

Loc.: South-Africa, Limpopo Province, Hoedspruit.

Travel: Airplane to Johannesburg and from there to Eastgate / Hoedspruit airport for pickup.

Dur.: 21 days / 3 weeks. It is a set programme.

Per.: Year round, 3 weeks per month.

L.term: Possibilities for longer stay depending on coordinator.

Age: 16 -55. Most volunteers are between 18 and 25.

Qualif.: No particular skills needed.

Work: Food preperation and feeding of animals. Helping out at centre.

Lang.: English.

Accom.: Huts with 2 beds per hut in a camp within a big 5 area with electricity and warm showers, bedding provided.

Cost: R 10,000 all inclusive (Approx. US$1,350 or GB£720).

Agents: African Conservation Experience

Applic.: E-mail accounts.students@campjabulani.org.za for application form.

Notes: Max. 10 students per session.

INTEGRATED COASTAL MANAGEMENT PROJECT, Malta
The Gaia Foundation
Elysium Visitor Centre and Tree Nursery
Ghajn Tuffieha Road, SPB 07
Tel.: ++35 (62) 158 4473
E-mail: admin@projectgaia.org
www.projectgaia.org

Desc.: A Mediterranean Coastal Management Project is welcoming volunteers to help in the conservation of protected areas, habitat restoration, organic farming, plant propagation (tree nursery) as well as office work. The Gaia Foundation exists since 1994 to protect the environment of the Maltese Islands and to promote sustainable living.

Spp.: Indigenous and endemic plant species, Aleppo Pine, Evergreen Oak, Maltese RockCentaury or Maltese Everlast.

Hab.: Mediterranean ecosystems, coastal area.

Loo.: Northwoot of Malta, Moditorranoan Soa.

Travel: Plane to Malta Airport; taxi or bus to apartment; bike or bus to work (20 min).

Dur.: Min. 1 month, up to 6 months.

Per.: Year round.

L.term: Volunteers can join the project for up to 6 months.

Age: Min. 20.

Qualif.: No particular skills required. Experience in environment, organic farming, fairtrade or graphic design welcome.

Work: Help in tree nursery, organic field, work on website, newsletters, brochures, infoboards 32hrs/week.

Lang.: English.

Accom.: Apartment with bathroom and kitchen. No sleeping bags required.

Cost: Lm15 (approx. EUR35 - US$45) per week including electricity, water, heating, use of bicycles.

Applic.: Download the application form from www.projectgaia.org/team/internships and sent it to admin@projectgaia.org

INTERNATIONAL CONSERVATION VOLUNTEER EXCHANGE, Nevada
Great Basin Institute
Mailstop 099 - University of Nevada Reno
Reno, Nevada 89557 USA
Tel.: ++1 (775) 784 1192 – Fax: ++1 (775) 327 2307
E-mail: powellj@unr.edu
www.greatbasininstitute.org click on "International Volunteering"

Desc.:	Over the past few field seasons, GBI has collaborated with numerous international environmental exchange programs, attracting over 100 students and young professionals from England, France, Sweden, New Zealand, and West Africa to serve on conservation projects throughout Nevada. Volunteers spent their time in the US working side-by-side with NCC members and GBI students at Lake Tahoe, Lake Mead, the Santa Rosa Mountains, and the Black Rock Desert, assisting with field research and restoration projects. In exchange for their service, ICVE volunteers are lead on educational trips, introducing them to premier spots in the west: central Sierra hot springs, Yosemite National Park, Big Sur coastal beaches, and high desert ranges.
Spp.:	Flora and fauna ecosystems ranging from low desert to mountains.
Hab.:	From deserts to high elevation mountain forests.
Loc.:	Projects in locations throughout the state of Nevada.
Travel:	By airplane to Reno or San Francisco (bus or train from S.F.).
Dur.:	1-6 months.
Per.:	Year round (see website for specific dates).
L.term:	Inquire with the organisation.
Age:	Min. 18 max.35.
Qualif.:	No qualifications required.
Work:	10 hour work days. 4 days in the field, with 3 days off or 8 days in the field with 6 days off. ICVE is not recommended for people with conditions that limit physical activity.
Accom.:	Camping during field work dormitory style cabin when off-time.
Cost:	Volunteers pay for travel, travellers' insurance and required gear. Food while in and out of the field is provided.
Applic:	Contact Joshua Powell, ICVE Program Coordinator.
Notes:	Projects change frequently and descriptions are provided for a general idea of what projects may entail.

IONIAN DOLPHIN PROJECT, Greece

Tethys Research Institute
c/o Civic Aquarium, Viale G.B. Gadio 2
20121 Milano Italy
Tel.: ++39 (02) 72001947/72013943 — Fax:++39 (02) 86995011
E-mail: tethys@tethys.org
www.tethys.org

Desc.: This is the first long-term project on cetaceans in Ionian Greece, initiated in 1993 by the Tethys Research Institute (see Organisation list), with the goal to study the socio-ecology of common and bottlenose dolphins that live in the coastal waters around the island of Kalamos. Common dolphins are now declining in the Mediterranean, owing to overfishing, by-catch and habitat degradation. By monitoring this community, researchers are promoting proper conservation measures. Methods of investigation include systematic surveys, individual photo-identification and behavioural sampling of free-ranging dolphins.

Spp.: Common dolphin (*Delphinus delphis*), bottlenose dolphin (*Tursiops truncatus*); sea turtles (*Caretta caretta*) swordfish (*Xiphias gladius*), manta rays (*Mobula mobula*) and monk seals (*Monachus monachus*) may be also observed.

Hab.: Coastal waters of the central Ionian Greece.

Loc.: Island of Kalamos, Greece.

Travel: Airplane to Athens or Preveza, then bus or taxi to Mytika. Transfer to Kalamos is provided by the researchers. Igoumenitsa and Patra can also be reached by ferry from the Italian ports of Venice, Ancona or Brindisi.

Dur.: 6 days.

Per.: May to October.

L.term: Consecutive shifts can be booked. Discount granted to university students less than 26 years old.

Age: Min. 18.

Qualif.: No particular skills are required. Volunteers should be interested and very motivated.

Work: The work consists of observations from inflatable craft during surveys at sea and long-lasting observations of dolphin groups found in two study areas (the area around Kalamos and the Amvrakikos Gulf). With bad weather volunteers stay at the base, entering and analysing data

147

and matching digital photos. Trips can also be organised. Daily lectures on dolphin research methods and conservation strategies are carried out by the researchers.

Lang.:   English, Italian.

Accom.:   The base is located in the village of Episcopi, on the island of Kalamos. The house has 4 bedrooms, 1 of which is for the volunteers. Everyone takes part in cooking and housekeeping. The base is equipped with computers, a basic scientific library, research archives, telephone-and fax.

Cost: EUR 500–830 (approx. GB£350–580) for 6 days, depending on the season, including food, membership and insurance. Fees do not include travel.

Agents: Tethys Research Institute (see Organisation list).

Applic.:   Request a standard application form to be completed and returned to the Tethys Research Institute. Early booking is suggested.

Notes: Only 5 volunteers can participate in each shift, depending on period. From 3 to 4 researchers reside at the field station with the volunteers. The small size of the boat and the low-noise engine allow an easy approach of the dolphins and their following at close range without modifications of their behaviour.

IRACAMBI ATLANTIC RAINFOREST RESEARCH AND CONSERVATION CENTER, Brazil

Fazenda Iracambi, Rosário da Limeira
36878–000 Minas Gerais Brazil
Tel.: ++55 (32) 3721 1436 – Fax: ++55 (32) 3721 0545
E-mail: iracambi@iracambi.com Skype ID: iracambi
www.iracambi.com

Desc.:	Iracambi is committed to making the preservation of the rainforest more attractive than its destruction. Its members are seeking ways that will not only arrest the rate of destruction, but reverse it, whilst providing at the same time a higher standard of living for the local farmers.
Spp.:	Inventories of flora and fauna are being carried out.
Hab.:	Semi-deciduous rainforest.
Loc.:	Southeastern Brazil in the State of Minas Gerais.
Travel:	Fly to Rio de Janeiro, bus to Muriaé and Rosário da Limeira.
Dur.:	Minimum 1 month.
Per.:	Year round.
L.term:	Visa allows max. 180 days. Longer stays require special visa.
Age:	Min.18, no max.
Qualif.:	General hands with no skills are welcome. IT, GIS and mapping specialists, carpenters, teachers (in Portuguese), tropical botanists and zoologists are especially needed.
Work:	There are a wide range of volunteer roles available. The work that volunteers do feeds into four defined research priority areas (land use management; forest restoration; income generating alternatives; community understanding and engagement) as well as work that improves the capacity of the Center. The work covers a wide range of areas, therefore volunteers with skills and expertise, as well as plenty of dedication and enthusiasm, are always welcome.
Lang.:	Portuguese and English.
Accom.:	Shared room in traditional farm cottages.
Cost:	US$550 for first month, US$525 for the second month and US$500 for third and subsequent months. This covers the costs of full board self cathering accomodation.
Applic.:	Send CV via e-mail. No deadlines or forms to fill in.

IRISH SEAL SANCTUARY, Ireland

Tobergregan, Garristown,
Co Dublin, Ireland
Tel ++353 (1) 835 4370
E-mail: emmahiggs@hotmail.com
www.irishsealsanctuary.ie

Desc.: The Irish Seal Sanctuary is Ireland's only full-time, 24 hour, wildlife rescue/ rehabilitation facility. It provides a service for the entire country and is sustained entirely by voluntary effort and in field conditions. The Sanctuary currently deals with more than 1,000 telephone calls per year reporting injured or distressed seals, or marine related incidents.

Spp.: Marine mammals, primarily pinnipeds, mainly the Grey Seal and the Harbour Seal. Occasionally other wildlife casualties e.g. cetaceans, birds and small mammals.

Hab.: Species rescued from anywhere on the 6,000 mile Irish coastline.

Loc.: North County Dublin, Ireland.

Travel: Short travelling distance from Dublin but there is no public transport to the Sanctuary itself. Pick up can be arranged in Dublin.

Dur.: Min. 3 months.

Per.: May - February.

L.Term: Suitable volunteers may be able to stay for 10 months.

Age: Min. 18.

Qualif.: Ability to work as part of a team. A driving license is essential. The work involves physical labour so volunteers must be fit. Training will be given. Veterinary experience useful but no essential.

Work: Full-time volunteers are required to make up a team of handlers to rehabilitate the seals. Duties will include cleaning seal pens, preparing food for the seals, force feeding sick pups, record keeping, general maintenance and seal rescues – collecting sick seals from around the country, and ultimately releasing them back into the wild.

Lang.: English.

Accom.: Small shared apartment.

Cost: Food and accommodation are provided free of charge. Volunteers must arrange their own transport to the ISS from their own country.

Applic.: Volunteer application form available from the website.

ISCHIA DOLPHIN PROJECT, Italy
DELPHIS Mediterranean Dolphin Conservation
Via Zaro 22
80075 Forio d'Ischia (NA) Italy
Tel./Fax: ++39 (081) 989 578 – Mob.:(on board) ++39 (349) 5749927
E-mail: info@delphismdc.org
www.delphismdc.org

Desc.:   The submarine canyon of Cuma is an important habitat where a particular pelagic fauna can be found very close to the coast. The presence of whales and dolphins, pelagic fishes and marine birds is related to the geological and ecological characteristics of the area. Primary research concentration is of a relic population unit of endangered short-beaked common dolphins. The island of Ischia was noted as 'critical habitat' for the species in the Mediterranean Sea by the IUCN. Pollution, prey depletion and by-catch are the main threats for cetaceans. Delphis MDC works to include the canyon into the perimeter of the future Marine Protected Area of Ischia, Procida and Vivara Islands proposed by the Italian Ministry of the Environment. The canyon represents a hot spot for other cetacean species, like striped, bottlenose and Risso's dolphins, pilot, sperm and fin whales. Management measures to protect cetaceans in this key area are urgently needed.

Spp.:   Common dolphin (*Delphinus delphis*), striped dolphin (*Stenella coeruleoalba*), bottlenose dolphin (*Tursiops truncatus*), Risso's dolphin (*Grampus griseus*), pilot whale (*Globicephala melas*), sperm whale *(Physeter macrocephalus)*, fin whale (*Balaenoptera physalus*).

Hab.:   Coastal and pelagic Mediterranean waters, submarine canyon.

Loc.:   Mediterranean sea, Ischia Island, Italy.

Travel: Airplane or train to Naples, then bus to Beverello, then ferry or hydrofoil to Ischia island.

Dur.:   1 week.

Per.:   June to October.

L.term: Maximum stay is 3 weeks with project's leader's approval.

Age: Min. 15.

Qualif.:   No particular skills required, just good physical health.

Work: All participants are required to help in data collection. In particular: watching, underwater camera monitoring, behavioural data collection, photo-identification will be shared between volunteers. The project relies on everybody's help even for navigation: steering, hoisting and folding the sails, helping with the mooring. Everybody on board will take part in all the duties. Everyone is expected to "mucks in" and help with the daily duties, including: cleaning the boat, shopping, cooking and washing the dishes.

Lang.:   English or Italian/French/Spanish.

Accom.:   On board of 'Jean Gab', a 17.70 m wooden cutter built in 1930 in Marseille, transformed in a laboratory on the sea, the boat is provided with a 15-year database and a recording system to collect bio-acoustic data and underwater videos. Available on board are books and scientific literature on cetaceans.

Cost: EUR720-820 (approx. GB£500–570). Price inlcudes: food and beverages, accommodation, insurance, fuel for the research vessel and the inflatable craft, port fees, lectures and training by Delphis researchers, membership fee, certificate of attendance. Travel and the first dinner are not included.

Agents: Delphis MDC.

Applic.:   Send and e-mail to above address. A 50% deposit to reserve the place is needed with the application.

Notes: Delphis MDC works in the area since 1991 thanks to the volunteers' help.

JATUN SACHA, Ecuador

Fundación Jatun Sacha
Eugenio de Santillán N34 –248 y Maurián
Casilla 17–12–867 Quito   Ecuador
Tel.: ++593 (2) 243 2173 – Fax: ++593 (2) 243 2240
E-mail: volunteer@jatunsacha.org
www.jatunsacha.org

Desc.: Jatun Sacha Foundation is an Ecuadorian NGO whose main objective is conservation of the environment. Jatun Sacha has 8 biological stations located in different areas of Ecuador: Amazon, coast and highlands, Galapagos Islands.

Spp.: Various species of Ecuadorian fauna and vegetation.

Hab.: Andean cloud forest, tropical rainforest, dry forest, premontane forest, humid forest, mangrove forest.

Loc.: Ecuadorian coast, highlands and Amazon, Galapagos Islands.

Travel: By airplane to Quito, bus or truck from Quito to the stations.

Dur: Min. 15 days.

Per.: Year round.

L.term: Possible, inquire with the organisation.

Age: Min. 18.

Qualif.: Volunteers must be dynamic and interested in conservation.

Work: Reforestation, agroforestry, organic agriculture and farming, community extension projects, general mainteinance, meteorological and other environmental data collection, trekking, visits to communities, aquaculture work.

Lang.: English, basic Spanish is recommended, but not required.

Accom.: Shared cabins, in some cases without electricity, with toilets outside.

Cost: Application fee US$35. Food and accommodation US$395 per month.

Applic.: Send by regular mail: CV, a cover letter, 2 passport size photos, medical certificate, police record, and a US$35 application fee.

KARUMBE' SEA TURTLES PROJECT, Uruguay

Karumbé: Sea turtles of Uruguay
Av.Giannattasio Km 30,500, Canelones, Uruguay.
Rocha state Uruguay
Tel.: ++ (598) 999 17 8
E-mail: maririos34@gmail.com
www.karumbe.org

Desc.:	Desc.: Karumbé is an NGO devoted to the conservation of the sea turtles of Uruguay. The organization combines conservation and research activities in different areas such as environmental education, monitoring sea turtles feeding areas and bycatch in artisanal and industrial fishing fleets.
Spp.:	Green (*Chelonia mydas*), Leatherback (*Dermochelys coriacea*) and Loggerhead (*Caretta caretta*) turtles.
Hab.:	Coastline and shallow rocky oceanic areas.
Loc.:	Barra de Valizas - Cabo Polonio, South Eastern Uruguay.
Travel:	Airplane to Montevideo or Ferry from Buenos Aires (Argentina) to Montevideo, where volunteers are met.
Dur.:	Min. 15 days, max. 2 months.
Per.:	Mid January to mid March.
Age:	Min. 18, max. 60.
Qualif.:	No specific qualifications are required. Veterinary or biology studies, and good physical condition helpful but not essential.
Work:	1) Sighting and capturing, with nets, juveniles of green turtle. 2) 12 km walk, searching for stranded sea turtles. 3) Help researchers with necropsies of dead turtles. 4) Collecting data of the artisanal fishery carried out locally, from onboard or at port. 5) Involvement in talks and workshops for the community and tourists.6) Rehabilitation of sick and weak sea turtles. 7) Help in the field station duties such us cleaning and cooking.
Lang.:	Spanish and English.
Accom.:	Shared room in a house or tent accommodation with indoor bathroom and shower, as well as electricity.
Cost:	US$15/day including: room, accommodation and simple meals.
Applic.:	Via e-mail with subject "Volunteer Barra de Valizas", in the text, include CV, photograph, letter of intents.

KIDO - WIDECAST SEA TURTLE NESTING MONITORING, Grenada

YWF-Kido Foundation
Carriacou, Grenada, West Indies.
Tel.: ++1 (473) 443 7936
E-mail: kido-ywf@spiceisle.com
www.kido-projects.com

Desc.: Leatherback and Hawksbill turtles conservation and monitoring project in Carriacou Island, Grenadines, Caribbean Sea. Volunteers will help to protect these critically endangered species and their eggs, still hunted and poached in this region and to collect data for their long-term survival.

Spp.: Leatherback turtle (*Dermochelys coriacea*), Hawksbill turtle (*Eretmochelys imbricata*).

Hab.: Tropical coasts.

Loc.: Carriacou Island, Grenadines of Grenada, West Indies.

Travel: Plane to international airport in Grenada; plane or ferry to Carriacou Island; 15min. bus to the project area.

Dur.: Minimum stay 1 month, maximum 8 months.

Per.: 1st of March-October 31st.

L.term: Volunteers can stay long term after the regular period.

Age: Min.18, max. 50. Younger with parents' permission, or older if fit.

Qualif.: Volunteers must be good swimmers, in excellent physical conditions and motivated to walk on soft sandy beaches all night and be keen on conservation and animal welfare.

Work: Night beach patrols with local guides, monitoring nesting/hatching activities, helping to measure/tag the turtle, egg counts, disguise turtle tracks and nests to prevent poaching and mapping nest location.

Lang.: English.

Accom.: Bunk beds in a Pagoda style accommodation, sheets or sleeping bags and bed mosquito net required.

Cost: US$15 per day for the first 60 days (including accommodation). For longer periods the daily cost is reduced. Minimum cost is US$450.

Applic.: A Volunteer Application Form to fill, CV, copy of passport, two references and travel insurance.

Notes: Ocean kayaks and motorboat - dinghy may be used for monitoring beaches during day and night time.

KLIPKOP WILDLIFE SANCTUARY, South Africa

P.O Box 76
Welbekend.
Gauteng 1517 South Africa
Tel.: ++27 (0) 11 964
E-mail: info@klipkop.co.za
www.klipkop.co.za

Desc.: Klipkop is a wildlife and environmental conservation initiative which seeks to preserve a high altitude grassland, Bankenveld. The wildlife sanctuary is home to over a dozen varieties of buck (antelope), many small mammals, and has nearly 200 varieties of bird on record (including wetland, savannah and grassland species).

Spp.: Primarily buck (antelope); lesser emphasis on smaller mammals and birds.

Hab.: Grassland.

Loc.: Gauteng, South Africa.

Travel: Volunteers are met at Johannesburg International Airport, or Pretoria Bus Station (if travelling overland).

Dur.: Minimum stay is 4 weeks. Stay as long as you can.

Per.: Year round.

L.term: Typical stay is 4-6 weeks; less often 2-3 months.

Age: Min. 18, max.70. Physical work is involved volunteers must be in good health.

Qualif.: No qualifications required. Full training provided.

Work: Mainly environmental conservation work and reporting; also birding and game assessment.

Lang.: English.

Accom.: Bunk-beds in home-style accommodation. Sleeping bags required.

Cost: US$1,250 for 1st month, then US$200 per week.

Applic.: The application form can be downloaded from Volunteer Programme on the website.

Notes: A comprehensive Volunteer Information Pack and FAQs is available from the website.

LA HESPERIA, Ecuador

La Hesperia Biological Station and Reserve, c/o Fundacion Jatun Sacha
Eugenio Santillan
N 34-248 y Maurian Quito, Ecuador
Tel.: ++593 (2) 243 2240   +593 (2) 243 2246 (EXT:113)
Fax: ++593 (02) 245 3583
E-mail: contact@la-hesperia.com   www.la-hesperia.com

Desc.: The western forests along the main highway between Quito and Santo Domingo, are a biologically rich mix of both Andean highland and coastal lowland species found together in one place. Besides conserving a significant piece of the forest, La Hesperia is developing reforestation work, a fish production pond, and a medicinal garden. Agroforestry alternatives will be developed with community participation.

Spp.: Currently 320 bird species have been identified in La Hesperia, 19 are endemic to the region and 7 are vulnerable or in danger of extinction.

Hab.: Tropical Cloud forest.

Loc.: Ecuador, Pichincha Province, Tropical Western Andes.

Travel: 2 hours bus ride from Quito.

Dur.: Minimum volunteer commitment of 2 weeks.

Per.: Year round.

L.term: All volunteers are welcome to extend their stay.

Age: Min.18.

Qualif.: A college degree is not required in order to participate in the volunteer program. Volunteers should have some interest in the topics of conservation, biodiversity, ecology, or nature.

Work: Volunteers can participate in the following activities: forestry program; sustainable agriculture; community integration; research; ecotourism program; hikes; COB workshops.

Lang.: English, Spanish and French are spoken by the station staff.

Accom.: Two volunteer houses, providing beds for up to 30 volunteers at a time. Both have a bathroom with hot shower, social areas and great views of the cloud forest. Laundry services free of charge.

Cost: US$395 monthly (for the first month) for foreigners. US$230 monthly for nationals. US$350 for the second month and on. To apply for the volunteer program, there is a one time application fee of US$ 35 .

Applic.: Contact form on website www.jatunsacha.org.

LEATHERBACK SEATURTLE TAGGING PROGRAMME, Grenada
Ocean Spirits Inc.
P.O. Box 1373, Grand Anse, St.George's, Grenada West Indies
Tel.: ++ (473) 403 4266
E-mail: volunteer@oceanspirits.org
www.oceanspirits.org

Desc.: Ocean Spirits Inc. is a non-profit NGO dedicated to the conservation of marine life and the marine environment. Through 3 programmes: Education, Research and Conservation and Community Development, the NGO is working to change attitudes towards the sustainable use of resources in Grenada.

Spp.: Leatherback sea turtle (*Dermochelys coriacea*); Hawksbill sea turtle (*Eretmochelys imbricata*).

Hab.: Tropical beaches.

Loc.: Grenada, Caribbean.

Travel: Plane to Grenada, volunteers are met at the airport.

Dur.: Volunteers must commit for a minimum period of 3 weeks.

Per.: April to August.

L.term: Volunteers may stay for more than1 period at reduced cost.

Age: Min. 18.

Qualif.: Previous experience of field work and data collection is an advantage but not essential. Good physical condition as the work involves long hours and in variable weather conditions. Must be enthusiastic and flexible.

Work: Night patrols for nesting turtles, applying tags and collecting other data. Morning beach surveys to determine other turtle nesting activity. Conducting educational field trips and school summer camps. Assist in accomodation mainteinance.

Lang.: English.

Accom.: Dormitory style accommodation, sheets and towels needed.

Cost: From GB£795/US$1,470 for 3 weeks. Price includes accommodation, food and airport transfers.

Applic.: Application form available via http: //www.workingabroad.com/page/24/ocean-spirits-grenada.htm

LEATHERBACK TURTLE CONSERVATION, Costa Rica and Panama
Endangered Wildlife Trust and Rainforest Concern
Rainforest Concern, Flat 3, 8 Clanricarde Gardens
London W2 4NA UK
Tel.: ++44 (207) 229 209
E-mail: info@rainforestconcern.org
www.turtleprotection.org

Desc.: Volunteers are needed at the Pacuare Reserve in Costa Rica and in Panama to help protect endangered Leatherback turtles. Volunteers assist with tagging, beach patrols, nest protection and monitoring of hatching success and all training is provided.

Spp.: Leatherback Turtles, Green Turtles, and Hawksbill Turtles.

Hab.: Tropical coasts.

Loc.: Pacuare Reserve, Costa Rica and Panama.

Travel: Plane to San José, buses and boat to Pacuare Reserve. Detailed directions provided on application.

Dur.: Minimum stay one week.

Per.: From mid March to the end of September.

Age: Min. 18. Children under 18 must be accompanied by a responsible adult.

Qualif.: No particular skills needed, but a keen interest in conservation required.

Work: Volunteers assist with tagging, beach patrols, nest protection and monitoring of hatching success and all training is provided.

Lang.: English and Spanish useful but not required.

Accom.: Shared accommodation in simple cabins with mosquito screens. No electricity.

Cost: Volunteers are reponsible for transportation to site. Prices include meals and accommodation.

Applic.: Volunteers are welcome to use the Green Volunteers Standard Application Form (see page 255).

LEATHERBACK TURTLE PROJECT, Costa Rica

Estación Las Tortugas
Matina, Region Mondonguillo, Costa Rica
Tel.: ++ (506) 396 0268 (Costa Rica, March-June)
  ++ 44 (1903) 244 134 (UK July-February)
E-mail: estacionlastortugas@yahoo.co.uk
www.estacionlastortugas.org or http://tortuga.is.dreaming.org/pub

---

Desc.: Each year the leatherback turtle visits the Caribbean coast of Costa Rica to nest. The biological station, Estación Las Tortugas is one of their most important nesting beaches. Since 2000, the project has been focusing on the conservation and protection of this now critically endangered species.

Spp.: Leatherback turtle (*Dermochelys coriacea*).

Hab.: Secondary coastal rainforest.

Loc.: Caribbean coast of Costa Rica (30 km north of Puerto Limon).

Travel: Airplane to San Jose, Costa Rica. Volunteers will be picked up at the airport and taken to Matina.

Dur.: 1 - 4 months.

Per.: March-June.

L.term: Long term opportunities might be available for research.

Age : Min. 18.

Qualif.: No specific skills required, just enthusiasm, willingness to work and ability to live in basic conditions and high humidity levels.

Work: Volunteers will assist researchers. Long distance walking without assistance is required, as 4-hour beach patrols will be carried out each night. Leatherback nests will be collected and translocated, together with environmental data. A few hours is also carried out in the day time.

Lang.: English or Spanish.

Accom.: Basic accommodation with rooms of 4-6 people and shared showers. Basic food of rice and beans provided 3 times a day.

Cost: Up to US$750/month which includes accommodation, 3 meals/day, transport from airport and accommodation in San Jose. Flights and travel insurance are not included.

Applic.: Contact Stamie at the above address for further information and application forms.

LIBANONA ECOLOGY CENTRE, Madagascar

BP 42, Fort Dauphin – 614 Madagascar
Tel.: ++ 261 (20) 922 1242
E-mail: libanonaecology@hotmail.com
www.andrewleestrust.org.uk/libanona.htm- www.libanonecology.com

Desc.: The Libanona Ecology Centre (LEC) is the first university program (BS) in southern Madagascar training future conservation and rural development experts. The Centre also acts as an NGO and has ongoing projects on: community forest management, GIS, conservation education, applied biodiversity, anthropological research and community tourism.

Spp.: Various endemic Malgasy flora and fauna.

Hab.: Malgasy spiny, littoral, humid and transitional forests, coastal ecosystem.

Loc.: Southern Madagascar.

Travel: Flight to Antananarivo and internal flight to Fort Dauphin.

Dur.: From a few weeks to 8–9 months.

Per.: Year round.

L.term: Possible, inquire with organisation.

Age: Min. 18, no max.

Qualif.: Capacity to teach university students in the fields of computers, ecological sciences, social sciences, or languages.

Work: In the following skill areas: GIS, eco tourism, conservation education, TEFL, apiculture, forestry, biodiversity research.

Lang.: French required for teaching jobs, English for field and office activities.

Accom.: Volunteers can have short-term accommodation only, local accommodation can be rented in Fort Dauphin.

Cost: A concrete contribution to a LEC development project is requested as a goodwill gesture. Volunteers should be self financing.

Applic.: Send CV and letter of interest via e-mail to Sylvain Eboroke. Specify area of expertise, availability and theme of interest.

Notes: The Centre also runs "Camp Namakia": a scout camp in a coastal zone, which is also an environmental education facility and a partner in the creation of a community managed park that includes terrestrial ecosystems, mangroves, and marine ecosystems including coral reefs. For further details, see www.campnamakia,org.

161

MANAGEMENT PLAN FOR PILOS LAGOON, Greece

Hellenic Ornithological Society (HOS)
Vas. Irakleiou 24, 10682 Athens   Greece
Tel.: ++30 (1) 822 8704/822 7937
Fax: ++30 (1) 822 8704
E-mail: mkalouli@ornithologiki.gr
www.ornithologiki.gr

Desc.:   The goal of the project is the implementation of a management plan for the Pilos lagoon. The goals are wetland restoration, providing visitor facilities and educating local people about the value of the site. A very important and sensitive section of the project is the research and protection of the African chameleon, found exclusively in this region.

Spp.:   African chameleon (*Chamaeleo africanus*).

Hab.:   Mediterranean coastal lagoon.

Loc.:   Greece, southwestern coast of the Peloponnese peninsula.

Travel: Airplane to Athens or by ferry from Italy to Patras; bus, train or airplane to Kalamata or Kiparissia; bus to Pilos.

Dur.:   1 - 2 months. Min. period of staying is 3 weeks.

Per.:   June to October.

L.term: Only with project leader's approval after regular period.

Age: Min. 20, max. 40, depending on the experience.

Qualif.:   No particular skills required.

Work: Beach patrolling to prevent collection and disturbance of the chameleons and helping with field research. Running information kiosk.

Lang.:   English, Greek.

Accom.:   In tents in a private campsite. Volunteers can bring their own tent. Sleeping bag and mat are a must.

Cost: Prticipation fee EUR60 (approx. GB£40).

Agents: Contact project leader Marilia Kalouli.

Applic.:   An application form needs to be filled out from www.ornithologiki.gr.

Notes: Field work and beach patrolling is hard work, especially during the summer. Volunteers must be motivated.

MANATEE RESEARCH PROJECT, Belize
Oceanic Society Expeditions
Fort Mason Center, Building E
San Francisco, CA 94123   USA
Tel.: ++1 (415) 441 1106 – (800) 326 7491 (toll free in N.America)
Fax: ++1 (415) 474 3395
E-mail: info@oceanic-society.org
www.oceanic-society.org

Desc.:	The goal of this project is to collect biological data necessary for manatee protection and habitat management. The research objectives are to determine distribution and abundance of manatees at Turneffe Atoll, their behavioural ecology, and environmental parameters of microhabitats used consistently.
Spp.:	Manatee (*Trichechus manatus*).
Hab.:	Tropical sea.
Loc.:	Turneffe Atoll, Belize.
Travel.	Volunteers can reach Belize by airplane using group airfare from some US gateway cities (Houston, Los Angeles, Miami).
Dur.:	8 days.
Per.:	June, July.
L. term:	Inquire with organisation.
Age:	Min. 18.
Qualif.:	No particular skills required.
Work:	By small boat, volunteers visit zones of manatee concentration, map positions, note individual markings, and log behavioural information.
Lang.:	English.
Cost:	US$1,790, excluding international flight.
Accom.:	Beachfront cabanas with porch, double rooms with private bath.
Applic.:	Request application form to be returned with a deposit of US$400.
Notes:	Max. group size is 8. Volunteer can have free time for beach snorkelling.

THE MARINE MAMMAL CENTER (TMMC), California USA

Marin Headlands, GGNRA
Sausalito, California 94965 USA
Tel.: ++1 (415) 289 7325 /979 4357 (volunteer inquiries)
Fax: ++1 (415) 289 7333
E-mail: volNteer@tmmc.org
www.tmmc.org – www.marinemammalcenter.org

Desc.:	The Marine Mammal Center is a leading rescue, rehabilitation and release facility for marine mammals. It treats almost 600 animals a year. Volunteer crews work on a 6-12 hour shift, both day and evening, 365 days a year.
Spp.:	Marine mammals, primarily pinnipeds.
Hab.:	Pacific coast.
Loc.:	Northern California (San Francisco).
Travel:	Airplane to San Francisco, then by car.
Dur.:	Not less than 3 weeks.
Per:	Volunteers are accepted year round but are most needed during high season (March to August).
L.term:	Volunteers can remain as long as they like.
Age.:	Min. 18.
Qualif.:	Ability to work as part of a team and with wild animals.
Work:	Volunteers prepare food, feed animals, restrain animals for tube feeds and physical exams, clean pens, wash dishes, do laundry, administer medication, weigh animals and chart all observations. The shifts run from 6–12 hours depending on the season. Training is provided.
Lang.:	English.
Accom.:	No accommodation available.
Cost:	Volunteers must provide accommodation, food and transportation. There is no public transportation to the site. Volunteers can reach the site by bicycle.
Applic.:	After admission volunteers must attend an orientation upon arrival and complete a liability waiver.
Notes:	This physically demanding work requires good health and a current tetanus shot is recommended.

MARINE TURTLES ADRIATIC ARCHE' PROJECT, Italy

A.R.C.H.E'. Research and Educational Activities for Chelonian Conservation
Via Mulinetto, 40/A-I   44100 Ferrara Italy
Tel.:/Fax: ++39 (0532) 767 852 – Mob.: ++39 (349) 393 7924
E-mail: archeturtle@tiscali.it
www.archeturtle.org

Desc.:	The research project focuses on interactions between marine turtles and fishing methods, tagging and recapture, migrations, rescue of injured animals, education program for fishermen and for tourists on marine turtles.
Spp.:	Loggerhead seaturtles (*Caretta caretta*).
Hab.:	Mediterranean coast.
Loc.:	Porto Garibaldi (Italy) Northwestern Adriatic Sea.
Travel:	Train from Bologna to Ostellato, then bus to Porto Garibaldi.
Dur.:	Min. 1 week.
Per.:	June, July, September.
L.Term.:	There is no limit for long-term stays.
Age:	Min. 18.
Qualif.:	No special qualifications, other than enthusiasm, adaptability, love for animals and willingness to work long hours.
Work:	Volunteers will carry on educational activities among tourists on the beach in the morning; in the afternoon when the fishing boat will come back to the harbour, they will start the work on the marine turtles accidentally captured by fishing nets and collecting data. Depending on fishing boats' availability, volunteers and researchers will go on board to experience a fishing day (for 12/14 hours).
Lang.:	English, basic Italian useful.
Accom.:	At a house with cooking and washing facilities in shared rooms.
Cost:	EUR300/week (approx.GB£ 210), with a reduction of 5% for students. Food, accommodation and insurance are included. Travel and personal expenses are not inlcuded.
Applic.:	Via e-mail or by completing the online application form.

MARINE TURTLE & YOUTH ENVIRONMENTAL EDUCATION, Mexico
Grupo Ecologico de La Costa Verde
827 Union Pacific
PMB 078–253, Laredo, Texas 78045–9452 USA
Tel.: ++52 (311) 258 84100
E-mail: grupo-eco@project-tortuga.org
www.project-tortuga.org

Desc.: Grupo Ecologico de la Costa Verde A.C. is a Mexican non-profit Civil Association dedicated to the protection of the natural environment, with special interest in the protection of the marine turtles and in Youth Environmental Education.

Spp.: Olive Ridley (*Lepidochelys olivacea*); leatherback (*Dermochelys coriacea*); eastern Pacific green turtle (*Chelonia agassizi*).

Hab.: Marine, tropical, coastal.

Loc.: Central Pacific coast of Mexico.

Travel: By airplane to Puerto Vallarta, where volunteers are met, or bus from Puerto Vallarta, to San Francisco or San Pancho.

Dur: 1 month minimum, although 5 would be ideal.

Per.: July 1 to November 15.

L.term: Inquire with organisation.

Age: Min. 18.

Qualif.: No special skills are required to work within the marine turtle program, although volunteers should be willing to work 5 to 7 nights a week in occasional heavy rain, and operate a Wolkswagen dune-buggy. Volunteers must be enthusiastic, efficient, willing to work as a part of a team, able to deal with the public and have a sense of humour.

Work: Collect and relocating marine turtle nests between 9am—6pm, 5—7 nights/week; maintain records, release hatchlings and teaching.

Lang.: English (with some Spanish) is needed for Marine Turtle Project. Spanish (with some English) for teaching.

Accom.: Houses for volunteers.

Cost: Volunteers are not required to pay any fee except for their own accommodation and living expenses. In some cases free lodging is available, or rooms rent for US$40/week, or single home US$400/month. Food: approx. US$35-40/week.

Applic.: By e-mail only on www.project-tortuga.org/volunteers.htm

MEDITERRANEAN MONK SEAL RESEARCH PROJECT, Turkey

Levant Nature Conservation Society
Merkez Ishani Kat:2 No:7 P.K. 10 Bozyazi
Mersin 33830
Tel.: +90 (324) 851 31
E-mail: contact@ecocilicia.org
www.ecocilicia.org

Desc.: The primary aims of this project are: a) to determine population size, preferred habitats, and the main threats; b) to increase awareness in the local people, fishermen and authorities;c) to organize educational programs for elementary and high schools;d) to elaborate proposals for mitigating conflicts between seals and local.

Spp.: Mediterranean Monk Seal (*Monachus monachus*) and Neptune's Sea Grass.

Hab.: Mediterranean coastal waters.

Loc.: South of Turkey.

Travel: Airplane to Adana or Antalya then to the project site by bus (approx. 5 hours).

Per.: All year round.

L.term: Available long term with project manager approval.

Age: 18 - 40.

Qualif.: Biologists or Biology students are preferred. Skin diving, computer skills are required.

Work: Volunteers will help recording and sorting out in-cave seal activities. Seal caves will be surveyed and fauna and flora around the seal habitats will be sampled, identified and processed.

Lang.: English or Turkish.

Accom.: Depending on the availability of the project house the volunteers may be accommodated in a house free of charge or otherwise in a low-cost pension.

Cost: EUR200 per week, accomodation and food included. Volunteers shall pay for their travel to project site. Students pay special rate based on their submitted proposal.

Applic.: Enclose a short CV underlining qualifications and skills useful to the project (please indicate gender).

MERGUI ARCHIPELAGO HORNBILLS PROJECT - Thailand and Myanmar

Europe Conservation Switzerland
via Bosconi 9
6983 Magliaso, Switzerland
Tel.: ++41 (91) 606 2383
E-mail: ecoswiss@hotmail.com

Desc.:   This conservation Project focuses on Hornbills, beautiful large birds of the Asian tropical forests of which at least 7 species live in the research area. Other wildlife is observed as well during a 12 days cruise organised monthly in Myanmar. The other two weeks the reserach observes Hornbills in nearby Thailand forests.

Spp.:   Great Hornbill, Wreathed Hornbill, Oriental Pied Hornbill, Brown Hornbill and other.

Hab.:   Coastal tropical rain forest and islands.

Loc.:   Base is in Ao Khoei, Thailand. Cruises to Myanmar.

Travel: Airplane to Bangkok or Phuket, bus to Ranong or location at Ao Khoei (Thailand).

Dur.:   Min 2 weeks; cruises to Myanmar every month, please enquire.

Per.:   November to April.

L.term: Yes. Enquire with Ecoswiss.

Age: Min. 18.

Qualif.:   Volunteers must be prepared to trek in hot and humid tropical forest. Sailing and scuba skills welcome.

Work: Observation treks, nest sites monitoring, bird species and vegetation identification, contacts with locals.

Lang.:   English (working), Italian, German and French are spoken.

Accom.:   In huts and tents above the beach, in cabins on board the research boat.

Cost: EUR600 at base for 2 weeks incl. 3 meals/day. Extra EUR30/day on Cruise and transport + visa EUR50.

Applic.:   Contact ecoswiss@hotmail.com

THE MONKEY SANCTUARY TRUST, England
Looe
Cornwall PL13 1NZ UK
Tel./Fax: ++44 (1503) 262 532
E-mail: info@monkeysanctuary.org
www.monkeysanctuary.org

Desc.: The Monkey Sanctuary is home to a colony of woolly monkeys and rescued capuchins. It was founded in 1964 as a reaction against the pet trade in primates. The Sanctuary is open to the public during the summer and the main emphasis is to encourage an attitude of caring and respect toward primates and the environment. The Sanctuary gardens and meadows contain many native species of plants and animals.

Spp.: Woolly monkeys (*Lagothryx lagothricha*) and capuchins.

Hab.: N/A.

Loc.: Looe, Cornwall, UK.

Dur.: 2–4 weeks.

Per.: Year round.

L.term: Invitation to stay long term if the initial visit proves successful.

Age: Min. 18.

Qualif.: No specific skills required, although applicants should have an interest in the field and practical skills are always welcome.

Work: Maintaining and cleaning the enclosures, preparing food for the animals, providing information to the public.

Lang.: English.

Cost: A voluntary donation for room and board is requested. Volunteers must provide transportation to the Sanctuary.

Applic.: Write for further details (please enclose international postage coupon or stamped SAE for UK residents), then fill out an application form. Owing to the large number of applicants, please apply at least 6 months in advance.

MONTE ADONE WILDLIFE PROTECTION CENTRE, Italy

Via Brento, 9
40037 – Sasso Marconi (Bologna) Italy
Tel./Fax: ++39 (051) 847 600
E-mail: info@centrotutelafauna.org
www.centrotutelafauna.org

Desc.: A voluntary non-profit institution working in the rescue and rehabilitation of wild animals found injured. Emergency service is active 24hrs/day. The Centre also takes care of different exotic animals found abandoned or others that have been confiscated from Government authorities. Guided visits for schools and families also play an important socio-educational role in the Centre's activities.

Spp.: Local wildlife (ungulates, mammals, raptors) and exotic fauna (primates, felines, reptiles, etc.).

Hab.: Temperate mountain woodland.

Loc.: Monte Adone, Sasso Marconi, near Bologna, Italy.

Travel: From Bologna by train to Pianoro or to Sasso Marconi.

Dur.: Min. 20 days, after a 1-week trial period.

Per.: Year round, busiest months during the spring (April to June).

L.term: To be arranged with Centre's Director after initial period.

Age: Min. 20.

Qualif.: A true love for animals, attitude to live and work in community, willingness to work in close contact with animals, goodwill and spirit of adaptation, sense of responsibility.

Work: Work (8–10hrs/day) depends on the season. Feeding, cleaning and caring of animals. Day and night rescuing operations of wounded fauna. Maintenance and building activities. Volunteers will give a little help in the housekeeping.

Lang.: Italian, English is also spoken by centre coordinators.

Accom.: In shared rooms in the Centre.

Cost: A EUR80 (approx. GB£55) payment is required to cover food and insurance for the first trial week. The Centre will offer free full board for the remaining period. Travel not included.

Notes: Anti-tetanus is required and B hepatitis is advised.

MUNDA WANGA WILDLIFE PARK AND SANCTUARY, Zambia

P.O. BOX 350068, Kafue Rd,
Chilanga Zambia
Tel.: ++260 (1) 278 456
Fax: ++260 (1) 278 529
E-mail: environment@zamnet.zm
www.mundawanga.com

Desc.:	Munda Wanga is a wildlife park and botanical garden. In the 1990s, due to the lack of funds and poor management, the park and gardens left to decay. Many animals died in their cages. In 1998 the estate was taken on by a new Munda Wanga Trust. Eight years on and the wildlife park has been rehabilitated, the gardens reshaped and an environmental programme developed. The facility now significantly contributes to conservation efforts in Zambia, both *in-situ* and *ex-situ*.
Spp.:	A variety of African birds and mammals, including wild dogs, lions, antelope and primates. Exotic species including a bengal tiger and black bear.
Hab.:	Wetland, woodland and grassland.
Loc.:	Approx.15km outside of Lusaka, the capital of Zambia.
Travel:	By plane to Lusaka, overland from southern/eastern Africa
Dur.:	3 weeks. Volunteers can stay for longer or shorter periods.
Per.:	Year round.
L.term:	Possible at reduced rate after approval from the project manager.
Age:	Min. 18, no max.
Qualif.:	Preference given to those with relevent experience; qualifications though all applicants welcome if they are prepared to work hard.
Work:	Designing enrichment an educational materials, monitoring animals, fundraising, hand-rearing orphaned animals, cleaning enclosures, construction, etc. Work is 6 days/week, 8 hours/day.
Lang.:	English.
Accom.:	Basic dorm style room, with bathroom and cooking area.
Cost:	US$750 (approx. GB£ 420) includes accommodation.
Applic.:	Request for a form via e-mail or fax.
Notes:	Volunteers' contributions help continual development of the park and staff capacity building.

MYSTERIOUS JAPAN AND ITS WONDROUS WETLANDS, Japan

BTCV
Sedum House
Mallard Way, Potteric Carr, Doncaster, DN4 8DB UK
Tel.: +44 (1302) 388 883
Fax: +44 (1302) 311 531
E-mail: information@btcv.org.uk International@btcv.org.uk
www.btcv.org.uk

Desc.: The project takes place in SE Hokkaido, home to important National Parks and remote wilderness. Volunteers are based at the farm of Genshi Sakakibaru, deep in the heart of the conservation area. The work involves wetland management; alongside Japanese volunteers, volunteers regenerate the area as well as build local and regional interest in volunteering.

Spp.: Japanese Crane, white tailed eagle, grey heron and Japanese snipe.

Hab.: Chokubetsu, Hokkaido, Japan.

Loc.: Kinashibetsu Nature Conservation Area.

Travel: Pick up at Kushiro Airport.

Dur.: 2 weeks.

Per.: June.

Age: Min 18.

Qualif.: No specific skills required.

Work: Wetland management, regeneration and restoration of vegetation, ponds and fences. Improvements of trail systems and visitor infrastructure, as well as encouraging local volunteering.

Lang.: English/Japanese welcome.

Cost: GB£690 (approx. EUR1000) excluding flight.

Applic.: GB£100 Deposit required. See www.btcv.org.

Notes: Conservation Holidays Brochure and further information available on request.

NAUCRATES CONSERVATION PROJECT, Thailand
Naucrates 'Conservation Biology'
Via Corbetta 11
22063 Cantù (Como) Italy
Tel.: ++39 (333) 430 6643 – Fax: ++39 (031) 716 315
E-mail: naucrates12@hotmail.com – naucrates12@tiscalinet.it
www.naucrates.org

Desc.: The Conservation project focuses on sea turtles' nest protection, reef and mangrove forest survey, educational programming for the local community and on conservation awareness activities for visitors.

Spp.: Olive ridley (*Lepidochelys olivacea*), leatherback (*Dermochelys coriacea*), green (*Chelonia mydas*) and hawksbill (*Eretmochelys imbricata*) turtles, reefs and mangroves.

Hab.: Tropical coast.

Loc.: Phra Thong Island, Phang-Nga province, Thailand.

Travel: Airplane to Phuket Island or to Ranong (via Bangkok), then bus or car to Kura Buri pier and boat to Phra Thong Island.

Dur.: Min. 10 days.

Per.: December to April.

L.term: Inquire with the organisation.

Age: Min. 18.

Qualif.: Volunteers must be prepared for long walks in hot and humid conditions on the beach. Research assistant position (unpaid) available based on academics and experience.

Work: Beach patrols (day or night) for turtle nest monitoring. Visits to the local schools for the educational programme. Lectures on biology and conservation are given to tourists. Rescuing turtles caught in fishing nets.

Lang.: English, Italian.

Accom.: In huts on the beach at the Golden Buddha Beach resort.

Cost: EUR 760 (approx. GB£520) in huts for 2 weeks including 3 meals per day. Travel expenses and insurance not included.

Agents: The Ecovolunteer Network (see organisation list).

Applic.: Contact the organisation or the Ecovolunteer Network (www.ecovolunteer.org) for an application form.

NKOMBI RESEARCH AND VOLUNTEER PROGRAMME, South Africa

P.O Box 20784
Protea Park, North West Province, 0305, South Africa
Tel.: ++27 (14) 558 3300
E-mail: nkombivolunteers@telkomsa.net
www.mankwewildlifereserve.com

Desc.:   Researching on a Wildlife Reserve in S.A. Oportunity to learn research techniques on projects such as nocturnal predator surveys, raptor population fluctuations, ecological links between large and small mammals, white rhino monitoring. Some reserve management tasks are also required eg. mammal counts, controlled burning, etc.

Spp.:   Brown hyaena, caracal, serval, white rhino, raptors, small mammals, Large herbivores.

Hab.:   Bushveld, savannah, grassland.

Loc.:   North West Province, South Africa.

Travel: Plane to Johannesburg International Airport, where volunteers are met.

Dur.:   Project runs for 2 or 4 weeks with option to extend further.

Per.:   Monthly, year round.

L.term: Option to extend after first month period with approval.

Age: Min. 17, max.75. Reasonable level of fitness necessary as a lot is spent on foot.

Qualif.:   No skills required as all training is given.

Work: Mainly research although at certain times of the year controlled burning, mammal counts, anti poaching patrols. etc.

Lang.:   English.

Accom.:   In 2 sleeper log cabins with beds, hot showers and flush toilets on site. Sleeping bag required.

Cost: Minimum GB£795 (US$1,400) maximum GB£1495 (US$1,800) including all accomodation, food, transport etc. Flights are excluded.

Applic.:   Standard Green Volunteers Form (see page 255) is acceptable although there is andemnity and health form to sign.

Notes: This is predominantly a research based project and not manual labour, with a lot of time in the field.

NOAH'S ARK, Greece

Supporters' Association for Animal Welfare on Crete Noah's Ark
Neritzer Weg 6, D 23867 Suelfeld Germany
E-mail: rschmid@archenoah-kreta.com
www.archenoah-kreta.com

Desc.: Noah's Ark is the name of the supporters' association for animal welfare on Crete, based in Germany, operating on donations and membership subscriptions only. The project is aimed at rescuing, treating, caring for and re-homing animals, as well as information and education programs for the locals and island-wide castration actions. Furthermore, the association meanwhile supplies 40 partners on the island with regular food donations.

Spp.: Domestic cats and dogs as well as donkeys.

Hab.: Mediterranean.

Loc.: Crete, Greece.

Travel: Plane to Chania airport, Heraklion, or Athens (then night boat to Chania or Heraklion).

Dur.: 2 weeks to 1 year.

Per.: Year round.

L.term: Long-term encouraged, inquire with organisation.

Age: Min.18, max. 60.

Qualif: Volunteers should love animals and be strong enough to handle the sight of animal cruelty, starvation, illness.

Work: Nursing cleaning, feeding, diet control, treating small animals under supervision.

Lang.: English, German, Greek.

Accom.: Local accommodation at reasonable rates.

Cost: Volunteers pay for accommodation. Noah's Ark's partners will assist in obtaining accommodation.

Agents: Contact Ms. Regina Schmid at: rschmid@archenoah-kreta.com.

Applic.: No official form needed, send letter of inquiry.

Notes: High summer is very hot; winter months are wet and muddy.

NORTH SEA CETACEAN MONITORING, UK and Norway

Organisation Cetacea
7 Ermin Close, Baydon, Marlborough
Wiltshire, England SN8 2JQ UK
Tel.: ++44 (0) 845 108
E-mail: secretary@orcaweb.org.uk
www.orcaweb.org.uk

Desc.: Monthly surveys onboard a ferry to record whale and dolphin sightings. Ferry runs between Newcastle, UK and Bergen, Norway. The surveys are the basis of a long-term monitoring project in the northern North Sea.

Spp.: Marine Mammals such as Harbour porpoise, Minke whale, White beaked dolphin, bottlenose dolphin.

Hab.: Coast, Sea.

Loc.: North Sea, UK.

Travel: Train/road to Newcastle if in the UK.

Dur.: Each trip lasts between 3-5 days.

Per.: Year-round.

L.term: Possible.

Age: Min. 18.

Qualif.: Previous field experience preferred but training is given.

Work: Observations of cetaceans onboard a large ferry. .

Lang.: English.

Accom.: Onboard ferry in shared cabin.

Cost: Travel and food. Accomodation costs onboard ferry covered by project.

Applic.: Letter and CV.

THE OCEANIA RESEARCH PROJECT, Australia
The Oceania Project
P.O. Box 646
Byron Bay NSW 2481 Australia
Tel.: ++61 (2) 668 58128 – Fax: ++61 (2) 9225 9176
E-mail: expedition@oceania.org.au
www.oceania.org.au

Desc.: The Oceania Project is a non-profit research and education organisation dedicated to raising awareness of Cetacea and the Ocean Environment through research and education. The Oceania Project is in the twelfth year of a long-term study of the abundance, distribution and behaviour of humpback whales in the Whale Management & Monitoring Area of the Hervey Bay Marine Park, off the northeast coast of Queensland, Australia. The study is being undertaken in conjunction with the Queensland Department of Environment & Heritage. The Hervey Bay research is conducted from a 12-metre power catamaran during 10 weeks of the annual humpback migration from August to October. Paying Eco-volunteers/Interns who join the expedition for a week at a time fund the research platforms. As well as participating in the on-board research programme, expedition participants are provided with in-depth interpretation and education programmes about cetaceans.

Spp.: Humpback whale (*Megaptera novaeangliae*), brydes tropical whale (*Balaenoptera edeni*), minke-piked whale (*Balaenoptera acutorostrata*), common dolphin (*Delphinus delphis*), bottlenose dolphin (*Tursiops truncatus*), Indo-pacific humpback dolphin (*Sousa chinensis*).

Hab.: Tropical coast/ocean bay/ancient sand island.

Loc.: Hervey Bay/Fraser Island, northeast coast of Queensland, Australia.

Travel: Airplane to Brisbane (capital of Queensland). The expedition departure point is Urangan Boat Harbour, Hervey Bay (approx. 400 km north of Brisbane, with access by car or daily bus, train or intrastate airline).

Dur.: 1–10 weeks, Sunday to Friday.

Per.: July to October.

L.term: Volunteers/Interns can join the expedition for a max. of up to 10 weeks.

Age: Min. 14.

Qualif.: No particular skills needed, previous field experience in marine mammal research useful. Common sense, a committed interest in whales and dolphins and willingness to work long hours as part of a small, highly motivated and focused field research team.

177

Work: Assist with humpback observations and with collection and collation of spatial and environmental data. General duties associated with daily operation aboard the vessel.

Lang.: English.

Accom.: Ship-style bunk. The present expedition vessel is a 12-metre catamaran. Information about what to bring, etc., will be provided to applicants.

Cost: Eco-Volunteers/Interns from 14–18 years of age pay AUS$950/week (approx. US$695). Graduate or post graduate students or teaching staff from an eligible educational institution are eligible to join as interns and pay AUS$1050/week (approx. US$842), otherwise AUS$1,350/week (approx. US$988). Cost includes living aboard the expedition vessel for 5 nights/6 days, all meals, participation in field research and on-board interpretation and education programmes. Transportation or accommodation to and from the departure point or personal insurance is not included.

Applic.: Application form is available online. See webiste for application and payment details.

Notes: The research programme is conducted and supervised by the expedition leaders, Trish and Wally Franklin. They are PhD Candidates at the Southern Cross University Whale Research Centre, see: http://www.scu.edu.au/research/whales/aboutus.html. Students or undergraduates may be able to receive credit towards marine science or environmental studies courses.

OKAVANGO DELTA LION MONITORING PROJECT, Botswana

Tau Consultants

Private Bag 83, Maun Botswana

E-mail: tau@dynabyte.bw

2tau@bushmail.net (text only, no attachments or pictures)

www.taucon.com

Desc.: Tau Consultants have been carrying out baseline survey data on the Okavango Delta lions since 1997. Much of the published data to date has come from the Serengeti Lion Population and the Okavango Delta lions are different in their behaviour and physiology. This is the fourth largest remaining lion population in Africa and is one of only 5 large populations left.

Spp.: Lion (*Panthera leo*).

Hab.: Seasonally flooded delta.

Loc.: South-West Okavango Delta south of Moremi Game Reserve.

Travel: Meeting in Maun for flight or drive into camp. Arrival in Maun must be synchronised with camp movements.

Dur.: 1 month to 3 months.

Per.: Year round except December.

L.term: Inquire with the organisation.

Age: Min. 20.

Qualif.: Graduates preferred. The camp is very remote and consists of a small team, volunteers must be responsible, hard working, and dependable. Field-work involves off-road driving.

Work: Radio tracking lions, lion identification, social and behavioural observations, herbivore, vegetation and flood monitoring.   Some maintenance work on camp or vehicles may be required along with computer and administrative work.

Lang.: English.

Accom.: Dome tent, shared bathroom. Need own sleeping bag.

Cost: US$1,500 for 1 month, US$2,500 for 2 months, $1,000 per month if 3 months or longer.

Applic.: Send application to both email addresses to ensure reception.

Notes: Max 2 volunteers at a time. 100% of fees goes directly into project. Volunteers need to arrange insurance and visas.

OPERATION OSPREY, Scotland
RSPB – The Royal Society for the Protection of Birds
The Lodge, Sandy
Bedfordshire SG19 2DL UK
Tel.: ++44 (1767) 680 551
Fax: ++44 (1767) 692 365
www.rspb.org.uk

Desc.: Within its Residential Volunteering Scheme, RSPB (see Organisation list) offers special projects, such as Operation Osprey, an opportunity for bird protection and conservation work. Ospreys are an endangered species in Scotland.

Spp.: Osprey (*Pandion haliaetus*).

Hab.: Scots pine woodland, lochs, moors.

Loc.: Abernethy Forest Reserve, Loch Garten, Scotland.

Travel: Travel details are given to selected applicants.

Dur.: Min. 1 week (Saturday to Saturday); max. 2 weeks.

Per.: Late March to early September.

Age: Min. 18.

Qualif.: Good spoken English and willingness to be part of a team.

Work: Osprey nest site protection and surveillance, information to visiting public.

Lang.: English.

Cost: Accommodation is provided free. Food and travel expenses are not included.

L.term: N/A.

Accom.: In chalets.

Applic.: Information and application form is available on www.rspb.org.uk/volunteering/residential or write to the Volunteer Department at the above address for further details and for an application form. Enclose a self-addressed label with 2 first class stamps (in the UK) or 2 International Postage Coupons.

ORANGUTAN FOUNDATION, Indonesia

7 Kent Terrace, London, NW1 4RP UK
Tel.: ++44 (20) 7724 2912
Fax: ++44 (20) 7706 2613
E-mail: info@orangutan.org.uk
www.orangutan.org.uk

Desc.:	The Orangutan Foundation is a charity that actively conserves the orangutan and its rainforest habitat in Indonesia and Malaysia. The Foundation conducts long-term research on the ecology of orangutans and operates a rehabilitation programme that returns orangutans to a life in the wild. The Foundation operates a volunteer programme in the Tanjung Puting National Park, Kalimantan.
Spp.:	Bornean Orangutan (*Pongo pygmaeus*).
Hab.:	Tropical rainforest.
Loc.:	Tanjung Puting National Park, Kalimantan, Indonesian Borneo.
Travel:	By airplane to Jakarta, train or flights to Semerang. From Semerang flight or boat to Pangkalan Bun.
Dur:	6 weeks.
Per.:	4 teams of 12 people, from April to November.
L.term:	Max 6 weeks.
Age:	Min. 18.
Qualif.:	Previous experience in the field is desirable but not necessary. Good health, physical fitness, team spirit and a willingness to do manual work.
Work:	The main area of the programme is Lamandau Reserve, an orangutan release site managed by the Foundation. Help is needed to build guard posts, mark out borders and assist with reforestation. The project operates in extremely remote conditions. There may be some lines of work around the original release site at Camp Leakey.
Lang.:	English or Indonesian.
Accom.:	Very basic. In huts on the floor or hammocks in the forest.
Cost:	GB£550 (approx. EUR 800) for food and accommodation, volunteers are responsible for their own travel arrangements.
Applic.:	Application form at www.orangutan.org.uk.

ORANGUTAN HEALTH, Indonesia

Dr Ivona Foitova – Principal Investigator
c/o Leuser International Foundation
Jl. Bioteknologi, Kampus USU, Medan 20155 Indonesia
E-mail: orangutanhealth@nusa.net.id
www.orangutan-health.org

Desc.: This unique project is investigating the special behaviours and ecological conditions necessary for the maintenance of health in wild orangutans. As part of a 14-day volunteer team, volunteers perform various research tasks necessary for the project's work. At the same time they have the chance to visit and experience a living, breathing rainforest in one of the most beautiful areas of the world.

Spp.: Orangutan (*Pongo pygmaeus*).

Hab: Tropical rainforest.

Loc.: Bukit Lawang, Sumatra, Indonesia.

Travel: By airplane to Medan via Jakarta, Kuala Lumpur, Singapore or Penang. Volunteers are met at the airport.

Dur.: Min. 14 days.

Per.: Year round.

L.term: Possible, inquire with the organisation.

Age: Min. 18.

Qualif.: A good level of fitness – able to hike 10km during 1 day in difficult terrain, without health problems, allergies or phobias. Volunteers are required to be patient and attentive.

Work: Work will be split between 3–4 day treks in the jungle, and computer/ lab work at base camp. This will be rotated and will depend on people's strength in certain areas.

Lang: English.

Accom.: Accommodation is very basic: a bed, a mosquito net and a basic Asian toilet. No shower, but a supply of water to wash.

Cost: US$1,289 (approx. GB£700) excluding travel.

Applic.: Request an application formvia e-mail.

Notes: There is no physical contact whatsoever with orangutans. A medical certificate of good health is mandatory.

ORANGUTAN TROPICAL PEATLAND PROJECT (OuTrop), Indonesia
Kampus UNPAR, Jl. Yos Sudarso,
Tunjung Nyaho, Palangka Raya,
C. Kalimantan 73112, Indonesia
Tel.: ++62 (536) 36 880
E-mail: info@orangutantrop.com
www.orangutantrop.com

Desc.:   Main research focuses on orangutan density and distribution, forest dynamics and biodiversity studies in the new Sabangau National Park, Indonesia. The project's research in last 10 years has benefitted orangutan and biodiveristy conservation in the area being instrumental in establishment of the Sabangau as a National Park in 2005.

Spp.:   Orangutans, gibbons, langurs, tarsiers, sun bears, birds and forest dynamics and seed dispersal research.

Hab.:   Tropical Rainforest peatlands.

Loc.:   Kalimantan, Indonesia (Island of Borneo).

Travel: Basecamp is 2 hours from Palangka Raya, the provincial capital. Travel to site is by car, boat.

Dur.:   Seven weeks expeditions.

Per.:   June-November.

L.term: If carrying out research for a B.Sc or MSc 10 week min.

Age: 18 - 40. Be fit and able to work in physically and mentally difficulty.

Qualif.:   Restricted to EU nationals, undertaking or have completed a bachelor's degree or relevant experience.

Work: Expected to assist with projects undertaken to gain essential field experience in biological/ecological surveys.

Lang.:   English.

Accom.:   At basecamp shared accommodation in style of traditional Dyak longhouse, mossie net and sleeping bags required.

Cost: GB£1300 including accommodation during expedition dates, transport to and from camp, at camp food, electricity.

Applic.:   Contact project for application forms to be submitted before 15th May.

Notes: Contact us for opportunities for Undergraduate and Masters students to carry out dissertation/thesis research.

PANDRILLUS FOUNDATION, Nigeria
Drill Rehabilitation & Breeding Center
H.E.P.O. Box 826 Calabar   Nigeria
Tel.: ++234 (87) 234 310
E-mail: drill@hyperia.com
(many websites describe the project: type"Pandrillus" in a search engine; see
http://limbewildlife.org for Limbe Wildlife Centre)

Desc.:   The centre (from 1991) recovers captive drill orphans and rehabs them into breeding groups: over 200 drills born to date. The project is closely involved in conservation of Afi Mountain Wildlife Sanctuary where wild drills, gorillas and chimps survive and where drills will be released. The project also maintains 25 non-breeding chimpanzees. Animals are kept in enclosures of natural habitat of up to 9 ha. Pandrillus also runs the Limbe Wildlife Center (Cameroon) where volunteers may apply.

Spp.:   Drill (*Mandrillus leucophaeus*), chimpanzee (*Pan troglodytes*).

Hab.:   Tropical rainforest.

Loc.:   Southeast Nigeria.

Travel: Flight to Lagos then to Calabar.

Dur.:   Min. 1 year.

Per.:   Year round.

L.term: Highly encouraged.

Age: Min. 25.

Qualif.:   Mature persons with 1) animal, veterinary or medical experience/skills or practical skills (carpentry, electrical, etc.); 2) appropriate educational background; 3) developing country experience; 4) sincere interest in conservation; 5) good human relations and teamwork ability ; 6) administrative or management experience.

Work: Staff management and training, animal management and record-keeping, administration, public relations, education, construction and maintenance. Versatility is a must.

Lang.:   English.

Accom.:   House at urban site, open-walled cabins at field site.

Cost: Room and board provided. Travel to project not provided.

Applic.:   Send CV with references, a photograph and a letter of intentions. Interview with an appointed person will follow.

PEACE RIVER REFUGE & RANCH, Florida USA

P.O. Box 1127
2545 Stoner Lane
Zolfo Springs, Florida 33890 USA
Tel.:++1 (863)-735-0804 – Fax: ++1 (863)-735-0805
E-mail: volunteer@peaceriverrefuge.org
www.peaceriverrefuge.org

Desc.: The sanctuary is dedicated to the lifetime care of abused, neglected, confiscated or unwanted exotic animals to prevent them from being destroyed. Animals rescued are not sold or transfered and they are not used for breeding. The highly trained staff ensures that their medical, nutritional, and emotional needs are well met. With help from supporters, the Sanctuary is able to provide permanent habitats for these animals on the 90-acre compound.

Spp.: Bengal tiger, leopard, cougar, bear, lynx, capuchin and spider monkey, cotton-top tamarin, grey wolf, jungle cat, african serval, bison, lemur.

Loc.: Florida, USA.

Travel: Plane to Tampa or Orlando, then car to project.

Dur.: Minimum 2 weeks, maximum 6 months.

Per.: Year round.

L.term: Only with project leaders approval after the regular volunteer period.

Age: Min. 21.

Qualif.: No particular skills needed, must have negative Tuberculosis test certification, and proof of health insurance. Students in animal-related educational track. Must be dedicated to working with animals.

Work: Wide range of duties: Sorting and cutting fruit for fruit bats and monkeys, feeding all of the animals and providing enrichment, cleaning enclosures, building habitats, maintaining the grounds and other chores.

Lang.: English.

Accom.: Shared living quarters with bunk beds, which are basic but comfortable with water, electricity and air conditioning. Meals are home-cooked and most of the cooking and cleanup duties are rotated among participants.

Cost: US$300 per week, including room and board. A fee of US$100 is charged (only upon request) for pick up and drop off at Tampa or Orlando Airports.

Applic.: Application and procedural forms will be given out upon request.

Notes: Independent room and board can be arranged, but a car is necessary.

PIONEER MADAGASCAR, Madagascar

Azafady UK
Studio 7, 1a Beethoven Street, London W10 4LG UK
Tel.: ++44 (20) 8960 6629
Fax: ++44 (20) 8962 0126
E-mail: mark@azafady.org – info@azafady.org
www.madagascar.co.uk

Desc: Pioneer Madagascar is run by the UK charity and Malagasy NGO Azafady, and is an opportunity for volunteers to gain on-the-ground experience in grass-roots sustainable development work. The programme focuses on integrated conservation and development, working closely with village communities.

Spp.: Primates, reptiles and birds, eg. brown collared lemur (*Eulemur fulvus collaris*), various botanical spp.

Hab.: Littoral forest (tropical coastal forest), coastal zone.

Loc.: Southeast Madagascar.

Travel: Airplane to Antananarivo, then to Fort Dauphin.

Dur.: Project placements are 10 weeks.

Per.: Year round; schemes start in January, April, July and October.

L.term: Long-term stay as a coordinator or specialist can be arranged.

Age: Min. 18, no max.

Qualif.: No special skills needed; enthusiasm and sensitivity are a must; practical and research experience welcome.

Work: Pioneers play an active part in ongoing health and sanitation, conservation and sustainable livelihoods projects, which may include surveying lemurs or collecting rare plant seeds in the littoral forest or building facilities in villages.

Lang.: English or French; intensive course in Malagasy is given.

Accom.: Basic camping facilities are provided throughout the scheme, although Pioneers do need to bring their own tent.

Cost: Successful applicants must cover live costs (flight, insurance, medical expenses, visa and equipment) and raise a minimum donation of GB £2,000 (less for non-UK applicants). All donations go to support the projects in Madagascar.

Applic.: Download an application form from the website.

PROJECT KIAL, Australia

AACE
PO Box 47 Marlborough
Queensland 4705
Australia
Tel.: ++61 (407) 62 377
E-mail: info@aace.org.au
www.aace.org.au

Desc.:	This is a community based conservation recovery program, focused on the endangered bridled bailtail wallaby.
Spp.:	Bridled nailtail wallaby (*Onychogalea fraenata*).
Hab.:	Semi-arid bushland.
Loc.:	Marlborough, Queensland, Australia.
Travel:	By plane or train: travel to Rockhampton. By Bus: travel to Marlborough.
Dur.:	Minimum stay 2 weeks.
Per.:	Year round.
L.term:	Only on approval of project coordinator.
Age:	Min 18. Younger only with consultation between parent and coordinator.
Qualif.:	No particular skills needed.
Work:	Being responsible for maintaining a high level of day to day animal husbandry and observation of animals behaviour.
Lang.:	English.
Accom.:	Bunk beds in rural shed, sleeping bag recomended for winter months.
Cost:	AU$10/day includes accomodation, food and pick up from Rockhampton/Marlborough.
Applic.:	Application form is required to be completed on confirmation of stay.

PROJECT "MEER LA GOMERA", Spain
M.E.E.R. e. V.
Bundesallee 123
12161 Berlin Germany
Tel./Fax: ++49 (30) 8507 8755
E-mail: praktika@m-e-e-r.de
www.m-e-e-r.de

Desc.: Observation of cetaceans. Scientific study aboard a small whale-watching vessel. Documentation of the behaviour of cetaceans and the kind of interaction between the vessel and the whales.

Spp.: Dolphins, whales, turtles, sharks.

Hab.: Coastal and offshore subtropical waters of the Atlantic Ocean.

Loc.: Southwest of La Gomera (Canary Islands, Spain).

Travel: Airplane to Tenerife, then ferry to La Gomera.

Dur.: 2 weeks.

Per.: Spring and autumn.

L.term: Not possible.

Age: Min. 18.

Qualif.: No particular skills needed. Previous experience in marine mammal research, photography or ethology are welcome.

Work: Volunteers participate in the whale-watching trips, gather data and enter it in a database. A full training programme, written working materials, scientific supervision and a certificate of attendance are provided.

Lang.: English, German.

Accom.: Tourist apartments (2–4 persons).

Cost: EUR875 (approx. GB£ 600). The cost includes accommodation, a donation to MEER e.V., all whale-watching trips and all other expenses related to the project. Travel costs are not included.

Applic.: Apply directly through praktika@m-e-e-r.de.

Notes: During the 14 days stay there are 7 whale-watching trips (4- hours trips and one 8-hour day trip). A detailed brochure on the courses can be downloaded at www.m-e-e-r.de.

PROJECTO JUBARTE DO CABO VERDE

Swiss Whale Society
Via Nolgio 3, CH–6900 Massagno Switzerland
Tel.: ++41 (91) 966 09 53
Fax: ++41 (91) 966 09 53
E-mail: beatricej@bluewin.ch
www.whales.ch

Desc.: The project's objective is to study the distribution and behaviour of Humpback whales around the Cabo Verde islands, and to identify the threats faced by the whales during their stay in the waters of the archipelago (fisheries, traffic, pollution, etc.).

Spp.: Humpback whale (*Megaptera novaeangliae*).

Hab.: Coastal waters and open ocean.

Loc.: Cabo Verde Islands, Atlantic Ocean.

Travel: Flight to island of Sal (international airport) and meet the ship or continue with domestic flight to another island where the ship may be located. Meeting point to be confirmed in advance.

Dur.: Min. 2 weeks.

Per.: March to May.

L.term: Max. length of stay is 2 months.

Age: Min.18.

Qualif.: No particular skills needed; photography welcome; relatively good physical condition to be able to live and work on a boat.

Work: Help in observation work; recording data on behaviour under supervision of scientists; photography.

Lang.: English, German, Italian (Portuguese is also spoken).

Accom.: On board a research ship.

Cost: About EUR1,400 (approx. GB£ 950) for 2 weeks on board the ship. Flight from Europe costs about EUR 700.

Agents: Travelchannel (Mr. Werner Bürer), Kohlrainstrasse 10, 8700 Küsnacht, Switzerland. Tel: ++41 (0)44 928 2020. Fax: ++41 (0)44 928 2031. E-mail: info@travelchannel.ch.

Applic.: Contact Beatrice Jann of the Swiss Whale Society or the agent.

PROYECTO CAMPANARIO, Costa Rica

Campanario Biological Reserve
Apdo. 263-1260 Escazu Costa Rica
Tel.: ++506 258 5778
Fax: ++506 256 0374
E-mail: volunteers@campanario.org info@campanario.org
www.campanario.org

Desc.: Founded in 1990, Proyecto Campanario maintains a tropical rainforest biological reserve in southwest Costa Rica. Through tropical ecology courses and eco-tourism, funds are generated to keep the reserve in its natural state. In addition, the programme offers opportunities for eco-tourists, student groups (of all ages) and researchers to learn more about the biodiversity and ecology of the Osa Peninsula to then promote the cause of rainforest protection in their own communities.

Spp.: Rainforest and tropical coastal flora and fauna.

Hab.: Tropical rainforest; mangrove forest, coastal zone.

Loc.: Osa Peninsula, southwest Costa Rica (near Corcovado National Park).

Travel: Flight to San Jose, bus to Palmar, then boat to Campanario.

Dur.: Min. 3 months.

Per.: Year round.

L.term: Possible with project leader's approval.

Qualif.: No particular skills are needed, only enthusiasm and a positive attitude. Every effort is made to utilize skills of volunteers. They should be able to swim, be able to work without supervision and be in good physical and emotional health.

Work: Variable; includes manual labour restoring trails, taking species inventories, building observation points, sometimes under hot or wet conditions.

Lang.: English, Spanish helpful but not essential.

Accom.: In a rustic field station (no hot water) or in a tent cabin close to the beach. Shared room or tent with at least 1 other volunteer.

Cost: Volunteers give a non-refundable US$25/day contribution for food, prior to arrival.

Applic.: Request application form via e-mail or fax.

Notes: A medical, accident and evacuation insurance is compulsory.

RAINSONG WILDLIFE SANCTUARY, Costa Rica

Apdo. 182-5361
Cobano de Puntarenas
Southern Nicoya Peninsula 5361 Costa Rica
Tel.: ++11 (506) 844 472
E-mail: rainsongwildlifesanctuary@gmail.com
www.rainsongsanctuary.com

Desc.: Wildlife rescue center and community wildlife refuge on the edge of Reserva Cabo Blanco, Cabuya, Costa Rica. Conservation education; reforestation (rare tropical hardwoods, native fruits); reintroduction of endangered animals and birds; biodynamic gardening/farming/landscaping; butterfly gardens. Native medicinals and edibles.

Spp.: Rainsong accepts all native species of animals and birds in the rescue center.

Hab.: Primary jungle, secondary jungle, tropical dry jungle.

Loc.: Southern tip of Nicoya Peninsula, Costa Rica.

Travel: San Jose; Puntarenas; ferry to Paquera; Montezuma; Cabuya. Direct shuttle available from San José Airport all the way to Rainsong.

Dur.: Minimum stay is one week no maximum.

Per.: Year round.

L.term: Long term desired.

Age: Min. 18, no max. Children with parents are welcome. Arrange in advance.

Qualif.: No skills required. Must be able to work in harmony within a group of people from diverse cultures.

Work: Animal and bird care in the sanctuary; reforestation; assist in Conservation Education events; garden tasks.

Lang.: No language requirements. Everyone helps with Spanish.

Accom.: Lodging options: sharing house, loft rooms, homestay, camphuts, local hotel(with big discount), or tent (during dry season).

Cost: US$5 day per person for lodging. Volunteers prepare their own meals. Fruits and produce gathered are gathered.

Applic.: E-mail to be sent one month before intended stay, with foreseen dates of stay.

Notes: Travel info : www.rainsongsanctuary.com

RE-AFORESTATION PROJECT, Ghana
Volunteer in Africa
P. O. Box AN 6552, Accra-North, Accra, Ghana
Tel.: ++233 (244) 761 050
E-mail: contact4@volunteeringinafrica.org
http://www.volunteeringinafrica.org/programs.htm

Desc.:	The purpose of the project is to plant trees on 75 acres of land, to restore a tropical rainforest destroyed by excessive lumbering for timber, firewood and charcoal production. An additional objective of the project is to protect the watershed and to restore the habitat for wildlife and birds through nursing and planting of trees.
Spp.:	Leucaena, acacia and mahogany trees.
Hab.:	Tropical rainforest, villages and farms.
Loc.:	Eastern region of Ghana, West Africa.
Travel:	Plane to Accra, bus to Suhum or AKim-Oda or Kade.
Dur.:	1 to 4 weeks.
Per.:	Year round.
L.term:	Volunteers can join for up to 12 weeks, with project leader's approval, after the regular volunteer period.
Age:	Min. 18, 16 with parents' permission, max. 60 or older if in good physical condition.
Qualif.:	No particular skills needed.
Work:	Volunteers work 4 days a week, 4 hours per day.
Lang.:	English.
Accom.:	In a house with water and electricity.
Cost:	US$700/month. Room and board are included. Volunteers walk a half kilometre to the project site.
Applic.:	Online form to be completed. There are no deadlines or membership requirements.
Notes:	There are many small villages near the project area where volunteers can visit on their free time for cultural exchange.

REEF CHECK GLOBAL CORAL REEF MONITORING

P;O. Box1057
17575 Pacific Coast Highway
Pacific Palisades, California 90272–1057 USA
Tel.: ++1 (310) 230 2371 – Fax: ++1 (310) 230 2376
E-mail: rcinfo@reefcheck.org
www.ReefCheck.org

Desc.: Reef Check is an international programme working with communities, governments and businesses to scientifically monitor, restore and maintain coral reef health. Reef Check objectives are to: educate the public about the coral reef crisis; to create a global network of volunteer teams trained in Reef Check's scientific methods who regularly monitor and report on reef health; to facilitate collaboration that produces ecologically sound and economically sustainable solutions; and to stimulate local community action to protect remaining pristine reefs and rehabilitate damaged reefs worldwide.

Spp.: Coral reef organisms, include fish, invertebrates and coral.

Hab.: Tropical and subtropical coral reefs.

Loc.: Volunteers are needed in all coral reef countries.

Travel: Travel arrangements are the responsibility of the participant.

Dur.: Min.1 week.

Per.: Year round.

L.term: To be arranged with Headquarters.

Age: Min. 18

Qualif.: Participants must be confident swimmers and comfortable with snorkeling for long periods of time. SCUBA may be used at some locations. Non-divers help organizing Reef Check activities, sponsorship, training sessions, etc.

Work: Volunteers will be trained in RC methods and carry out coral reef surveys in water no deeper than 10m.

Lang.: Language used in country of choice.

Accom.: Accommodations vary with location.

Cost: Cost vary with location.

Applic.: See website or contact e-mail address above for information.

RE-HYDRATION OF THE EARTH, Kenya

Westerveld Conservation Trust

Flevolaan 34, 1399 HG Muiderberg The Netherlands

Tel.: ++31 (294) 261 457

Fax: ++31 (294) 262 080

E-mail: development@planet.nl

www.westerveld.nu

Desc.: Re-hydration and water conservation project. Recreation of water catchments and rehabilitation of sunken water table.

Spp.: Various East African Savannah species.

Hab.: Semi-arid area in sub-saharan Africa; bush country.

Loc.: Bufferzones of national parks, among others Tsavo and Amboseli National Park, Kenya and Manyara N.P., Tanzania.

Travel: By air to Nairobi, Kenya or other airport near project location. Meeting point will be discussed before travel.

Dur.: Min. 2 weeks.

Per.: Year round.

L.term: Possible. Students and initiatives from engineers, biologists, etc. welcome. Volunteers must cover their stay.

Age: Min. 18.

Qualif.: Good health and physical condition. Willing to work in the field for long hours with hot temperatures.

Work: Assist staff of the local partner NGO's and Self Help Groups with construction of water catchments and agroforestry and biofuel projects.

Lang.: English.

Accom.: Simple camps or lodges nearby project location.

Cost: Volunteers pay for their own accomodation and meals. Estimated cost EUR 800 (approx. GB£550) for 2 weeks and EUR 315 (approx. GB£210) for every extra week. Transport to and from project and during fieldwork are included. Entry and camping fees for the National Parks included if the project is located within the national park boundaries. WCT membership, EUR 15/person, is required.

Applic: Westerveld Conservation Trust for information and booking.

Notes: Dates must be arranged in advance. Individual insurance required. Projects can be visited for one day only by safari parties. Arrangements should be made well in advance through WCT.

RESERVA PACUARE, Costa Rica

Avenida 10 (entre calle 27 y29) N.2550
San José, Costa Rica
Tel.: ++ (506) 224 85 68
E-mail: *fdezlaw@racsa.co.cr* – *c.fernandez@turtleprotection.org*
www.turtleprotection.org

Desc.: Reserva Pacuare is a 800ha tropical rainforest area in Costa Rica owned by the NGO Endangered Wildlife Trust where conservation, education and research projects are carried out.

Spp.: Leatherback, green and hawksbill sea turtles, howler, whitefaced and spider monkeys, 211spp of birds, 17spp of amphibians, 70spp of butterflies, occasionally peccary, anteater, paca, jaguarundy. Crocodiles and caiman are often seen in the canals, iguanas and basiliscs near the cabins.

Hab.: Lowland rainforest, coastal and freshwater lagoons and canals

Loc.: Province of Limón, on the Caribbean Coast, South of the mouth of the Pacuare River, Costa Rica.

Travel: Airplane to San José, bus to Matina, taxi to the canal dock, where boat transportation will be provided to the Reserve.

Dur.: Min. 1 week.

Per.: March to end September.

L. term: There is no limit of time for long-term stays.

Age: Min. 18.

Qualif.: No qualifications needed except for research assistants, just good physical condition to be able to walk the soft sandy beach.

Work: Assistance on all conservation and research projects carried out at the reserve. Walking the beach at night to monitor the turtles and nests, and during the day for nest excavations.

Lang.: Spanish and English are spoken.

Accom.: Cabins with shared bathrooms and showers.

Cost: US$140/week (research assistants do not pay) includes boat transportation, room and board.

Applic.: Via e-mail, preferred dates must be indicated.

Notes: Positions for long term Research Assistants in Costa Rica and Panama are available. Independent research must be carried out.

RHINO RESCUE PROJECT, Swaziland

The Ecovolunteer Network
Meyersweg 29, 7553 AX Hengelo The Netherlands
Tel.: ++31 (74) 250 8250
Fax: ++31 (74) 250 6572
E-mail: info@ecovolunteer.org
www.ecovolunteer.org

Desc.: Hands-on participation in various activities such as the daily monitoring of endangered species, a regular check of the fence enclosing the Reserve, maintenance work and assist with anti-poaching activities.

Spp.: White rhinoceros (*Ceratotherium simum*), black rhinoceros (*Diceros bicornis*); many other species such as elephants, buffaloes, antelopes, crocodiles, hyppopotamus, zebra, giraffes, monkeys, leopards, etc, can be observed.

Hab.: African savannah.

Loc.: Swaziland, Africa.

Travel: Airplane to Mbabane; a visa and a passport valid for at least 6 months after leaving Swaziland are necessary.

Dur.: Min. 2, max. 5 weeks.

Per.: Year round.

L.term: Max. 5 weeks.

Age: Min. 18.

Qualif.: Volunteers must be able to walk long distances and tolerate heat. Some knowledge of wildlife and birds is helpful.

Work: Participation in daily monitoring of endangered species, nightly detecting of poaching activities from watchtowers, animal surveys, maintenance work. Most working days start before sunrise. Cooking and cleaning tasks are rotated.

Lang.: English.

Cost: 2 weeks US$1200; 3rd week US$260; 4th week US$160, 5th week free. Flights, visa, local taxes and insurance not included.

Accom.: Simple huts or tents close to the working area. Overnight camping is very primitive with cold-water shower and pit latrine.

Applic.: The Ecovolunteer Network (see Organisation list).

Notes: Volunteers can visit nearby parks. Malaria treatment required.

RIVER OTTER PROJECT, Brazil

The Ecovolunteer Network
Meyersweg 29   7553 AX Hengelo The Netherlands
Tel.: ++31 (74) 250 8250 – Fax: ++31 (74) 250 6572
E-mail: info@ecovolunteer.org
www.ecovolunteer.org

Desc.: Hands-on participation in biological field research on South American otters on an attractive island in southern Brazil. Most of the work consists in fieldwork, but also some laboratory analysis is involved.

Spp.: American river otter (*Lutra longicaudis*).

Hab.: Streams and lakes, estuaries, coastal lagoons, mangroves.

Loc.: Piri Lake, Island of Santa Catarina, Atlantic Ocean, about 1,000 km south of Rio, Brazil.

Travel: Flight to Florianopolis, Santa Catarina State.

Dur.: Min. 1 week.

Per.: Year round.

L.term: Long-term encouraged; price decreases for longer stays.

Age: Min. 18.

Qualif.: Good health and physical condition. Willing to work in the field for long periods under varying weather conditions. Able to walk for long periods and spend evenings in the forest at wildlife observation posts.

Work: Activities vary and include analysis of the otter's frequency at the shelters, monitoring of nests, ethological studies and food habits. Most of volunteers' work is in the field, but also some laboratory analysis is involved. Work involves treks through the Atlantic forest, dunes, use of canoes and kayaks and nocturnal observations. Approx. 10 hours/day.

Lang.: English, Portuguese, Spanish.

Accom.: Research bases have toilets and hot water; 2 meals per day.

Cost: US$53/night for the first and second week; US$48/night for the third week; US$43/night for the fourth week; US$37/night for every extra week.

Applic.: The Ecovolunteer Network (see Organisation list).

THE SANWILD WILDLIFE TRUST, South Africa

PO Box 418
Letsitele, 0885 South Africa
Tel.:: ++27 (15) 318 7900 – Fax: ++27 (15) 318 7901
Mob.: ++27 (83) 310 3881
E-mail: sanwild@pixie.co.za
www.sanwild.org – www.afritrust.com

Desc.:   SanWild is an NGO devoted to the rehabilitation of animals and release into it's own reserve. Often animals have been rescued from malpractices like the canned hunting industry.

Spp.:   African wild dog, lion, white rhino, cheetah, impala, kudu, blue wildebeest, Burchell's zebra, eland, brown hyena, waterbuck, red hartebeest, giraffe, common reedbuck, mountain reedbuck, common duiker, steenbok, nyala, bushbuck, klipspringer, baboons, vervet monkey, warthog, bush pig, pangolin, aardvark, caracal, serval, genet, mongoose, civet, aardwolf, and various birds of prey.

Hab.:   Mixed broadleaf woodland/thornveld type bush, riverine forest and open grasslands, alternating flat plains, hills and ridges.

Loc.:   16 km south of Gravelotte, between Tzaneen and Phalaborwa.

Travel: Flight to Johannesburg, then flight to Phalaborwa or by bus to Tzaneen. Transportation from Airport or Bus-station provided.

Dur.:   Min. 1 week.

Per.:   Year round.

L.term: There is no limit of time for long-term stays.

Age: Min. 20.

Qualif.:   Good physical condition.

Work: Feeding the animals, cleaning enclosures, maintenance, resources management.

Lang.:   English.

Accom.:   Shared dome-tents in a bush-camp with all daily living facilities.

Cost: US$550/week. Occasionally there are special offers on the website. Includes accommodation, meals and soft-drinks, 3 lectures /week, e-mail access, 2 trips to Tzaneen or Phalaborwa, daily game drive or bush-walks, airport pick-up.

Applic.:   Via e-mail volunteers@sanwild.org.

Notes: Health insurance and anti-malarial tablets mandatory.

SANTA LUCIA, Ecuador

Cooperativa Santa Lucia
Apartado Postal 17-07-9414, Quito Ecuador
Tel.: ++593 (2) 215 7
E-mail: info@santaluciaecuador.com
www.santaluciaecuador.com

Desc.:	Conservation and sustainability project in the heart of Ecuadorian cloud forest reserve. Cooperativa Santa Lucia is a community-owned and community-run organisation that seeks to conserve the forest while earning a sustainable living for its members.
Spp.:	Birds including antpittas and white-faced nunbird. Orchids.
Hab.:	Cloud forest.
Loc.:	Northwest Ecuador.
Travel:	Plane or overland to Quito, two hour bus/car journey to meeting place, truck and one/two hour hike to lodge.
Dur.:	Minimum commitment of two weeks.
Per.:	Year round.
L.term:	Volunteers welcome up to 3 mths or longer if specialists.
Age:	Min 16. Children with parents, teenagers alone with parental permission
Qualif.:	No particular skills needed but most of the work requires reasonable level of health/fitness.
Work:	Mix of activities: i.e. treeplanting, orchid monitoring project, organic gardening, agroforestry, trail maintenance.
Lang.:	English; some Spanish useful but not essential.
Accom.:	Shared rooms in ecolodge in forest, all bedding supplied. The option to stay with local host family weekends.
Cost:	US$105 per week incl. all food and accommodation. Transport not included.
Applic.:	No application form. Volunteers can apply directly via email or use the Green Volunteers Standard Application Form (see page 255).

SANTA MARTHA RESCUE CENTERS, Ecuador

Santa Martha, Tambillo, Pichincha Ecuador

Tel.: ++ 593 (9) 709 8542

E-mail: santamartha@mail.com

www.santamartharescue.org

Desc.:   Santa Martha Rescue Center is an animal sanctuary in the Andes, which rescues wild animals victims of animal-trafficking or mistreatment from unhealthy and illegal situations. Santa Martha Flor de la Amazonía is a new animal rehabilitation and release center in the Amazon jungle of Ecuador. It works in partnership with an indigenous Indian community and, amazingly, manages over 1,000 private hectares of primary Amazon forest within which, if possible, rescued animals are released.

Spp.:   Over 100 animals staying within the centers at any given time .

Hab.:   Andean farmland or Amazon rainforest.

Loc.:   Tambillo, one hour south of Quito. The Amazon, one hour from Puyo.

Travel: Airplane to Quito, then bus to Tambillo or Puyo.

Dur.:   Min. 2 weeks.

Per.:   Year round.

L.term: There is no limit of time for long-term stays.

Age: Min. 18.

Qualif.:   No special qualifications required for volunteers other than being enthusiastic, hardworking, and have a genuine love for animals and a desire and passion to see them back in their natural environments.

Work: Volunteers are responsibler for the well-being and daily upkeep of all the animals in the centers, for the feeding of the animals and the cleaning of the enclosures daily while also trying to improve their living conditions.

Lang.:   English, with any comprehension Spanish a bonus.

Accom.:   Comfortable detached houses with all of the desired facilities: hot showers, TV, stereo, DVD player, and fully equipped kitchen. Each house hosts 6 volunteers, enjoying a great communal living experience.

Cost: US$85/week. Food is not included and the volunteers contribute US$10-15/week each to shop at the local market and cook together as a flat.

Applic.:   Via e-mail specifying: age, nationality, interests, experience, qualifications, goals, etc. and the dates.

SCOTTISH WHALE & DOLPHIN PROJECT, Scotland UK
The Hebridean Whale and Dolphin Trust, HWDT
28 Main Street, Tobermory
Isle of Mull, Argyll PA75 6NU Scotland UK
Tel. ++44 (1688) 302 620
E-mail: volunteercoordinator@hwdt.org – admin@hwdt.org
www.hwdt.org

Desc.:	The Trust conducts land and boat based educational and research projects on whales, dolphins and porpoises inhabiting the waters of western Scotland.
Spp.:	Whales, dolphins, porpoises, seals, otters, basking sharks.
Hab.:	Temperate sea and coast.
Loc.:	Western Scotland.
Travel:	Train or bus to Oban; ferry from Oban to Isle of Mull.
Dur.:	From 10 days to 1 year.
Per.:	Year round.
L.term:	Long-term positions possible for outstanding volunteers.
Age:	Min. 18.
Qualif.:	Tailored to projects: e.g. education experience for education projects; administration/marketing/fund-raising skills for discovery centre projects; student/graduate for research projects. Volunteers must be enthusiastic, efficient, friendly, willing to work as part of a team and able to converse confidently with the public.
Work:	Boat based projects involve visual and acoustic monitoring of marine mammals. Other projects involve research and education of marine mammals coupled with working in the discovery centre.
Lang.:	English.
Accom.:	Accommodation is on the boat for 10 day projects. Volunteer arranges own accommodation for longer projects.
Cost.:	No cost for office based projects in the discovery centre. However volunteers are responsible for their own living costs approx. GB£75-100/week (EUR110-150). Refer to the website for costs of boat based projects.
Applic.:	Apply through the website using the online application form, or send a CV and covering letter by post or e-mail.

SCOTTISH WILDLIFE RESCUE, Scotland UK

Hessilhead Wildlife Rescue Trust
Hessilhead, Gateside, Beith Ayrshire KA15 1HT Scotland UK
Tel.: ++44 (1505) 502 415
E-mail: info@hessilhead.org.uk
www.hessilhead.org.uk

Desc.: Rescue, care, rehabilitate and release all native species of wild birds and mammals. Hand rearing, cleaning and feeding animals; maintenance and construction work and monitoring the casualties after release. Some groups of birds will be ringed, and hopefully some species will be radio-tracked.

Spp.: All Scottish wild birds and mammals.

Hab.: Urban, woodland, farmland, coast, moorland.

Loc.: West central Scotland.

Travel: The Centre is within easy travelling distance from Glasgow.

Dur.: Min. 2–3 weeks.

Per.: March to October.

L.term: Suitable volunteers may be able to stay for 6 months or more.

Age: Min. 18.

Qualif.: Ability to work as part of a team. Training will be given. Experience of radio tracking could be useful. Veterinary experience useful.

Work: Volunteers may help with all aspects of the Trust's work. This includes rescue, treatment, feeding, cleaning, preparing of birds and animals for release and post-release monitoring. Educational work with the public may be possible.

Lang.: English.

Accom.: Log cabins.

Cost: GB£10 (approx. EUR 15) per week for cabins. Food must be provided by the volunteer. Volunteers must arrange their own transport, though can be collected from Glasgow.

Applic.: Apply directly to HWRT with relevant details and a contact number or address. More information will be supplied.

SEA TURTLE CONSERVATION PROGRAM, Cost Rica

Asociación ANAI

Apdo. 170–2070

Sabanilla de Montes de Oca, San José   Costa Rica

Tel.: ++ (506) 224 3570/224 6090 – Fax: ++ (506) 253 7524

E-mail: volunteers@racsa.co.cr

www.anaicr.org

Desc.: Asociación ANAI has over 20 years of experience working in the Caribbean coastline of Costa Rica, mainly in the region of Talamanca; one of the biologically richest areas of the planet with over 2% of the entire world's biodiversity. The Sea Turtle project was started in 1986 in Gandoca Beach and the success of that project has led to its expansion in year 2000 to cover Playa Negra. Before an unknown beach for sea turtles nesting, now the most important beach for the Hawksbill sea turtle, which is critically endangered worldwide.

Spp.: Seaturtles: Leatherback (*Dermochelys coriacea*), Hawksbill (*Eretmochelys imbricata*), Loggerhead (*Caretta caretta*) and Green (*Chelonia mydas*).

Hab.: Caribbean, tropical coast.

Loc.: Gandoca, Puerto Vargas and Playa Negra Beaches, region of Talamanca, Caribbean coastline of Costa Rica.

Travel: Airplane to San Jose, then bus to Talamanca.

Dur.: Min. 1 week, max. 6 months.

Per.: Gandoca, Playa Negra: March to July; Puerto Vargas: March to October.

L.Term.: Generic volunteers can stay for the entire nesting season. Professional volunteers typically come for 8–12 months.

Age: Min. 18.

Qualif.: ANAI has 2 kinds of volunteers: generic and professional. For generic volunteers no specific skills are required, but a strong motivation is a must. Ability to walk long hours at night and to withstand hot tropical temperatures. Professional volunteers have skills in fields such as economy, business administration, accounting, agriculture, and forest management and in developing new skills and experiences.

Work: Generic volunteers help patrol the beach to protect the turtles, assist with the scientific monitoring of the species, guard nests and work with the hatchlings on their journey to the ocean. Professional volunteers will put their skills at the disposal of the organisation while helping in the tasks of generic volunteers.

Lang.: English, Spanish useful but not necessary.

Accom.: In Gandoca with local families; in Playa Negra and Puerto Vargas in the project accomodations.

Cost: There is a registration fee of US$35. Full room and board at Gandoca for volunteers range from US$7/day with own tent in camping area (food can be bought in the community) to US$18/day in private cabins or local family. Playa Negra and Puerto Vargas volunteers pay US$15/day. Professional volunteers stay with staff at the ANAI facilities for US$10/day. Optional services include US$10/night lodging in ANAI office in San José upon arrival and US$30/35 airport pick-up.

Agents: Contact Asociación ANAI directly.

Applic.: Use on-line application form.

Notes: Gandoca Beach is in the Gandoca-Manzanillo Wildlife Refuge, a protected area that also includes mangrove, coral reefs and tropical rainforest. Playa Negra and Puerto Vargas are within the Cahuita National Park. Volunteers at both projects sites will be able to explore the amazing marine and land wildlife of the region during their stay.

SEA TURTLE CONSERVATION PROJECTS, Costa Rica
PRETOMA - Sea Turtle Restoration Program of Costa Rica
Apdo. 1203-1100 Tibás
San José Costa Rica
Tel.: ++ (506) 241-5227 – Fax: ++ (506) 236-6017
E-mail: info@tortugamarina.org – tortugas@tortugamarina.org
www.tortugamarina.org

Desc.:	Each year Olive ridley sea turtles nest on the beaches of Punta Banco, Costa de Oro and San Miguel, Costa Rica. Participants study nesting sea turtles and protect their nests in hatcheries.
Spp.:	Olive ridley sea turtle (*Lepidochelys olivacea*).
Hab.:	Topical and subtropical coast.
Loc.:	Several small beach communities on Pacific coast of Costa Rica.
Travel:	Flight to San José, then bus to site.
Dur.:	From 2 weeks to 5 months.
Per.:	July to December.
L.term:	Long-term stays are encouraged to better know the project and local communities.
Age:	No age restrictions. Inquire for younger than 18.
Qualif.:	No qualifications required. Volunteers should be in good health.
Work:	Beach patrols for nesting turtles, transfer eggs to hatchery and optional participation in environmental education programmes in small local schools. Tag and measure turtles, record data on hatching success and work with community and local biologists.
Lang.:	Spanish helpful but not necessary.
Accom.:	Station house and cabins operated by local community members, homestays.
Cost:	US$530/2wks, US$930/4weeks,US$1,730/8 weeks. Longer stays available, prices include meals and lodging; transportation not included, travel assistance available.
Applic.:	Contact tortugas@tortugamarina.org.
Notes:	Leisure activities include: jungle hikes, swimming, surfing, viewing abundant wildlife, Spanish practice, interaction with local community.

SEA TURTLE RESCUE CENTRE, Greece
Archelon – Sea Turtle Protection Society of Greece
3rd Marina Glyfada, GR-16675 Athens Greece
Tel./Fax: ++30 (210) 898 2600
E-mail: stps@archelon.gr
www.archelon.gr

Desc.: Archelon is a non-profit organisation that conducts sea turtle conservation projects in Greece with the support of international volunteers. This project focuses on treatment and rehabilitation of injured, sick or weak turtles. Raising of public awareness is part of the activities, as well as expanding and improving the Sea Turtle Rescue Network in Greece.

Spp.: Sea turtles.

Hab.: Mediterranean coast.

Loc.: Glyfada, about 20 km from Athens, Greece.

Travel: Airplane to Athens. Inquire with the organisation for further instruction.

Dur.: Min. 4 weeks.

Per.: Year round.

L.term: After the initial stay of 4 weeks.

Age: Min. 18.

Qualif.: A strong motivation.

Work: Treatment of turtles, construction and maintenance work, painting, building, cleaning.

Lang.: English. German and Greek are useful.

Accom: At the Centre.

Cost: Participation fee is approximately EUR150 (approx.GB£110). Volunteers must also pay for their own travel expenses and pay a min. of EUR9/ day to cover food costs.

Applic.: Prospective volunteers must fill out an application form.

Notes: Participation fee includes a 1-year subscription to the newsletter *Turtle Tracks* as a Archelon supporter. Volunteers must carry international health insurance.

SEA TURTLE SUMMER FIELD WORK, Greece

Archelon – Sea Turtle Protection Society of Greece
3rd Marina Glyfada, GR-16675 Athens Greece
Tel./Fax: ++30 (210) 898 2600
E-mail: stps@archelon.gr
www.archelon.gr

Desc.:	Archelon is a non-profit organisation that conducts sea turtle conservation projects in Greece with the support of international volunteers. Summer field work includes monitoring turtle nesting activities on the beaches, tagging nesting female turtles, protecting nests and raising public (visitor and local) awareness.
Spp.:	Loggerhead sea turtle *(Caretta caretta)*.
Hab.:	Mediterranean coast.
Loc.:	Peloponnesus and the islands of Zakynthos and Crete, Greece.
Travel:	Airplane to Athens, then bus or ferry boat.
Dur.:	Min. 4 weeks.
Per.:	May to October.
L.term:	Volunteers applying for long-term are particularly welcome.
Age:	Min. 18.
Qualif.:	On site training provided. Tolerance for hot weather necessary.
Work:	Based upon project requirements; include beach surveys, nest relocations, on-site nest protection as well as tagging nesting female turtles at night and raising public awareness through information stations, slide shows and beach patrolling.
Lang.:	English. German, Italian, Dutch, Swedish and Greek useful.
Accom:	Designated free campsites in tents. Basic sanitary and cooking facilities with limited water supply.
Cost:	Participation fee is approximately EUR150 (approx.GB£110) plus a min. EUR10/day to cover food costs. Travel expenses paid by volunteer.
Applic.:	Prospective volunteers must fill out an application form.
Notes:	Participants receive a 1-year subscription to *Turtle Tracks* newsletter. International health insurance required. Groups (over 2 persons) not accepted for the same area.

SIBERIAN/EAST RUSSIAN VOLUNTEER PROGRAM, Russia
Building the Great Baikal Trail – Earth Island Institute
300 Broadway, Suite 28, San Francisco, California 94133 USA
Tel.: ++1 (415) 788 3666
Fax: ++1 (415) 788 7324
E-mail: baikalwatch@earthisland.org
www.earthisland.org

Desc.:	Earth Island and Great Baikal Trail Association are building the first national hiking trail in Russia. The Great Baikal Association will lead some 1,600 km around Lake Baikal, through 3 national parks and 3 nature reserves. Every year multiple teams of volunteers are organised to help build the trail. Teams are international, with many local Siberians mixing with foreign participants. At least 25 project sites are planned. Examples would be: 1) in Zabaikalski National Park, where a 40-mile trail extension needs to be constructed from the foot of the Barguzin Mountains, along the shores of Baikal, to the wooden Siberian village of Ust-Barguzin; 2) in Baikalski Nature Reserve, where a 3-mile trail needs improving from the Reserve's visitor centre up into an old-growth forest and right up to the edge of a secluded waterfall; 3) along the southern shores of Baikal, where the Round Baikal Railroad is now being partially converted to a hiking and biking trail, leading through tunnels, gables, and many cliff-front passages that face Baikal. For more information on all the work sites for volunteers in the summer, please see www.greatbaikaltrail.ru/index_en.html.
Spp.:	Varies greatly: along the trail one might see Baikal seal, bears, eagles, sable or red deer. Divers may see many exotic species of fish and even coral.
Hab.:	Lakeshore habitat, temperate mountain forests, wetlands and meadowlands.
Loc.:	Lake Baikal region of south central Russia, near the Mongolian border.
Travel:	Airplane to Irkutsk (via Moscow or the Far East) or the Trans-Siberian train, which takes 3 days of travel from Moscow.
Dur.:	2–4 weeks.
Per.:	Summer, from May to September.
L.term.:	Opportunities for volunteering for several projects around Baikal are available for those who wish to stay on longer.
Age:	Min.18.

Qualif.: Helpful (but not required) trail-building experience. Good health and ability to do hard work are a must, since some heavy tools will be used, with training provided.

Work: Mostly physical, all outdoors, with opportunities to assist the design and strategy teams as they choose the best sites and methods for building each trail.

Lang.: Some knowledge of Russian would be helpful but not required. At least one English-language interpreter will be working on every team.

Accom.: Field work involves sleeping on boats or in tents; sleeping bag required.

Cost: Earth Island charges no fees for referring to the trail-building crews. However, the Association is a non-profit group and will depend on international volunteers to pay for their own travel and food costs at Baikal: US$250 for each 2-week project. Volunteers should also bear the cost of insurance and accommodations in Russia before and after the work period.

Agents: Prospective volunteers can communicate directly with Earth Island's staff (at baikalwatch@earthisland.org) or with the Russian partners at the national parks and nature reserves, through their colleagues at the Association (ariadna_gbt@mail.ru) who are fluent in English.

Applic.: No application form to fill out, simple inquiries will be sufficient.

Notes: There are many other volunteer and internship opportunities with Siberian environmental groups available, where knowledge of Russian is a requirement. For more information on these programmes, contact Earth Island Institute.

SKAFTAFELL NATIONAL PARK, Iceland

BTCV
Sedum House
Mallard Way, Potteric Carr, Doncaster, DN4 8DB UK
Tel.: +44 (1302) 388 883 – Fax: +44 (1302) 311 531
E-mail: information@btcv.org.uk International@btcv.org.uk
www.btcv.org.uk

Desc.:	A dramatic landscape of green oasis surrounded by black sand, dark rivers and white glaciers. Since the park was opened to the public erosion from tourists has become a serious problem. Constructing footpaths directs visitors to certain areas and helps conserve this unique landscape.
Spp.:	Subarctic species of flora and fauna (ptarmigan, arctic fox).
Hab.:	Glacier area, subarctic tundra.
Loc.:	Skaftafell National Park, southeast Iceland.
Travel:	Pick up at Reykjavik BSI.
Dur.:	1 to 2 weeks.
Per.:	Summer.
L.term:	Contact organisation for details.
Age:	Min. 18.
Qualif.:	Strenuous work: a reasonable level of fitness required.
Work:	Footpath construction and repair.
Lang.:	English.
Cost:	GB£480 (approx. EUR750/US$ 950). Flights approx. GB£600.
Agents:	Contact BTCV directly. International@btcv.org.uk
Applic.:	Deposit of GB£100 required.
Notes:	Conservation Holiday brochure available on request.

SOUTHWESTERN RESEARCH STATION, Arizona USA
American Museum of Natural History
P.O. Box 16553 Portal, Arizona 85632 USA
Tel./Fax:++1 (520) 558 2396
E-mail: swrs@amnh.org
http://research.amnh.org/swrs/

Desc.: The volunteer programme offers students in biological sciences outstanding opportunities to observe and become involved with scientists doing field research. Food and lodging are provided to volunteers in exchange for 24 hours per week of routine chores, with the remaining time available for research activities. The program is open to both undergraduate and graduate students; the latter may pursue their own research projects. The program is open to non-students as well, particularly in the spring and fall.

Spp.: Birds, reptiles, amphibians, mammals, insects, plants.

Hab: Five life-zones are encountered, from desert to alpine.

Loc.: Portal, southeastern Arizona.

Travel: Airplane to Tucson, then shuttle to Douglas (meeting place).

Dur.: Generally 6-week commitment, although shorter commitments are allowed in spring and fall.

Per.: Mid-March through the end of October.

L.term: Possible with the Station director's approval, after initial period.

Age: Min. 18, no max.

Qualif.: Some biological background is helpful, but not necessary.

Work: Volunteers work 24 hours on routine Station chores, e.g., housekeeping, grounds keeping, assisting in the kitchen/dining room, in exchange for room and board. Remaining time is available for research activities.

Lang.: English.

Accom.: Shared rooms are provided. All linens are provided. Meals are in a common dining room.

Cost: There is no cost to volunteers, other than transportation.

Applic.: Contact Volunteer Coordinator, P.D.Hulce, dhulce@amnh.org. An application must be submitted with letter(s) of reference.

SPANISH DOLPHINS, Spain

Earthwatch (Europe)
267 Banbury Road
Oxford OX2 7HT   UK
Tel.: ++44 (1865) 318 831 – Fax: ++44 (1865) 311 383
E-mail: projects@earthwatch.org.uk
www.earthwatch.org/europe

Desc.: Monitoring the distribution and dynamics of cetaceans, in particular the declining common dolphin populations in the region, using photo-ID and bio-acoustic surveys. Research is carried out onboard the *Toftevaag*, an old 1910 Norwegian fishing boat converted into a research vessel.

Spp.: Common dolphin (*Delphinus delphis*), striped and bottlenose dolphins, long-finned pilot whales, Risso's dolphins.

Hab.: Temperate sea (Mediterranean Sea).

Loc.: Southeast Spain.

Travel: Airplane to Almería; bus or taxi to the ship (Almerimar).

Dur.: 10 days.

Per.: Throughout the year.

L.term: Volunteers can join the project for more than 1 period.

Age: Min. 18.

Qualif.: No particular skills needed.

Work: Volunteers share all duties with the research crew, including navigation, helping with the feeding of computer data, lookout watch, water sampling and analyses and bio-acoustic watch. Volunteers, depending on their experience, can participate in other activities such as inflatable-boat driving, photo-ID and underwater filming. During days of bad weather researchers will show slides, videos and publications.

Lang.: English.

Accom.: In bunks aboard research vessel.

Cost: Approx. GB£ 1,250 (approx. US$ 2,200) including food, accomodation, trainig.

Agents: Contact the Earthwatch (Europe) (see Organisation list).

Applic.: Apply on-line at www.earthwatch.org/europe/.

SUSTAINABLE LIVELIHOOD DEVELOPMENT ASSOCIATION, Sri Lanka

No 258, Moragoda Road, Mudungoda,
Gampaha Sri Lanka
Tel.: ++94 (33) 222 9003
E-mail: damilda@sltnet.lk

Desc.: An NGO involved in conserving and propagating lesser known traditional food plants beneficial to rural communities. The organisation is active in running native plant nursery and arboretum for the purpose of conservation and distribution of plants such as medicinal, wild fruits, yam and herbal drinks. Volunteers are able to involve in the nursery in the arboretum and at community level. Volunteers' posts are mainly community based and provide a unique opportunity to understand the local culture and values.

Spp.: Low impact sustainable crops.

Hab: Hilly tropical farmland.

Loc.: Western province of Sri Lanka.

Travel: Airplane to Colombo then bus to project area.

Dur.: Depending on the time availability of the volunteers.

Per.: Year round, but rainy season (Apr. -Jul./Oct. - Dec.) preferable.

L.term: Volunteers can stay as long as they want.

Age: Above 25 years. Elderly people are welcome.

Qualif.: No particular skills required; initiative, adaptability, compassion for nature and traditional knowledge are important requisites.

Work: Regeneration of traditional environmental values by practically implementing the programmes with hands on experience at family level in rural areas. Volunteers will learn from a mentor who will look after them during their stay.

Lang.: English.

Accom.: With local families: basic, but clean and comfortable.

Costs: Volunteers pay fro their living expenses US$ 10/day. They receive food and lodging and are free to make a contribution.

Applic.: Send a detailed CV to the above e-mail address.

Notes: Expect a genuine hospitality by a local Sri Lanka family.

TAMBOPATA RESIDENT NATURALIST PROGRAM, Peru
Peruvian Safaris
Alcanfores #459 Miraflores
Lima 18 Perù
E-mail: safaris@amauta. rcp.net.pe
www.geocities.com/resident_naturalist/

Desc.: The Explorer's Inn, a tourist lodge and research station along the Tambopata River, offers a Resident Naturalist (RN) programme. RNs are volunteers at the lodge and help undertake numerous simple scientific-based tasks associated with an ongoing environmental monitoring programme. RNs also help train resident Peruvian guides in European languages and tropical natural history interpretation.

Spp.: Tropical rainforest species.

Hab.: Sub-tropical moist forest.

Loc.: Tambopata region, Peru southeast province of Madre de Dios.

Travel: Airplane to Lima, then to Puerto Maldonado, then river boat.

Dur.: Min. 3 months; 6 months preferred.

Per.: Year round. Applicants should arrive 1 week earlier for training.

L.term: RNs who wish to stay at least 6 months are preferred.

Age: Min. 22.

Qualif.: Graduates in natural sciences, biology or related disciplines.

Work: RN duties include: training Peruvian staff in languages and natural history; recordings of weather data; maintaining wildlife sightings logs; monitoring giant otters, macaws and parrots; helping maintain the trail system; giving natural history lectures to guests; writing monthly reports to RN Co-ordinator.

Lang.: English, priority to people with working knowledge of Spanish.

Accom.: Shared room in one of the lodge bungalows.

Cost:: Free room and board in return for undertaking RN activities. RNs pay for their travel to Puerto Maldonado.

Applic.: Contact Peruvian Safaris (via e-mail).

Notes: RNs may also undertake their own research during their stay with approval of RN Co-ordinator and Reserve Administrator (INRENA).

TILOS PARK ASSOCIATION, Greece
Livadia
GR-85002 Tilos   Greece
Tel.: ++30 (22460) 70880
Fax: ++30 (22460) 70892
E-mail: tilopark@otenet.gr
www.tilos-park.org

Desc.: Tilos Park is an NGO devoted to the conservation of wildlife on the island of Tilos, Dodecanese, Greece. Tilos and its fourteen islets are classified as a Special Protection Area for the birds (SPA) and a Natura 2000 site under EU laws.

Spp.: 126 bird species have been recorded on Tilos with 27 of them classified in Annex 1 of the Bird Directive of the European Union as being under threat of extinction. 377 flora species and many reptile species have also been recorded.

Hab.: Coastal Mediterranean with 16 different types of biotopes.

Loc.: The Greek island of Tilos is located in the Dodecanese Archipelago of the Aegean Sea in the Eastern Mediterranean.

Travel: By airplane to Rhodes, bus to the Rhodes port, ferry or high speed hovercraft to the Livadia port of Tilos.

Dur.: Minimum 1 month, subject to renewal every 3 months.

Per.: Year round.

L.Term: There is no limit of time for long-term stays.

Age: Min. 18 with no upper age limit.

Qualif.: Ability to work in a team, experience in mountain trekking can be useful, ornithological or veterinary experience and/or construction experience also helpful.

Work: Assistance with the ecological programmes, wildlife record keeping and observation, assistance on wildlife rehabilitation, facility and nature trail maintenance.

Lang.: English and/or Greek.

Acccom.: Room in a house with indoor bathroom and shower.

Cost: EUR50 non-refundable, payable at registration.

Applic.: Via e-mail with subject : 'Volunteer program'; applicants must send CV, letter of intentions and possible dates.

TOLGA BAT HOSPITAL, Australia

Tolga Bat Rescue & Research, Inc.

P.O. Box 685 Atherton 4883 Australia

Tel.: ++61 (7) 4091 2683

Fax: ++61 (7) 4091 2683

E-mail: enny@tolggabathospital.org

www.tolgabathospital.org

Desc.:	Tolga Bat Hospital works mainly with spectacled flying foxes and their habitat, but is also involved in education and research. An education centre will open to the public in late 2007.
Spp.:	Spectacled flying fox (Pteropus conspicillatus), Little Red flying fox (*Pteropus scapulatus.*), several species of microbat.
Hab.:	Tropical rainforest.
Loc.:	Atherton, near Cairns, Australia.
Travel:	Airplane to Cairns, then bus to Atherton.
Dur.:	Minimum 4 weeks in busy season; 1 week for rest of year.
Per.:	Year round but especially from October to February.
L.term:	A stay of 2-3 months in the busy season is welcome.
Age:	Min. 21 years, no max.
Qualif.:	Ability to work well in teams and for long hours. Experience with bats not necessary, though experience with wildlife, veterinary or zoo work is a plus. Cooks and Vets are welcome.
Work:	Extremely varied in busy season: it involves searching the colony daily for tick paralysis bat; hospital treatments; feeding babies; preparing food for adults and babies; cleaning; washing; cooking; weighing and measuring bats; computer work. In low season there are about 100 bats, but work is less hands-on. May include work in the vegetable and bush gardens
Lang.:	English necessary.
Accom.:	Excellent accommodation. Single, twin or triple room available. Some form of 'soft volunteering' is possible where people can pay more and work less.
Cost:	AUS$30-50 per day for food and accommodation.
Applic.:	Application form online.
Notes:	Vaccination for rabies is mandatory from October to February, although Australian Bat Lyssa Virus is rare in Spectacled flying foxes.

TREE PLANTERS FARM, Australia
Willing Workers on Organic Farms
2 Deserio Rd., Cedar Pocket, Gympie
Queensland 4570 Australia
Tel.: ++61 (7) 5486 6147
E-mail: forest@spiderweb.com.au
www.spiderweb.com.au/~forest

Desc.:	This privately owned organic working farm aims to establish rainforest tree species through rainforest regeneration and tree planting on former rainforest sites. Special interest on the farm is in rare rainforest tree species. Adjoining the state forest, the farm has large rainforest trees, walking trails, swimming holes, a creek, a camping cave, an isolated visitors hut and an small orchard of tropical fruit trees.
Spp.:	Rainforest trees.
Hab:	Rainforest.
Loc.:	Southeast Queensland.
Travel:	Train or bus to Gympie, about 160 km north of Brisbane, the meeting point.
Dur.:	2 nights to make sure that both parties are happy and after that by negotiation.
Per.:	Any time of the year.
L.term:	Longer terms can perhaps be arranged.
Age:	Min. 18.
Qualif.:	No specific qualifications required, just enthusiasm.
Work:	To assist with the establishment of the forests and perhaps some other farm jobs.
Lang:	Only English is spoken but the project manager will assist those that wish to improve their English.
Accom.:	Either in a spare bedroom in the house or a self-contained old converted dairy behind the house. Sleeping bags required.
Cost:	No cost. Work is done in return for keep.
Applic.:	Contact Bob Whitworth, owner, directly either by telephone or writing to the above address.

TREES FOR LIFE, Scotland UK

The Park, Findhorn Bay, Forres, IV36 3TZ, Scotland UK
Tel.: +44 (1309) 691 292
Fax: +44 (1309) 691 155
E-mail: trees@findhorn.org
www.treesforlife.org.uk

Desc.: Trees for Life is an ecological restoration charity, working with volunteers to restore the Caledonian Forest to the Highlands of Scotland.

Spp.: Tree planting weeks may include Scots pine, silver and downy birch, hazel, willow, alder and juniper. Fauna inlcudes red or roe deer, red squirrel, black grouse, many small birds and, occasionally, capercaille or pine marten.

Hab.: Caledonian Forest.

Loc.: Highlands of Scotland, west of Inverness.

Travel: Transport is provided from Inverness station.

Dur.: Min. 1 week, Saturday to Saturday.

Per.: March – June and September – October.

L.term: Long-term opportunites are possible.

Age: Minimum 18 years.

Qualif.: None required, although volunteers would need to be reasonably fit to take part.

Work: Tree planting, removing redundant fences, small scale stock fencing and tree tubing, wetland restoration, felling non-native trees and seed collection.

Lang.: English.

Accom.: Simple but comfortable, ranging from a renovated croft house to well appointed bunkhouse with all facilities.

Cost: GB£90 (GB£55 unwaged: ie students, unemployed, pensioners), includes accommodation, vegetarian food and transport from Inverness.

Applic.: Via e-mail or online.

Notes: The website has testimonials and experiences from volunteers.

TURTLE CONSERVATION PROJECT (TCP), Sri Lanka

11, Perera Mawatha, Madakumbura, Panadura, Sri Lanka
Tel.: ++94 (777) 810 508/9, ++94 (38) 567 0168,
Fax: ++94 (38) 223 3106
E-mail: turtle@sltnet.lk
Website: www.tcpsrilanka.org

Desc.:	TCP is an NGO devoted to the conservation of marine & Coastal resources in Sri Lanka through Community participation.
Spp.:	Green (*Chelonia mydas*), hawksbill (*Eretmochelys imbricata*), loggerhead (*Caretta caretta*), olive ridley (*Lepidochelys olivacea*) and leatherback turtles (*Dermochelys coriacea*).
Hab.:	Tropical – marine and coastal.
Loc.:	Marine and coastal areas of Sri Lanka.
Travel:	Airplane to Colombo. Transportation to project site provided.
Dur.:	Minimum 2 weeks, a minimum of 3 months is preferred.
Per.:	Year round.
L.term:	There is no limit of time for long-term stays.
Age:	Min. 18.
Qualif.:	No special skills required. A degree of stamina is required for the long shifts and occasional variations in climate. Volunteers must be enthusiastic, efficient, willing to work as part of a team and have a strong adaptability.
Work:	Measuring turtles, beach patrols and mapping, conduct education programmes, environmental hotel presentations, English teaching in monasteries and schools, office administration, fundraising, IT development work, promotion of responsible nature tourism.
Lang.:	English.
Accom.:	The type of accommodation will vary and may include basic standards of living compared to Western standards.
Cost:	US$ 750, US$ 1100, US$ 2800, US$ 4200, for 2 weeks, 1, 3 or 6 months respectively; includes accommodation, food, visa depending on the duration, airport pickup and any transport incurred through TCP work. A local family will provide all required meals.
Applic.:	Contact the organization by e-mail for Application Form.

TURTLE PROJECT KEFALONIA, Greece

Katelios Group for the Research and Protection of Marine and Terrestrial Life
28086 Kefalonia
Greece
Tel.: ++30 (26) 710 8100
E-mail: info@kateliosgroup.org
www.kateliosgroup.org

Desc.: Local project for the conservation of the Loggerhead sea turtle (*Caretta caretta*) in Greece. Main volunteer activities: nesting beach patrols, turtle monitoring, data collection, environmental education and awareness raising. Project runs during turtle nesting season (May to October).

Spp.: Loggerhead sea turtle (*Caretta caretta*).

Hab.: Mediterranean sea, coast and beach sand dunes.

Loc.: Kefalonia, Greece.

Travel: Airplane to Athens, then bus or ferry boat. Or direct charter flight to Kefalonia.

Dur.: Minimum stay 4 weeks, longer stay (up to whole summer) welcome.

Per.: May to October.

L.term: Long term volunteers are particularly welcome.

Age: Min 18. No upper age limit.

Qualif.: No specific skills or background required. For beach patrols good fitness is essential.

Work: Nesting beach patrols, turtle monitoring, data collection, environmental education and awareness raising.

Lang.: English. Greek and any other European language welcome.

Accom.: Free in basic campsite with showers, toilet and kitchen facilities.

Cost: Participation fee is EUR 120. Travel, food and insurance paid by volunteer. Free accommodation in campsite.

Applic.: Prospective volunteers must send CV and cover letter. There is no deadline but places fill up in spring.

Notes: Volunteers need to show strong motivation and committment. For beach patrols good fitness is essential.

TURTLES OF TORTUGUERO, Costa Rica
Caribbean Conservation Corporation
4424 NW 13th Street, Suite A-1
Gainesville, Florida 32609 USA
Tel.: ++1 (352) 373 6441 – Fax: ++1 (352) 375 2449
E-mail: resprog@cccturtle.org – ccc@cccturtle.org
www.cccturtle.org

Desc.: Caribbean Conservation Corporation (CCC) has been tagging and monitoring the green turtles of Tortuguero for nearly 50 years. CCC is now gathering information also on leatherback turtles, which nest at Tortuguero Beach in impressive numbers.

Spp.: Green turtles (*Chelonia mydas*).

Hab.: Tropical coast.

Loc.: Tortuguero, Costa Rica.

Travel: Airplane to San José, Costa Rica.

Dur.: 1–2 weeks.

Per.: June to September.

L.term: Volunteers can stay longer than 2 weeks with prior approval.

Age: Min. 18.

Qualif.: Volunteers must be in good physical condition, be able to live in rustic setting and tolerate harsh weather.

Work: Volunteers assist researchers with tagging turtles and collecting data on size, tag numbers, nest location, etc.

Lang.: English. Spanish may be useful.

Accom.: Volunteers stay at CCC's research Station in Tortuguero.

Cost: US$1,599 for 1 week; US$2,149 for 2 weeks. Cost includes 2 nights in San José, transfers to Tortuguero, all room, meals and training while at Tortuguero. A deposit is required. Flight to San José not included.

Agents: Holbrook Travel, tel. 1 (800) 451 7111 in North America.

Applic.: Contact Daniel Evans at CCC or agent to confirm dates.

THE UNIVERSITY OF GEORGIA SAN LUIS RESEARCH STATION, Costa Rica

Apdo.108, Santa Elena de Monteverde, Puntarenas, Costa Rica
Tel.: ++ (506) 206 5133
Fax: ++ (506) 206 5134
E-mail: sofiarce@uga.edu fabricio@uga.edu
www.uga.edu/costarica

Desc.: The University of Georgia San Luis Research Station, which is a satellite campus of the University of Georgia, is dedicated to research, education, ecotourism, conservation and the community. Field courses, academic programmes and the public are served. Volunteers include Interns and Resident Naturalists.

Spp.: Cloud forest flora and fauna, crop species.

Hab.: Tropical cloud forest, tropical agricultural landscape.

Loc.: San Luis de Monteverde, Northwestern Costa Rica.

Travel: Bus from San Jose to Monteverde; then taxi to the Station.

Dur.: Interns: min. 3 months. Resident Naturalists: min. 6 months.

Per.: Year round.

L.term: Preferred for Resident naturalists (6 months or longer).

Age: Min. 20.

Qualif.: Interns: excellent physical condition, able to interact with scientists, students and the public. Resident Naturalists: Minimum bachelors' degree in Environmental Sciences or related topics, tropical experience, natural history background.

Work: Working as part of a team in: leading hikes, horseback tours, birdwalks, slide shows, community service; helping with logistics; designing educational programmes; participating in research, education, ecotourism and conservation missions.

Lang.: English; conversational Spanish is preferable for Resident Naturalists. Intensive language study can be arranged on site at $280/week, including homestay.

Accom.: Bunkhouse or rustic one-room casitas. Bedding provided.

Cost: Interns pay initial US$450; Resident Naturalists pay no fee. All volunteers receive free room and board.

Applic.: Send e-mail to request application form and further details.

Notes: Intensive training in flora and fauna provided. Good research potential.

VOLUNTEER IN VILCABAMBA, Ecuador
"Rumi Wilco" Nature Reserve & Ecolodge
Vilcabamba, Loja, Ecuador
E-mail: rumiwilco@yahoo.com
www.rumiwilco.com

Desc.:	Created and run by Alicia and Orlando Falco, biologists, ex-Galápagos naturalist guides, the Rumi Wilco Nature Reserve is a self-sustainable conservation project, on private lands with several owners. The Ecolodge -adjacent to it- provides housing for international tourism and roughly a third of the profits, plus the help given by volunteer workers, to the Reserve needs. Rumi Wilco provides volunteer outdoor activities for travellers as well as students who have an interest in nature, learning practical skills and scientific research.
Spp.:	117 species of birds recorded, 400 of plants, 67 spp of butterflies. Other animals observed: opossums, bats, squirrel, rabbit, fox, weasel, red brocket deer, snakes and frogs.
Hab.:	Wilco-dominated forest remnants, open woodlands and grasslands.
Loc.:	Vilcabamba is located 45 km south of Loja City, in Ecuador.
Travel:	Airplane to Quito or Guayaquil, bus to Loja then mini-bus to Vilcabamba.
Dur.:	From one week to several months.
Qualif.:	No specific skills required for volunteers in general. Students in particular fields may perform their research and leave copies for future reference.
Work:	Volunteers work 5 days/week 4 hours per day. The rest of the day is usually spent reading, relaxing, walking around, taking Spanish lessons, etc. Work includes trail maintenance, reforestation, riverbank repair, gardening, minor construction, shaded-grown coffee picking/processing, making marmalades, etc. For scientific research, adequate knowledge is required depending on the subject (i.e. taxonomy, ecology, etc.).
Lang.:	English, Spanish, French, Italian.
Accom.:	In the Ecolodge with other guests. Rooms are shared, perhaps private; there are 2 well-furnished kitchens, 4 bathrooms with hot water showers, laundry facilities. Restaurant service is not included.
Cost:	US$4/day. Many kinds of food/ingredients are easy to find in Vilcabamba village. Indivudal Spanish lessons are available in town for US$4/hour.
Applic.:	Via e-mail. Arrival must be confirmed at least one week in advance.

VOLUNTEER PETEN, Guatemala

Parque Nueva Juventud
San Andres, Peten, Guatemala
Tel.: ++ (502) 5711 0040/5496 2276
E-mail: volunteerpeten@hotmail.com
www.volunteerpeten.com

Desc.:	Volunteer Peten is a small independent non-profit organization dedicated to: 1) protect and manage a 150-acre ecological reserve in San Andres, Peten; 2) provide environmental education programs to all the schools in the San Andres area; 3) assist and develop small sustainable community projects; 4) provide quality volunteer opportunities for international travellers and students.
Spp.:	Volunteer Peten has identified in the area over 160 bird species, 120 medicinal plant species, 95 tree species, and countless insect and reptile species in the park.
Hab.:	Semi-humid, deciduous tropical rain forest.
Loc.:	Northern Guatemala. San Andres, Peten.
Travel:	San Andres is 30 min. by bus from Santa Elena\Flores.
Dur.:	Volunteers can stay for one month to one year.
Per.:	Year round.
L.term:	Volunteers can stay for as long as they want.
Age:	Min. 18.
Qualif.:	No specific skills required.
Work:	Volunteers work Monday though Friday from 8-12. Most work is outside and includes trail management, reforestation, gardening, minor construction, environmental education, and making arts and crafts.
Lang.:	English, basic Spanish is highly desirable.
Accom.:	With local families, which provide food and accommodations.
Cost:	US$ 350/650/950 for 4, 8 or 12 weeks respectively; includes all food, housing (with local family), training, activities, and resources for projects. Spanish lessons available at US$3/hour.
Appl.:	Via e-mail by confirming date of arrival at least one week in advance.

WAKULUZU: FRIENDS OF THE COLOBUS TRUST, Kenya

Colobus Trust
P.O. Box 5380, Diani Beach 80401 Kenya
Tel./fax: ++ (254) 40 320 3519
E-mail: info@colobustrust.org
www.colobustrust.org

Desc.:	The Colobus Trust is committed to saving the endemic Angolan colobus monkey and preserving its threatened coastal forest habitat.
Spp.:	Primates: Angolan black-and-white colobus (*Colobus angolensis palliatus*), yellow baboons, sykes, vervets, bush babies.
Hab.:	Tropical coral rag forest.
Loc.:	Diani Beach, south of Mombasa, Kenya.
Travel:	Flight to Mombasa via Nairobi or direct.
Dur.:	3 months.
Per.:	Year round.
L.term:	Subject to prior approval.
Age:	Min. 22.
Qualif.:	Preferably undergraduates or graduates with experience in conservation, education, zoology, journalism, ecology, veterinary medicine, marketing, fundraising.
Work:	Primate rescue and rehabilitation, practical conservation activities (construction and repair of monkey road-crossing bridges, tree planting, invasive scrub clearance, removal of snares from forests, etc.), assisting with education workshops, ecological and primate surveys, maintenance work, office work.
Lang.:	English. Swahili, German, Dutch, Italian, French, useful but not essential.
Accom.:	Basic but clean accommodation in shared rooms at the Trust headquarters. Bed linen provided but volunteer must bring own mosquito net and towel.
Cost:	EUR425/month including accommodation. Food extra (costs approx. EUR15/week).
Applic.:	There is a standard form to be completed from the website www.colobustrust.org.

WDCS WILDLIFE CENTRE, Scotland
Research, Education & Conservation
WDCS - The Whale and Dolphin Conservation Society
Spey Bay, Moray, Scotland IV32 7PJ   UK
Tel.: ++44 (1343) 820 339 – Fax: ++44 (1343) 829 065
E-mail: volunteering@wdcs.org
www.wdcs.org/

Desc.:   Volunteering opportunities are extremely varied at WDCS's Wildlife Centre. Tasks include interpretation at the Wildlife Centre, helping with events, school visits, guiding wildlife-watching holidays & dolphin research (boat and shore-based).

Spp.:   Bottlenose dolphin (*Tursiops truncatus*).

Hab.:   North Sea coast.

Loc.:   Northeast Scotland.

Travel: Airplane (or bus or train) to either Aberdeen or Inverness; bus or train to Fochabers. Spey Bay lies 5 km north of Fochabers.

Dur.:   Min. 1 month.

Per.:   Year round.

L.term: Long term volunteering preferable; accomodation and living expenses available.

Age: Min. 18.

Qualif.:   Biology background preferred. Experience working with the public useful. Ability to work as part of a team.

Work: Photo-ID work, update records, supervise volunteers, public interpretation. Support volunteers: assist project officer; shore monitoring and estuary wildlife surveys.

Lang.:   Excellent written and spoken English essential. Other languages (especially German) helpful.

Accom.:   House on-site at the Wildlife Centre.

Cost: Longer term volunteers get accomodation and living expenses paid.

Applic.:   Download, complete and return an application form available on the website www.wdcs.org .

Notes: More opportunities during summer months (March-September).

THE WHALE CENTER OF NEW ENGLAND, Massachusetts USA

PO Box 159
Gloucester, 01930
Massachusetts North Shore
Tel.: ++1 (978) 281 6351
E-mail: info@whalecenter.org
www.whalecenter.org

Desc.: A conservation education position for volunteers who are willing to give of themselves. As the overseer of the exhibit which includes a 2 year old humpback whale skeleton, volunteers are responsible for public education of visitors and staffing a small gift shop.

Spp.: Marine mammals, focusing on humpback, fin and North Atlantic Right Whales.

Hab.: The Gulf of Maine, Jeffrey's Ledge and Stellwag.

Loc.: Massachusetts, USA.

Travel: The Whale Center is easily accessible by car or train.

Per.: Year round.

Age: Min. 17.

Qualif.: A willingness to learn.

Work: Volunteers will greet visitors, answer visitor's questions, and run a small gift shop.

Lang.: English.

Accom.: No accommodation provided.

Cost: There is no cost except for transportation to and from The Whale Center of New England.

Applic.: Involves an interview (can be over the phone) and an application. The Green Volunteers Standard Application form (page 255) is accepted. Interested applicants should call or e-mail for further information.

WHALE RESEARCH IN THE ST.LAWRENCE ESTUARY, Canada

Swiss Whale Society, Niederwilerstr. 12, CH-5524 Nesselnbach, Switzerland
Centre Mériscope, 64 rue du Barrage, Longue-Rive, Québec, Canada
Tel.:++1 (418) 231 2033 (summer)/++41 (76) 530 9192(winter)
Fax:++1 (418) 231 2033 (summer)/++41 (56) 426 0609(winter)
E-mail: info@whales.ch dany@whales.ch
www.whales.ch

Desc.: The 'Mériscope' is a small research base on the North shore of the St. Lawrence estuary. Research projects include bioacoustics of minke, finback and blue whales, habitat utilisation, social behaviour and feeding behaviour of baleen whales. Work is conducted with 2 rigid-hulled inflatable boats; day trips typically last 5–6 hours. Slide talks and land excursions complete the courses in marine biology.

Spp.: Baleen whales: blue, finback, minke, and humpback whales. Toothed whales: belugas, sperm whale, harbour porpoises.

Hab.: Subarctic estuary (coastal waters).

Loc.: St. Lawrence estuary, about 350 km northeast of Québec City.

Travel: Flight to Montreal or Quebec, then bus to Portneuf-sur-Mer.

Dur.: Courses last 2 weeks, 7 courses per summer, 10 people max.

Per.: June to October.

L.term: Biologists may join for 2-4 months.

Age: Min.18 (younger participants only accompanied by parents).

Qualif.: No particular skills needed; reasonably good physical condition (living in prospector tents and working on board inflatable boats for several hours); manual and computer skills welcome.

Work: All work under supervision of staff biologists: data collection at sea; observation and identification of marine mammals; behavioural sampling; navigation (GPS); sound recording; photo-ID, video. Data entry, matching and sound analysis in the lab.

Lang.: English, German and French.

Accom.: 4 prospector tents by the sea; cooking in a big kitchen tent.

Cost: US$1,250; students US$1,110. Includes food and accommodation, lectures and thermo suit.

Agents: Contact Dany Zbinden, project coordinator directly.

Applic.: A standard form is also available from the website.

WHALES AND DOLPHINS OFF CôTE D'AZUR, France

Swiss Cetacean Society (SCS)
Max-Olivier Bourcoud
PO Box 1430, CH–1001 Lausanne Switzerland
Tel.: ++41 (21) 403 2114
E-mail: scs1@vtxnet.ch
www.swisscetaceansociety.org

Desc.:	Study of the distribution, abundance and dynamics of cetaceans in the Mediterranean Sea, between Côte d'Azur and Corsica.
Spp.:	Cetaceans.
Hab.:	Mediterranean French coast.
Loc.:	South of France (Provence-Côte d'Azur).
Travel:	Airplane to Nice; bus or train to St. Mandrier (Toulon).
Dur.:	Min. 6 days.
Per.:	June to September.
L.term:	Negotiable (max. 4 months).
Age:	Min. 18.
Qualif.:	Strong interest in cetacean research and conservation, strong willingness to work and learn, navigation experience, photography, good hearing and sight, ability to swim and not prone to seasickness.
Work:	Scanning the horizon for whales and dolphins; assisting the researchers with bioacoustic survey, photo-ID, skin and faces sampling, recording specific data, etc. cooking, dishwashing and ship upkeep.
Lang.:	French (good knowledge required).
Accom.:	On the ship. Volunteers must bring sheets or sleeping bags.
Cost:	Approx. EUR780 (approx. GB£ 540/US$ 1,000) for 6 days and nights for accommodation and food.
Applic.:	E-mail a short CV and a statement of purpose.

WILD BIRD REHABILITATION, Bulgaria
BTCV
Sedum House
Mallard Way, Potteric Carr, Doncaster, DN4 8DB UK
Tel.: +44 (1302) 388 883 - Fax: +44 (1302) 311 531
E-mail: information@btcv.org.uk International@btcv.org.uk
www.btcv.org.uk

Desc.: The project is carried out in association with the local conservation group the "Green Balkan". Its priorities are: treatment, rehabilitation, breeding and release of wild, rare and threatened species in the wild.

Spp.: Dalmatian pelican, red-breasted goose, imperial and golden eagle, Egyptian and griffon vulture.

Hab.: Eastern European Boreal Forest.

Loc.: Stara Zagora Wildlife Rehabilitation & Breeding Centre, Bulgaria.

Travel: Pick up at Bourgas airport.

Dur.: 2 weeks.

Per.: June - September.

L. term: Contact organisation for details.

Age: Min. 18.

Qualif.: No specific skills required.

Work: Construction/repair of specialised cages to increase capacity; bird care, fencing and pond making. The experience allows volunteers to observe birds from close and to assist to activities related to their rehabilitation and release.

Lang.: English.

Accom.: Hotel.

Cost: GB£640 (approx. EUR950) excluding flight.

Agents: BTCV.

Applic.: GB£100 deposit required. Go to: www.btcv.org.

Notes: Conservation Holidays brochure available on request.

THE WILD DOLPHIN PROJECT, Bahamas
The Wild Dolphin Project
P.O. Box 8436
Jupiter, Florida 33468 USA
Tel.: ++1 (561) 575 5660 – Fax: ++1 (561) 575 5681
E-mail: wdpcindy@earthlink.net
www.wilddolphinproject.org

Desc.: The Wild Dolphin Project (WDP) has been studying a specific pod of Atlantic spotted and bottlenose dolphins, in the Bahamas, since 1985. WDP is a non-profit organization dedicated to research, education and conservation. While continuing to collect long-term baseline data WDP researches many other aspects of dolphin society, including behavior, communication, vocalizations, social structure, genetics and habitat. Participants will assist the researchers in various tasks and get to snorkel with the dolphins and may also visit other snorkel spots, such as coral reefs and shipwrecks. .

Spp.: Spotted dolphins (*Stenella frontalis*) and Bottlenose dolphins (*Tursiops truncatus*).

Hab.: Shallow sandbanks 40 miles offshore (offshore anchorage).

Loc.: Northern Bahamas.

Travel: Airplane to Grand Bahama Island.

Dur.: 9 day and 6 day trips.

Per.: Field season: May-September (contact WDP for trip dates).

Age: Minimum 18 without parent.

Qualif.: Volunteers must be able to swim and snorkel safely.

Work: Help with routine data collection and dolphin watches. Observe (while snorkeling) the wild spotted and bottlenose dolphins underwater, in addition to surface observations.

Lang.: English.

Accom.: All food and sleeping accommodations are provided aboard a 62 feet (20m) power catamaran, 2 to 4 to a room.

Cost: US $2,495 for 9 days, US $1,795 for 6 days, airfare to and from Florida and/or Grand Bahama Island not included.

Applic.: Inquire about trip dates and request application form.

Notes: Portion of trip price is tax deductible for US citizens.

WILDLIFE REHABILITATION INTERNSHIP, Connecticut USA
Wildlife In Crisis
P.O. Box 1246
Weston, CT 06883 USA
Tel.: ++1 (203) 544 991
E-mail: wildlifeincrisis@snet.net
www.wildlifeincrisis.org

Desc.: Resident Intern for wildlife rehabilitation program. Seeking dedicated, hard working individuals with a passion for caring for injured and orphaned wildlife. This internship is unpaid.

Spp.: Primarily birds and mammals native to Northeastern USA.

Hab.: Suburbia.

Loc.: Weston, Connecticut USA.

Travel: Plane to New York City, Train to Connecticut.

Dur.: Negotiable.

Per.: Year round.

L.term: Long term is welcome.

Age: Min. 21. Prefer college graduates.

Qualif.: Passion for wildlife.

Work: Animal care, cage repair/building, answering phone and volunteer management.

Lang.: English.

Accom.: Free shared housing.

Cost: Housing is free, only the cost of food.

Applic.: E-mail Standard Application plus resume, photo and 3 references.

Notes: WIC is a volunteer run organization.

INDICES

TABLE OF ORGANISATIONS AND PROJECTS BY GEOGRAPHIC LOCATION AND COST

(cost is intended approximately per week, with or w/o food, travel to project site is always not included)

	Africa	Asia	Europe	Mediterranean	Centr. America	South America	North America	Oceania	US$ 0-100	US$100-500	US$ 500-1500	Over US$ 1500
A' Pas de Loup	X		X			X			X			X
African Conservation Experience	X											X
American Bear Association							X		X			
Appalachian Trail Conservancy							X		X			
ARCAS – Asociación de Rescate y Conservación de Vida Silvestre				X	X				X			
ASVO – Asociacion de Voluntarios para el Servicio en las Area Protegidas				X	X	X			X			
Biosphere Expeditions	X	X	X	X	X	X	X	X			X	
Les Blongios			X						X			
Blue Ventures	X								X			
Brathay Exploration Group	X	X	X	X				X			X	X
BTCV	X	X	X	X			X	X		X	X	
Carapax – European Center for Conservation of Chelonians			X	X					X			
Centre for Alternative Technology			X						X			
Chantiers de Jeunes Provence Cote d'Azur			X							X		
Coral Cay Conservation		X			X					X	X	
Cotravaux				X					X			
CTS - Centro Turistico Studentesco e Giovanile			X	X					X			
CVA - Conservation Volunteers Australia/Conservation Volunteer New Zealand				X				X	X	X		
CVG - Conaervation Volunteers Greece			X	X					X			
Earthwatch	X	X	X	X	X	X	X	X			X	
Ecovolunteer Network	X	X	X	X	X	X	X	X				
EUROPARC Deutschland			X						X	X		
Frontier	X	X			X	X	X	X		X	X	X
Geography Outdoors	X	X	X		X	X	X	X	X	X	X	
Global Service Corps	X	X			X	X			X		X	X
Global Vision International	X			X	X					X	X	X
Go Xplore	X										X	
Greenforce	X	X	X		X			X	X			X
Hellenic Ornithological Society		X	X						X			

234

TABLE OF ORGANISATIONS AND PROJECTS BY GEOGRAPHIC LOCATION AND COST

(cost is intended approximately per week, with or w/o food, travel to project site is always not included)

Organisation	Africa	Asia	Europe	Mediterranean	Centr. America	South America	North America	Oceania	US$0-100	US$100-500	US$500-1500	Over US$1500
Iceland Conservation Volunteers	×	×	×						×			
i to i	×	×	×			×		×	×			
International Otter Survival Fund	×		×								×	
Involvment Volunteers Association	×	×	×	×	×	×	×	×		×		
IUCN – The World Conservation Union	×	×	×	×	×	×	×	×		×		
Legambiente			×	×						×		
LIPU Italian League for Protection of Birds			×	×						×		
Mingan Island Cetacean Research Expeditions							×				×	
The National Trust			×		×				×			
The Nature Corps							×		×			
NZTCV - The New Zealand Trust for Conservation Volunteers								×				×
Oceanic Society Expeditions			×		×	×	×	×			×	
Oceanus Onlus				×	×						×	
Operation Wallacea	×	×			×			×			×	
Raleigh International	×	×			×	×					×	
RSPB – The Royal Society for the Protection of Birds			×						×			
SANCCOB – South African Foundation for the Conservation of Coastal Birds	×								×			
SCA – Student Conservation Association							×	×	×			
SCI – Service Civil International			×				×	×	×			
Tethys			×	×						×		
Trekforce Worldwide					×	×			×			
United Nations Volunteer (UNV)	×	×			×	×	×		×			
USDA Forest Service							×		×			
US Fish and Wildlife Service							×		×			
US National Park Service							×		×			
Volunteer fo Nature							×		×			
Volunteers for Outdoor Colorado							×		×			
Wilderness Foundation, the	×		×				×			×	×	
WWF Italy	×		×	×		×			×	×		

TABLE OF ORGANISATIONS AND PROJECTS BY GEOGRAPHIC LOCATION AND COST

(cost is intended approximately per week, with or w/o food, travel to project site is always not included)

PROJECTS	Africa	Asia	Europe	Mediterranean	Centr. America	South America	North America	Oceania	US$ 0–100	US$100–500	US$ 500–1500	Over US$ 1500
YCI - Youth Challenge International	X				X	X		X			X	X
ACE- American Conservation Experience							X		X			
Adriatic Dolphin Project				X						X		
African Conservation Trust	X									X		
African Impact Lion Rehabilitation Programmes, Zimbabwe	X										X	
African Wild Dog Conservation (AWDC), Zambia	X									X		
Amigos de las Aves					X				X			
Andean Bear Research Project, Ecuador						X			X			
ARFA – Asociacion de Rescate de Fauna						X			X	X		
Asociación Salvemos las Tortugas de Parismina (ASTOP), Costa Rica					X				X	X		
BDRI - Bottlenose Dolphin Research Institute, Italy				X							X	
Bimini Lemon Shark, Bahamas					X					X		
Birds of Tortuguero, Costa Rica					X					X		
Black Rhino, Kenya	X										X	
Black Sheep Inn, Ecuador						X			X			
Blue-fronted Parrot Project, Argentina						X			X			
Bohorok Environmental Center, Indonesia		X									X	
Bottlenose Dolphin Project, Belize					X					X		
Brown Bear Project, Russia			X								X	
California Wildlife Center, California USA							X		X			
Cano Palma Biological Station, Costa Rica					X					X		
Cape Tribulation Tropical Research Station, Australia								X		X		
Cardigan Bay Marine Wildlife Centre, Wales UK			X						X			
Caretta Research Project, USA							X			X		
Cats of Rome, Italy			X						X			
Centre for Dolphin Studies (CDS), South Africa	X									X		
Centre for Rehabilitation of Wildlife (CROW), South Africa	X									X		

TABLE OF ORGANISATIONS AND PROJECTS BY GEOGRAPHIC LOCATION AND COST

(cost is intended approximately per week, with or w/o food, travel to project site is always not included)

	Africa	Asia	Europe	Mediterranean	Centr. America	South America	North America	Oceania	US$ 0-100	US$100-500	US$ 500-1500	Over US$ 1500
CERCOPAN, Nigeria	X								X	X		
Cetacean Research & Rescue Unit (CRRU), Scotland UK			X								X	
Cetacean Sanctuary Research, Italy and France				X							X	
Charles Darwin Foundation, Galapagos						X						X
Cheetah Conservation Fund, Namibia	X									X		
Cheetah Conservation, Botswana	X								X			
Cochrane Ecological Institute (CEI), Canada							X		X			
Comunidad Inti Wara Yassi, Bolivia						X			X			
Community Integrated Conservation Project at Tofu Beach, Mozambique	X									X		
Conservation Project Utila Iguana (CPUI), Honduras					X				X			
Conservation Volunteering in St. Lucia, Caribbean					X				X			
CREES Volunteers Programme, Peru						X				X		
Dolphin Observation, Greece				X						X		
Dolphin Research Center, Florida, USA							X			X		
Dolphins and Sea Life around the Maltese Islands, Malta				X					X			
Donkey Sanctuary, the Netherlands Antilles					X					X		
East African Whale Shark Trust, Kenya	X								X			
Ecology and Conservation of Deer in Patagonia, Argentina						X				X		
Ecuadorian Reptile and Amphibian Research Expeditions, Ecuador						X			X			
El Eden Flora y Fauna: Animal Rescue and Rehabilitation, Argentina						X			X			
Elephant Nature Park, Thailand		X								X		
Flat Holm Island, Wales UK			X						X	X		
Forest Restoration, USA							X		X	X		
Gibbon Rehabilitation Project, Thailand		X								X		
GoEco, Israel				X								
Great Whales in their Natural Environment, Canada							X				X	
Grey Whales Research Expeditions, Canada and Mexico					X		X				X	
Grey Wolf Project, USA							X		X			
Griffon Vulture Conservation Project, Croatia				X						X		

237

TABLE OF ORGANISATIONS AND PROJECTS BY GEOGRAPHIC LOCATION AND COST

(cost is intended approximately per week, with or w/o food, travel to project site is always not included)

	Africa	Asia	Europe	Mediterranean	Centr. America	South America	North America	Oceania	US$ 0-100	US$100-500	US$ 500-1500	Over US$ 1500
Grupo Lobo, Portugal			X						X			
Hawaiian Forest Restoration Project, USA							X		X			
Hellenic Wildlife Hospital, Greece				X					X			
Hoedspruit Endangered Species Centre, South Africa	X									X		
Integrated Coastal Management Project, Malta				X					X			
International Conservation Volunteer Exchange, Nevada USA							X		X			
Ionian Dolphin Project, Greece				X							X	
Iracambi Atlantic Rainforest Research and Conservation Center, Brazil						X			X			
Irish Seal Sanctuary, Ireland			X						X			
Ischia Dolphin Project, Italy				X							X	
Jatun Sacha, Ecuador						X			X			
Karumbé Sea Turtles Project, Uruguay						X			X			
Kido - WIDECAST Sea Turtles Nesting Monitoring, Grenada					X				X			
Klipkop Wildlife Sanctuary, South Africa	X								X			
La Hesperia, Ecuador						X			X			
Leatherback Seaturtle Tagging Programme, Grenada					X					X		
Leatherback Turtle Conservation, Costa Rica and Panama					X					X		
Leatherback Turtle Project, Costa Rica					X					X		
Libanona Ecology Centre, Madagascar	X								X			
Management Plan for Pylos Lagoon, Greece				X					X			
Manatee Research Project, Belize					X				X			
Marine Mammal Center, the (TMMC), California USA							X				X	
Marine Turtle Adriatic ARCHE' Project, Italy				X					X			
Marine Turtle & Youth Environmental Education, Mexico					X				X			
Mediterranean Monk Seal Research Project, Turkey				X						X		
Mergui Archipelago Hornbills Project, Thailand and Myanmar		X								X		
Monkey Sanctuary, the, England			X						X			
Monte Adone Wildlife Protection Centre, Italy			X						X			
Munda Wanga Wildlife Park and Sanctuary, Zambia	X									X		

238

TABLE OF ORGANISATIONS AND PROJECTS BY GEOGRAPHIC LOCATION AND COST

(cost is intended approximately per week, with or w/o food, travel to project site is always not included)

Project	Over US$ 1500	US$ 500-1500	US$ 100-500	US$ 0-100	Oceania	North America	South America	Centr. America	Mediterranean	Europe	Asia	Africa
Mysterious Japan and its Wondrous Wetlands, Japan		X									X	
Naucrates Conservation Project, Thailand			X								X	
Nkombi Research and Volunteer Programme, South Africa			X									X
Noah's Arc, Greece				X					X			
North Sea Cetacean Monitoring, UK and Norway				X						X		
Oceania Research Project, the, Australia		X			X							
Okavango Delta Lion Monitoring Project, Botswana			X									X
Operation Osprey, Scotland UK				X						X		
Orangutan Foundation, Indonesia			X								X	
Orangutan Health, Indonesia		X									X	
Orangutan Tropical Peatland Project (OuTrop), Indonesia			X								X	
Pandrillus Foundation, Nigeria				X								X
Peace River Refuge & Ranch, Florida USA			X			X						
Pioneer Madagascar, Madagascar			X									X
Project Kial, Australia				X	X							
Project «MEER La Gomera», Spain		X										X
Proyecto Jubarte do Cabo Verde		X										X
Proyecto Campanario, Costa Rica			X					X				
Rainsong Wildlife Sanctuary, Costa Rica			X					X				
Re-Aforestation Project, Ghana				X								X
Reef Check Global Coral Reef Monitoring, USA				X	X	X					X	
Re-Hydration of the Earth, Kenya			X									X
Reserva Pacuare, Costa Rica			X					X				
Rhino Rescue Project, Swaziland			X									X
River Otter Project, Brazil			X				X					
San Wild Wildlife Trust, the, South Africa		X										X
Santa Lucia, Ecuador				X			X					
Santa Martha Rescue Centers, Ecuador				X			X					
Scottish Whale and Dolphin Project, Scotland UK				X						X		

239

TABLE OF ORGANISATIONS AND PROJECTS BY GEOGRAPHIC LOCATION AND COST

(cost is intended approximately per week, with or w/o food, travel to project site is always not included)

	Africa	Asia	Europe	Mediterranean	Centr. America	South America	North America	Oceania	US$ 0-100	US$100-500	US$ 500-1500	Over US$ 1500
Scottish Wildlife Rescue, Scotland UK			X						X			
Sea Turtle Conservation Program, Costa Rica					X				X			
Sea Turtle Conservation Projects, Costa Rica					X					X		
Sea Turtle Rescue Center, Greece				X					X			
Sea Turtle Summer Field Work, Greece				X					X	X		
Siberian–East Russian Volunteer Program, Russia		X							X	X		
Skaftafell National Park, Iceland			X									
Southwestern Research Station, Arizona USA							X		X			
Spanish Dolphins, Spain				X								X
Sustainable Livelihood Development Association, Sri Lanka		X							X			
Tambopata Resident Naturalist Program, Peru						X			X			
Tilos Park Association, Greece				X					X			
Tolga Bat Hospital, Australia								X	X			
Tree Planters Farm, Australia								X	X			
Trees For Life, Scotland UK			X						X	X		
Turtle Conservation Project (TCP), Sri Lanka		X							X			
Turtle Project, Kefalonia, Greece				X					X			
Turtles of Tortuguero, Costa Rica					X				X			X
University of Georgia San Luis Research Station, the, Costa Rica					X				X			
Volunteering in Vilcabamba, Ecuador						X			X			
Volunteer Peten, Guatemala					X				X			
Wakuluzu: Friends of the Colobus Trust, Kenya	X								X			
WDCS Wildlife Centre, Scotland UK			X						X			
Whale Center of New England, the, Massachusetts USA							X			X		
Whale Research in the Saint Lawrence Estuary, Canada							X			X	X	
Whales and Dolphins of Cote D'Azur, France				X							X	
Wild Bird Rehabilitation in Bulgaria			X							X		
Wild Dolphin Project, Bahamas							X					X
Wildlife Rehabilitation Internship, Connecticut USA							X		X			

240

TABLE OF ORGANISATIONS AND PROJECTS BY SPECIES OR GROUP OF SPECIES

(species or group of species are indicated with common names)

Organisation / Project	Various Spp.	Trees/Vegetat.	Birds	Sea Turtles	Amph./Reptile	Corals	Sharks	Seals	Whales/dolph.	Oth. Mammals	Wolves/Canids	Felines	Primates	Bears	Bats	Africa Herbiv.
A' Pas de Loup				×				×			×					×
African conservation experience		×	×		×	×										×
American bear association														×		
Appalachian Trail Conservancy	×															
ARCAS – Asociación de Rescate y Conservación de Vida Silvestre	×	×	×	×	×					×		×	×	×		
ASVO - Asociación de Voluntarios para el Servicio en las Area Protegidas	×	×	×	×	×					×	×	×	×			
Biosphere Expeditions	×	×	×							×						×
Les Blongios		×														
Blue Ventures						×										
Brathay Exploration Group	×															
BTCV	×	×	×		×					×			×			
Carapax – European Center for Conservation of Chelonians				×	×											
Centre for Alternative Technology	×															
Chantiers de Jeunes Provence Cote d'Azur	×															
Coral Cay Conservation	×					×										
Cotravaux	×															
CTS - Centro Turístico Studentesco e Giovanile	×	×	×	×		×			×	×	×	×	×	×		
CVA – Conservation Volunteers Australia/ Conservation Volunteer New Zealand	×	×	×						×	×		×	×	×		
CVG – Conservation Volunteers Greece	×	×	×	×	×											
Earthwatch	×	×	×	×	×				×	×	×					×
Ecovolunteer Network	×	×	×	×				×	×	×	×	×	×	×		×
EUROPARC Deutschland	×	×	×													
Frontier	×					×										
Geography Outdoors																
Global Service Corps	×	×														
Global Vision International	×		×			×			×	×						×
Go Xplore												×	×			×
Greenforce	×	×	×		×	×										
Hellenic Ornithological Society			×													

241

TABLE OF ORGANISATIONS AND PROJECTS BY SPECIES OR GROUP OF SPECIES

(species or group of species are indicated with common names)

Organisation / Project	Various Spp.	Trees/Vegetat.	Birds	Sea Turtles	Amph./Reptile	Corals	Sharks	Seals	Whales/dolph.	Oth. Mammals	Wolves/Canids	Felines	Primates	Bears	Bats	Africa Herbiv.
Iceland Conservation Volunteers	X	X	X													
i to i	X	X														
International Otter Survival Fund										X						
Involvment Volunteers Association	X															
IUCN – The World Conservation Union	X	X														
Legambiente	X															
LIPU - Italian League for the Protection of Birds			X													
Mingan Island Cetacean Research Expeditions									X							
The National Trust	X	X														
The Nature Corps	X	X														
NZTCV - The New Zealand Trust for Conservation Volunteers	X	X														
Oceanic Society Expeditions	X			X		X			X	X			X			
Oceanus Onlus	X			X			X		X	X						
Operation Wallacea	X		X	X	X	X						X	X		X	
Raleigh International			X													
RSPB – The Royal Society for the Protection of Birds			X													
SANCCOB – South African Foundation for the Conservation of Coastal Birds			X													
SCA – Student Conservation Association	X	X														
SCI – Service Civil International	X	X														
Tethys Research Institute									X							
Trekforce Worldwide	X	X														
United Nations Volunteer (UNV)	X	X														
USDA Forest Service	X	X														
US Fish and Wildlife Service	X	X	X													
US National Park Service	X	X														
Volunteer fo Nature	X	X														
Volunteers for Outdoor Colorado	X	X														
Wilderness Foundation, the				X										X		
WWF Italy			X						X	X						

242

TABLE OF ORGANISATIONS AND PROJECTS BY SPECIES OR GROUP OF SPECIES

(species or group of species are indicated with common names)

PROJECTS	Africa Herbiv.	Bats	Bears	Primates	Felines	Wolves/Canids	Oth. Mammals	Whales/dolph.	Seals	Sharks	Corals	Amph./Reptile	Sea Turtles	Birds	Trees/Vegetat.	Various Spp.
YCI - Youth Challenge International															X	X
ACE- American Conservation Experience																
Adriatic Dolphin Project								X							X	X
African Conservation Trust	X														X	
African Impact Lion Rehabilitation Programmes, Zimbabwe					X											
African Wild Dog Conservation (AWDC), Zambia						X										
Amigos de las Aves														X		
Andean Bear Research Project, Ecuador			X													
ARFA – Asociación de Rescate de Fauna				X	X		X					X		X		
Asociación Salvemos las Tortugas de Parismina (ASTCP), Costa Rica													X			
BDRI – Bottlenose Dolphin Research Institute, Italy								X								
Bimini Lemon Shark, Bahamas										X						
Birds of Tortuguero, Costa Rica														X		
Black Rhino, Kenya	X															
Black Sheep Inn, Ecuador			X											X	X	
Blue-fronted Parrot Project, Argentina														X		X
Bohorok Environmental Center, Indonesia				X											X	
Bottlenose Dolphin Project, Belize								X								
Brown Bear Project, Russia			X													
California Wildlife Center, California USA						X	X					X		X		
Cano Palma Biological Station, Costa Rica				X		X	X							X	X	
Cape Tribulation Tropical Research Station, Australia		X					X		X							
Cardigan Bay Marine Wildlife Centre, Wales UK								X						X		X
Caretta Research Project, USA													X			
Cats of Rome, Italy					X											
Centre for Dolphin Studies (CDS), South Africa								X								
Centre for Rehabilitation of Wildlife (CROW), South Africa	X			X								X		X		X

243

TABLE OF ORGANISATIONS AND PROJECTS BY SPECIES OR GROUP OF SPECIES

(species or group of species are indicated with common names)

Organisation	Various Spp.	Trees/Veget.	Birds	Sea Turtles	Amph./Reptile	Corals	Sharks	Seals	Whales/dolph.	Oth. Mammals	Wolves/Canids	Felines	Primates	Bears	Bats	Africa Herbiv.
CERCOPAN, Nigeria													X			
Cetacean Research & Rescue Unit (CRRU), Scotland UK									X							
Cetacean Sanctuary Research, Italy and France									X							
Charles Darwin Foundation, Galapagos	X	X	X	X	X		X	X	X							
Cheetah Conservation Fund, Namibia												X				
Cheetah Conservation, Botswana												X				
Cochrane Ecological Institute (CEI), Canada											X					
Comunidad Inti Wara Yassi, Bolivia	X	X	X		X					X	X	X	X			
Community Integrated Conservation Project at Tofu Beach, Mozambique				X												
Conservation Project Utila Iguana (CPUI), Honduras					X											
Conservation Volunteering in St. Lucia, Caribbean	X	X	X							X					X	
CREES Volunteer Programme, Peru	X	X	X		X					X		X	X			
Dolphin Observation, Greece									X							
Dolphin Research Center, Florida USA									X							
Dolphins and Sea Life around the Maltese Islands, Malta			X	X		X	X		X							
Donkey Sanctuary, the Netherlands Antilles										X						
East African Whale Shark Trust, Kenya							X									
Ecology and Conservation of Deer in Patagonia, Argentina										X						
Ecuadorian Reptile and Amphibian Research Expeditions, Ecuador					X											
El Eden Flora y Fauna: Animal Rescue and Rehabilitation, Argentina	X	X	X							X		X	X			
Elephant Nature Park, Thailand										X						
Flat Holm Island, Wales UK			X													
Forest Restoration, USA																
Gibbon Rehabilitation Project, Thailand													X			
GoEco, Israel			X													
Great Whales in their Natural Environment, Canada									X							
Grey Whales Research Expeditions, Canada and Mexico									X							
Grey Wolf Project, USA											X					
Griffon Vulture Conservation Project, Island of Cres, Croatia	X		X													

244

TABLE OF ORGANISATIONS AND PROJECTS BY SPECIES OR GROUP OF SPECIES

(species or group of species are indicated with common names)

Organisation / Project	Various Spp.	Trees/Vegetat.	Birds	Sea Turtles	Amph./Reptile	Corals	Sharks	Seals	Whales/dolph.	Oth. Mammals	Wolves/Canids	Felines	Primates	Bears	Bats	Africa Herbiv.
Grupo Lobo, Portugal											X					
Hawaiian Forest Restoration Project, USA		X														
Hellenic Wildlife Hospital, Greece	X		X							X						
Hoedspruit Endangered Species Centre, South Africa	X		X								X	X				X
Integrated Coastal Management Project, Malta	X															
International Conservation Volunteer Exchange, Nevada USA	X	X														
Ionian Dolphin Project, Greece									X							
Iracambi Atlantic Rainforest Research and Conservation Center, Brazil	X	X	X		X					X						
Irish Seal Sanctuary, Ireland								X								
Ischia Dolphin Project, Italy									X							
Jatun Sacha, Ecuador	X	X	X		X					X						
Karumbé Sea Turtles Project, Uruguay				X												
Kido - WIDECAST Sea Turtles Nesting Monitoring, Grenada				X												
Kilpkop Wildlife Sanctuary, South Africa	X		X													
La Hesperia, Ecuador	X		X		X											
Leatherback Seaturtle Tagging Programme, Grenada				X												
Leatherback Turtle Conservation, Costa Rica and Panama				X												
Leatherback Turtle Project, Costa Rica				X												
Libanona Ecology Centre, Madagascar													X			
Management Plan for Pylos Lagoon, Greece	X	X	X		X											
Manatee Research Project, Belize										X						
Marine Mammal Center (TMMC), California USA								X								
Marine Turtles Adriatic ARCHE' Project, Italy				X												
Marine Turtle & Youth Environmental Education, Mexico				X												
Mediterranean Monk Seal Research Project, Turkey								X								
Mergui Archipelago Hornbills Project, Thailand and Myanmar			X													
Monkey Sanctuary, the, England													X			
Monte Adone Wildlife Protection Centre, Italy	X		X		X					X		X	X			
Munda Wanga Wildlife Park and Sanctuary, Zambia	X		X							X		X	X	X		X

(species or group of species are indicated with common names)

Organisation / Project	Africa Herbiv.	Bats	Bears	Primates	Felines	Wolves/Canids	Oth. Mammals	Whales/dolph.	Seals	Sharks	Corals	Amph./Reptile	Sea Turtles	Birds	Trees/Vegetat.	Various Spp.
Mysterious Japan and its Wondrous Wetlands, Japan											X			X	X	
Naucrates Conservation Project, Thailand													X			X
Nkombi Research and Volunteer Programme, South Africa	X					X	X							X		X
Noah's Arc, Greece							X									X
North Sea Cetacean Monitoring, UK and Norway								X								
Oceania Research Project, the, Australia								X								
Okavango Delta Lion Monitoring Project, Botswana					X											
Operation Osprey, Scotland UK														X		
Orangutan Foundation, Indonesia				X												
Orangutan Health, Indonesia				X												
Orangutan Tropical Peatland Project (OuTrop), Indonesia				X												
Pandrillus Foundation, Nigeria				X												X
Peace River Refuge & Ranch, Florida USA				X	X	X	X									
Pioneer Madagascar, Madagascar				X			X					X				
Project Kial, Australia													X			
Project «MEER La Gomera», Spain								X		X						
Projecto Jubarte do Cabo Verde								X								
Proyecto Campanario, Costa Rica				X	X		X					X				
Rainsong Wildlife Sanctuary, Costa Rica				X	X		X					X				
Re-Aforestation Project, Ghana															X	
Reef Check Global Coral Reef Monitoring, USA											X					
Re-Hydration of the Earth, Kenya	X			X	X	X	X							X	X	X
Reserva Pacuare, Costa Rica												X	X	X	X	X
Rhino Rescue Project, Swaziland	X															
River Otter Project, Brazil							X									
San Wild Wildlife Trust, the, South Africa	X			X	X	X	X					X		X	X	X
Santa Lucia, Ecuador												X		X	X	X
Santa Martha Rescue Centers, Ecuador			X	X	X		X							X		X
Scottish Whale and Dolphin Project, Scotland UK							X	X	X							

TABLE OF ORGANISATIONS AND PROJECTS BY SPECIES OR GROUP OF SPECIES

(species or group of species are indicated with common names)

Organisation / Project	Various Spp.	Trees/Vegetat.	Birds	Sea Turtles	Amph./Reptile	Corals	Sharks	Seals	Whales/dolph.	Oth. Mammals	Wolves/Canids	Felines	Primates	Bears	Bats	Africa Herbiv.
Scottish Wildlife Rescue, Scotland UK			X							X						
Sea Turtle Conservation Program, Costa Rica				X												
Sea Turtle Conservation Projects, Costa Rica				X												
Sea Turtle Rescue Center, Greece				X												
Sea Turtle Summer Field Work, Greece				X												
Siberian-East Russian Volunteer Program, Russia	X	X	X							X	X					
Skaftafell National park, Iceland	X	X	X		X					X						
Southwestern Research Station, Arizona USA		X			X					X						
Spanish Dolphins, Spain									X							
Sustainable Livelihood Development Association, Sri Lanka	X	X	X		X					X		X	X			
Tambopata Resident Naturalist Program, Peru	X	X	X							X		X	X			
Tilos Park Association, Greece		X	X													
Tolga Bat Hospital, Australia															X	
Tree Planters Farm, Australia		X														
Trees For Life, Scotland UK		X														
Turtle Conservation Project (TCP), Sri Lanka				X												
Turtle Project, Kefalonia, Greece				X												
Turtles of Tortuguero, Costa Rica				X												
University of Georgia Ecolodge San Luis Research Station, the, Costa Rica	X	X	X		X					X		X	X		X	
Volunteering in Vilcabamba, Ecuador	X	X	X		X					X	X	X	X			
Volunteer Peten, Guatemala	X	X	X		X					X		X	X			
Wakuluzu: Friends of the Colobus Trust, Kenya													X			
WDCS Wildlife Centre, Scotland UK									X							
Whale Center of New England, the, Massachusetts USA									X							
Whale Research in the Saint Lawrence Estuary, Canada									X							
Whales and Dolphins off Cote D'Azur, France									X	X						
Wild Bird Rehabilitation, Bulgaria			X													
Wild Dolphin Project, Bahamas									X							
Wildlife Rehabilitation Internship, Connecticut USA	X		X							X						

ORGANISATION ALPHABETICAL INDEX

PROJECT ALPHABETICAL INDEX

THE *GREEN VOLUNTEERS* PHOTO CONTEST

Good photographs of wildlife and people together are extremely rare, especially those that give the idea of involvement and participation, which is what *Green Volunteers* is all about. *Green Volunteers* is therefore launching a contest among all its readers and active volunteers. We are looking for good pictures of wildlife together with people (possibly volunteers) to be published in our website and to be chosen as the cover picture (such as the picture on the current cover) for future issues of the Guide.

If your pictures get published, you will not be paid by Green Volunteers but you will have the opportunity of helping your favourite project by allowing it to receive more exposure and therefore more volunteers, and you will have the satisfaction to see your picture published in our website. *Green Volunteers* will award US$ 100 to the pictures that will be chosen for covers of next issues of the Guide. Please send your pictures exclusively via e-mail (possibly in low density) to: green@greenvolunteers.org. No picture will be used for publication without prior permission of the photographer. If the picture is selected, you will be contacted, and asked if your picture can be added to our website. **Make sure, however, that for taking your pictures of volunteers in action you don't interfere with the work of the project. We look forward to seeing your great pictures. Good luck with your Green Volunteering!**

The *Green Volunteers Hostel* is opening soon! Hiking, canoeing, sailing, climbing, mountain biking and good food at an affordable price in the spectacular Lake District in the foothills of the Alps! See **www.greenvolunteers.org** for details.

STANDARD APPLICATION FORM
Green Volunteers © 2007

To be photocopied enlarged, retyped or downloaded from the **Green Volunteers Database** (ask for a User ID and password to access it, see contacts at www.greenvolunteers.org). This is not an official application form; many organisations have their own, others may accept this. (Please print)

Last name: .... First name: ....

Nationality: .... Date of birth: .... Passport n°: ....

Occupation: ....

Address for correspondence: ....

Tel.: .... Fax: .... E-mail: ....

Next of kin (name, address and tel. number): ....
....

If you are a student, write the name and address of the school, College or University:
....

Mother tongue: .... Other languages spoken:
excellent: .... very good: .... good: .... basic: ....

Education: ....

Indicate your experience in volunteering (also in other fields) or in participating in environmental projects, wildlife rescue centres, fieldwork, camping, backpacking or other outdoor activities:
....
....
....

Skills which may be useful to the project:
....
....
....

Are you a member of any environmental organization? If yes, specify:
....

Do you have any health problems? If yes, specify:
....

Indicate your preferences for project's dates and location:
....

Any additional relevant information (feel free to add additional pages):
....
....
....

Date: ..... / ..... /...... Signature: ....

From the same publisher

(available from your bookstore or from the website www.greenvol.com)

Green Volunteers   The World Guide
to Voluntary Work in Nature Conservation
Over 200 projects worldwide for those vho want to experience active conservation work as a volunteer. Projects are worldwide, year round, in a variety of habitats, from one week to one year or more. From dolphins to rhinos, from whales to primates, this guide is ideal for a meaningful vacation or for finding thesis or research opportunities.
Price £ 10.99   € 16.00 $ 14.95   Pages: 256

World Volunteers   The World Guide
to Humanitarian and Development Volunteering
Nearly 200 projects and organizations worldwide for people who want to work in international humanitarian projects but don't know how to begin. Opportunities are from 2 weeks to 2 years or longer. An ideal resource for a working holiday or a leave of absence. A guide for students, reitrees, doctors or accountants, nurses or agronomists, surveyors and teachers, plumbers or builders, electricians or computer operators... For everyone who wants to get involved in helping those who suffer worldwide.
Price £ 10.99   € 16.00 $ 14.95   Pages: 256

Archaeo-Volunteers   The World Guide
to Archaeological and Heritage Volunteering
Listing 200 projects and organizations in the 5 continents for those who want to spend a different working vacation helping Archaeologists Placements are from 2 weeks to a few months. For enthusiastic amateurs, students and those wanting hands-on experience. Cultural and historical heritage maintenance and restoration and museum volunteering opportunities are also listed. The guide also tells how to find hundreds more excavations and workcamps on the Internet.
Price £ 10.99   € 16.00 $ 14.95   Pages: 256